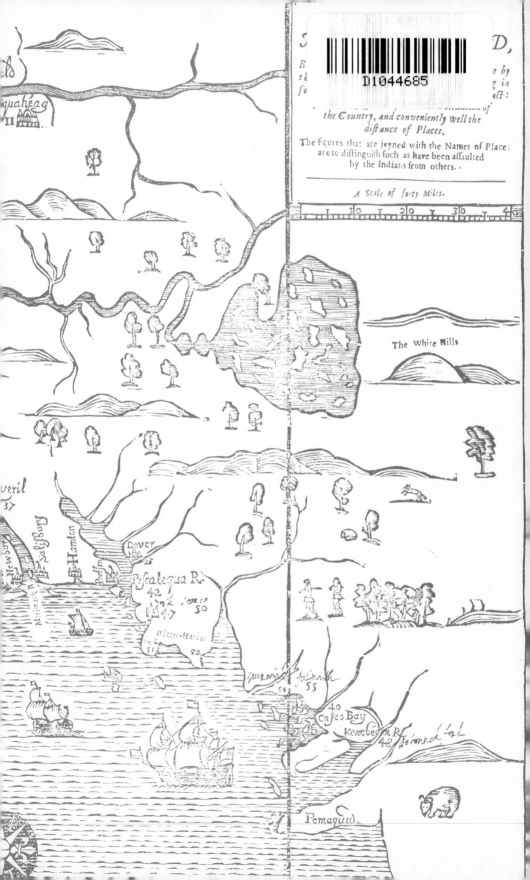

The Heart Prepared
Grace and Conversion
in Puritan Spiritual Life
by Norman Pettit

No other point in New England theology was more significant for spiritual
well-being than the question of how
much a man could do to prepare himself for saving grace and, in turn, to
what degree his preparation would pre-
dispose God to save him. Uncertainty
could and often did lead to agonizing
tension of the soul, and if the preaching
of preparation encouraged sound con-
versions in some, it provoked from
others critical questions in a series of
searching controversies that virtually
molded the New England mind.

This investigation traces the emergence of the concept of preparation
within the framework of experiential
religion and covenant theology and its
development by such Reform theologi-
ans as Heinrich Bullinger and John Calvin. The author describes the debates
centering around it, especially the An-
tinomian Controversy in Massachusetts, and explores the problem that
arose when preparation became a requirement for church membership.

*Yale Publications in
American Studies, 11.*

"His approach is strikingly concrete
and . . . convincingly serious. In a prose
whose clarity belies the volumes of
cobwebbed tracts he has suffered
through, he renders penumbral nuances
of theology distinct, gives personality
to a dozen divines, and somewhat
sweetens our impression of Puritan
tenets."—*The New Yorker.* $5.75

Printed in the U.S.A.

Symbols of American Community, 1735–1775
by Richard L. Merritt

When did the eighteenth-century American colonists break their symbolic ties with England? When did American affairs start to interest them more than London court politics and continental intrigues? When did the colonists begin to think of themselves as Americans, rather than as His Majesty's subjects or English colonists? Mr. Merritt explores these questions through a quantitative content analysis of the colonial press. He describes the growing patterns of communication throughout the prerevolutionary colonies and casts doubt on some long-held theories of the causes of the Revolution. The study is of substantive as well as methodological value, for the political integration of colonial America offers comparisons and parallels to modern efforts to unite separate groups.

"A unique and pioneering contribution to early American history and symbol analysis. . . . The author—a political scientist—has made our knowledge of the emergence of American nationalism far more precise than historians ever imagined possible."—*Choice*. $6.00

The Poems of Edward Taylor
edited by Donald E. Stanford
Foreword by Louis L. Martz

"This first complete collection of the poems of America's finest colonial poet is scrupulously edited. In addition to having the usual apparatus, it benefits from an excellent brief foreword by Louis L. Martz, who settles Taylor in his literary context, and a very helpful glossary. A useful introduction to Taylor and to Puritanism in New England."—*The Key Reporter*.

"Professors Stanford and Martz have performed a most praiseworthy service in presenting the largest single collection of America's finest colonial poet."—*William and Mary Quarterly*.

"Nothing has been spared by the editor to assemble what must long stand as the definitive edition of Edward Taylor's verse."—*Books Abroad*.   cloth $10.00; paper $2.95

YALE UNIVERSITY PRESS   **YA LE**   NEW HAVEN AND LONDON

Pilgrim Colony
A History of New Plymouth
1620–1691

by George D. Langdon, Jr.

While the story of the Pilgrims and the landing at Plymouth is a familiar part of American history and legend, the subsequent history of the first Puritan settlement in North America has long awaited its first chronicler. Mr. Langdon, in the first full-scale and scholarly history of New Plymouth Colony, shows how seventeenth-century Plymouth developed independently of neighboring Massachusetts. Challenging the view that policy at Plymouth reflected that in Massachusetts, he systematically delineates patterns of religious, political, and economic growth which contributed to the uniqueness of the Plymouth experiment. He further contests the assumption that political democracy thrived in the American climate, and sheds new light on such familiar figures as William Bradford and members of the Winslow family. Of particular importance to students of colonial history and religion, the book should interest anyone concerned with early America.

Mr. Langdon is assistant professor of history at Vassar College.

"A thoughtful and persuasive discussion of a subject that strangely has been one of the neglected subjects in American history."
                    —*Wesley Frank Craven.*

*Yale Publications in
American Studies, 12.*

Yale Publications in American Studies, 12

Published under the direction
of the
American Studies Program

PILGRIM COLONY

A HISTORY OF NEW PLYMOUTH

1620 - 1691

by George D. Langdon, Jr.

New Haven and London: Yale University Press

NOTE ON THE ENDPAPERS

John Foster's Woodcut Map of New England is the first known printed American map, done for the Boston edition of Hubbard's *Narrative of the Troubles with the Indians* (1677). The impression reproduced here is from the Beinecke Rare Book and Manuscript Library, Yale University. Manuscript annotations (Westfield, Warwick, York, etc.) are of an unknown eighteenth–century hand.

For Patty

Contents

Preface

WRITING nearly three centuries ago, Nathaniel Morton, secretary and magistrate of the New Plymouth Colony, explained why he had given his time and energy to writing a history of the colony: "To the Right Worshipful, Thomas Prence Esq.; Govenour of the Jurisdiction of New Plimoth . . . Right Worshipful, The consideration of the weight of Duty that lieth upon us to Commemorize to future Generations the memorable passages of Gods Providence to us and our Predecessors in the beginning of this Plantation hath wrought in me a restlessness of spirit . . ." Morton's history, *New Englands Memoriall*, published in Cambridge in 1669, is one of numerous books about Plymouth.

Like most of the historians who have followed him, however, Morton was chiefly interested in the early years of the colony, and like them he carried the story of Plymouth beyond 1630 only in a perfunctory way. It is not difficult to understand why. To Morton, as to many of his successors, the high excitement and drama of Plymouth lay in the epic of the Pilgrim Fathers and their fight for survival on the edge of the world. Once that fight was won and the settlement of Massachusetts had taken place, what happened in Plymouth Colony seemed less important.

Because most writers have been primarily concerned with the years of early settlement at Plymouth, many people who know that the Pilgrims landed in 1620 do not know that Plymouth was a separate colony for most of the seventeenth century. Those who have known it have generally assumed that even before the absorption of the colony by Massachusetts in 1692, Plymouth was little more than an appendage of the Bay Colony. In many respects, of course, Plymouth was similar to Massachusetts. Both colonies were settled by Englishmen, and in both the men controlling the government were Puritans. The conjunction of Puritan dedication and English heritage meant that the same philosophical goals were often shared. But the means used to obtain these goals sometimes differed, for, at least in respect to the leadership of the colony, Plymouth and Massachusetts were settled by different men at different times and for somewhat different reasons. It is therefore, I think, valid to reexamine the history of Plymouth Colony and ask about it some of the questions other scholars have recently asked about Massachusetts.

Because the questions I have asked often seemed to have little relationship to one another, I have not attempted to find a single underlying theme. Rather, I have tried only to tell the story of the colony as best I was able. Yet, while I have no major thesis to propound, the more familiar I have become with seventeenth-century Plymouth—and no one now can become very familiar—the more convinced I have become that one consideration stands out beyond all others. In the opportunities to hold political office, to vote in elections, to gain church membership, and to obtain land, the people who settled before 1640 seem, in retrospect, to have enjoyed marked advantages over their successors.

In the writing of this book I owe a great debt to all of the people who have helped me. The staffs of the Massachusetts State Archives and of the Massachusetts Historical Society extended me every courtesy, as did W. W. Austin of the Old Colony Historical Society in Taunton. The custodians of Pilgrim Hall in Plymouth generously took their manuscripts and books from the usual showcases and made them available to me. I am grateful to John Alden of the Boston Public Library and E. K. Timings of the Public Record Office in London for giving so freely of their time and patience. A grant from the American Philosophical Society made it possible for me to visit England and much of the material used in Chapter 14 was found in the course of that trip. The town clerks of southeastern Massachusetts and southeastern Rhode Island almost without exception permitted me to use their records and provided me with a place to work. These records, in many instances preserved from the first settlement of the town, are a mine for early New England history, and they are, at least collectively, virtually unused. I also wish to thank the various custodians of early church records for their help in tracking down and making available the very few volumes that have survived. Some of the material in Chapter 7 was first published in the October 1963 issue of the *William and Mary Quarterly*. A grant from the Vassar College Class of '59 Fund helped to underwrite the expense of typing the manuscript. I could not have written this book without the vast resources of the Yale Library and the courtesy and the competence of the Library Staff.

David Potter, Rodman Paul, Robert Middlekauff, Paul Baker, and John Bumsted have read parts of the manuscript, and I have profited from their suggestions. Norman Holmes Pearson has given counsel and direction in making important revisions. To Edmund S. Morgan I owe a special obligation: teacher and friend, he has never been too busy to talk or read about Plymouth.

Poughkeepsie, New York George D. Langdon, Jr.
March 15, 1966

I

"The Very Root and Rise of the Same"

O_N a clear fall day in early November 1620 a small ship tacked toward the shore of eastern Cape Cod. Aboard ship men and women, cramped and weary after ten weeks at sea, strained for their first view of the land which would become their new home.

Their transatlantic crossing had begun in August. Twice, the *Mayflower*, in company with her smaller consort, the *Speedwell*, had sailed from England, but twice leaks in the *Speedwell* had forced both ships to return. Finally, on September 6th, the *Mayflower* departed alone for America. Off the British Isles the weather had been favorable; but in mid-passage the sea had begun to make up, and the ship had encountered the gales that race across the North Atlantic in the autumn. During one great storm a beam had cracked under the strain and several among the crew questioned the wisdom of continuing. Believing his ship still sound, Captain Jones, master of the *Mayflower*, ordered the beam braced and the westerly course maintained. In spite of the hardships and terror of the voyage, of 102 passengers unaccustomed to the rigors of life at sea, only one had died. A year earlier, another company 180 strong had sailed for Virginia, and before the ship anchored in Jamestown, 130 were said to have perished.[1] The Pilgrims were familiar with that statistic but it had not affected their resolution to settle in America.

1. William Bradford, *History of Plymouth Plantation 1620–1647*, W. C. Ford, ed., The Massachusetts Historical Society (2 vols. Boston, 1912), *I*, p. 87. All references to Bradford's *History* are to this edition unless otherwise indicated.

On the morning of November 9, a conference took place on the quarterdeck of the *Mayflower*. A decision had to be reached at once where the Pilgrims would settle. Captain Jones knew that the land in sight was Cape Cod; he also knew that the Pilgrims had left England with a patent allowing settlement within the Virginia Company's grant, and that the Company's grant extended only to latitude forty-one degrees north. Landfall was almost a degree north of this line. Because the Pilgrims were anxious to settle with full legal right to begin a plantation, and because their patent was useless above the forty-first parallel, Jones and the Pilgrim leaders decided to sail for the mouth of the Hudson River which lay within the Virginia grant. Jones ordered the ship put about and set the *Mayflower* on a south south-west course which he hoped would weather the Cape.

But the Pilgrims' expectations of skirting the tip of the Cape and settling Manhattan were not to be realized. Below what is now Chatham, sand bars lying a few feet beneath the surface of the sea reach southeasterly into the Atlantic. By mid-afternoon of the 9th, the *Mayflower* was among these shoals and surrounded by the roar of white water. With night coming on, the ship was in danger of grounding and breaking up, and Captain Jones insisted that he had no alternative but to turn back. The following day he sailed the *Mayflower* north along the eastern shore of the Cape, and on the morning of November 11, the ship rounded the beaches of Race Point and dropped anchor in Provincetown Harbor. Some of the Pilgrims went ashore and fell on their knees to give thanks to God.

For a few of the Pilgrims the dislocation climaxed by their arrival in America in 1620 had begun fourteen years earlier in Scrooby, England. Scrooby Manor, formerly a hunting lodge and travelers' rest house, by 1606 a post station for the crown, lay on the great road between Edinburgh and London about fifty miles south of the old Roman fortress town of York. Margaret Tudor, journeying to Scotland to marry James IV, stopped there with her entourage in 1503. A century later when her great-grandson, James VI of Scotland, became King of England as James I, the manor house belonged to the Archbishop of York. Either because of a lack of funds, or from a lack of interest, the archbishop had allowed the property to deteriorate. In August 1603, when James tried to purchase the manor house as a place to rest in his travels between London and Scotland, it was in considerable disrepair.[2] William Brewster was then resident at the manor house as master of the post and receiver and bailiff for the archbishop.

The Brewster family association with Scrooby Manor had begun three decades earlier. Brewster's father, William Brewster Sr., had become receiver and bailiff for the archbishop in 1576 when his son was about ten years old. Four years after his father's appointment, Brewster left for Peterhouse College, Cambridge, to begin university life. How long he studied at Peterhouse is uncertain, but he did not take a degree. Some time before 1585, Brewster became an attendant to William Davison, a diplomatic troubleshooter for Queen Elizabeth, and in 1585 and 1586 traveled with Davison in the Low Countries. After Davison fell from favor he returned to Scrooby to assist his aging father and in 1590, upon the elder Brewster's death, succeeded to his father's responsibilities. Until 1608 Brewster continued to act for the archbishop and as master of the post at Scrooby. But while he remained in the service of a high officer of the Anglican Church, Brewster himself became a Puritan.

Since the middle of the sixteenth century, the progress of the Reformation had given increasing concern to many in England. Henry VIII had broken with the Pope in 1531, but more for dynastic than ecclesiastical reasons, and while doctrinal reforms had developed after the split, in the opinion of some men these reforms had not gone nearly far enough. By the middle of the century, to accommodate this group, the established church had framed *The Thirty-Nine Articles,* which purposely stated the doctrines of the Church in such general terms that it was hoped everyone could accept them.[3] *The Thirty-Nine Articles* achieved their purpose at least temporarily; but efforts to quiet protest over church polity, something quite different from doctrine, were not so successful. A growing number of men wanted to purge the ceremonies of the English Church of all "papal trappings" and hierarchy. By 1582 this group of "purifyers," or Puritans, had found a leader in Thomas Cartwright, and the struggle between conformist and nonconformist was joined. Most Puritans thought it better to reform the existing structure, and battled for

2. *Calendar of State Papers, Domestic Series, 8, James I, 1603–1610,* M. A. E. Green, ed. (London, 1857), p. 33.
3. Perry Miller, *Orthodoxy in Massachusetts* (Cambridge, 1933), p. 18.

their cause within the framework of the established church. But a few did not, abandoned the English Church and its corruptions altogether, and formed so-called separating churches. Brewster, whose attachment to Puritanism may have started while he was at Cambridge, was one of the separatists, and early in the seventeenth century he joined in gathering a separatist church at Scrooby.

Evidence of the date of organization of the Scrooby Church does not exist. Richard Clyfton, its first minister, had taken the parish of Babworth, a few miles south of Scrooby, before 1590, but it is not known when he left Babworth for Scrooby. About ten miles east of Scrooby, in Gainsborough, a separatist church had begun to meet in 1602, and four years later moved to Amsterdam, Holland. The Pilgrim historian William Bradford, one of the original members of the Scrooby group, states that both separatist churches met concurrently in England, which would date formation of the Scrooby Church before the departure of the Gainsborough Church. But Bradford also says that when the Scrooby separatists left for Holland in 1607 they had worshipped together about a year.[4] Possibly the decision by a majority in the Gainsborough Church to leave England prompted the gathering of a church at Scrooby. Bradford himself may have been an early Gainsborough communicant.

Before Cromwell's soldiers forced recognition of the right to dissent in 1653, the crown, and later Parliament, required all Englishmen to belong to and support the established church. Membership in a separatist church was a high crime against the state, and even during Elizabeth's reign, when mere nonconformity was not the target of aggressive persecution, two prominent separatist ministers were executed for their beliefs. After the succession of James I to the throne in 1603, and the concurrent rise to power of a generation of churchmen who knew the Establishment as a continuing institution, both separating and non-separating Puritans became the targets of increasing harassment by the crown.[5]

By 1607 separatism at Scrooby had come to the attention of civil authority. In November, Gervase Neville, a Scrooby separatist, was imprisoned in the castle at York. The following month the Court of High Commission summoned three of the

4. Bradford, *History, I,* pp. 25–26.
5. Miller, *Orthodoxy,* pp. 38–42.

congregation including Brewster. In April each was fined £20 for failure to appear before the Court.[6] The Scrooby separatists had previously agreed that they could not continue to worship together in England and, in spite of the difficulties involved in dislocation, determined to leave their homes to live as exiles in the Netherlands.

For some of them, the first attempt to leave England in the autumn of 1607 ended in failure. After engaging a ship to take them from Boston, they were betrayed by the ship's captain and seized by law enforcement officers of the crown. Apprehended on suspicion of illegal exit from the country, they were first subjected to close personal search for money—in the case of the women, further "than became modestie"—and then taken into magistrate's court, and from there to jail. Upon the expiration of thirty days, all but seven who were bound over to appear in superior court were released and sent home.[7]

A second effort to reach Holland in the spring of 1608 was scarcely more successful. To diminish the likelihood of arrest, a rendezvous was arranged with a Dutch ship off a deserted strip of coast between Grimsby and Hull. The men came to the appointed meeting place by land; the women and children in a small bark. Rough seas, however, interfered with the scheduled transfer of passengers to the bigger ship and, wet and seasick, the women persuaded the captain of the bark to put into a small creek to await an improvement in the weather. There, as the tide fell, the bark grounded. On the following day, while waiting for high tide to float the bark, the Dutch captain sent a boat ashore to ferry the men out to his anchorage. No sooner had the first boatload reached the ship than a party of armed men, some on foot and some mounted, appeared in the distance. Cursing this turn of events, the Dutch captain raised his sails and departed the coast, leaving the women and children without their men to fend for themselves as best they could.

In spite of these frustrations, most of the Scrooby Church eventually arrived in the Netherlands. They chose Holland because of the freedom of worship then accepted in the United Provinces and found nowhere else in the Western World. In the sixteenth and early seventeenth centuries, Charles V and his suc-

6. Henry M. Dexter and Morton Dexter, *The England and Holland of the Pilgrims* (Cambridge, 1906), pp. 392, 401–02.
7. Bradford, *History, I*, p. 31; Dexter, *England and Holland*, pp. 401–02.

cessor to the Spanish throne, Philip II, had attempted to exterminate Protestantism in Spain's Dutch provinces. Out of their attempts came war, and finally, in 1609, a truce and consent to the temporary establishment of an independent Dutch republic. From Spanish repression also arose a unique toleration of Protestant sectarianism and a refuge for English dissenters.

The flight of English separatists to Holland began in 1593 when a church which had gathered in London moved to Amsterdam after royal authorities had seized and imprisoned the minister and some of the members. Known in 1607 as the Ancient Church, the London group had chosen Francis Johnson and Henry Ainsworth to minister to them. In 1606 a second company of separatists, the Gainsborough Church, had arrived in Amsterdam. Perhaps because of the accessibility of Amsterdam from England and perhaps because of the friendliness shown the earlier English exiles, the Scrooby congregation also settled there. With the arrival of their minister, Richard Clyfton, one of the last to come over, they began again in the summer of 1608 to worship together.

Within a year the Scrooby Church decided to move to Leyden. The determination to move again grew from troubles that were breaking out in the other separatist churches in Amsterdam. The Gainsborough Church under John Smyth already had fallen into contention by renouncing infant baptism and dissolving the existing church fellowship. More disheartening for the Scrooby Church were signs of trouble within the Ancient Church. Although the Scrooby congregation had preserved its integrity after arrival in Amsterdam, contact was apparently so close between the two that trouble in one came to involve the other.[8] To forestall internal quarreling of their own, the Scrooby congregation seemed to have no alternative but to leave and settle elsewhere, but they left without their minister. Spent from the harassment and uprooting of the past two years, Clyfton decided to stay in Amsterdam and transfer to the Ancient Church. John Robinson took Clyfton's place as minister.

Robinson graduated from Cambridge in 1596 and the following year he was elected a fellow of Corpus Christie College. In 1604 he left Cambridge to become minister of St. Andrew's Parish, Norwich, but within a year his Puritan sympathies

8. Bradford, *History, I,* p. 38; for a detailed account of dissension in the separatist churches in Amsterdam, see Dexter, *England and Holland,* pp. 421–69.

caused his dismissal. He returned to Sturton-le-Steeple, his boy-hood home a few miles east of Scrooby, where he became a member of the Scrooby Church. In 1608 he joined in the removal to Holland, and with his succession to the ministry in 1609 soon became one of the principal spokesmen of the separatist cause. Well-educated, flexible when he thought that basic principles were not at stake, Robinson tempered the separatist impulse to escape from the world and taught his church to seek accommodation with other godly men. Although he himself never reached America, his teachings gave a direction to the Plymouth settlement that remained long after his death in 1625.

From 1609 until 1620 the Scrooby group lived at Leyden. William Bradford's later memories of the city were pleasant, and he wrote that, by working hard, the English separatists managed to make a comfortable living. Many were apparently engaged in cloth making; Bradford himself was a fustian maker, Brewster a printer. For some of them, however, Leyden was not and could not be a permanent home, and by 1617 some of the Church had resolved to go to America. There is no evidence that ill-treatment by the Dutch influenced this decision and Bradford, corresponding with the Dutch settlers of New Netherland, recalled in 1627 the courtesy shown to the Pilgrims in Holland.[9] Yet they were exiles there. The language barrier alone testified to that. Moreover, if they valued their English heritage, and it is clear they did, an indefinite stay in the Netherlands meant their children either would remain aliens or become Dutchmen; neither alternative appealed to the Pilgrims. And although they were able to make a living, economic opportunities were limited. Bradford's economic status probably compared favorably with most of the Pilgrims, but he too met with financial difficulties in Holland.[10]

For those searching for more inspired reasons for removal, greater opportunity existed in America for advancing the gospel. The Pilgrims were not missionaries. Their immediate concern was for themselves, not for the heathen, nor yet for the rest of the civilized world. They never stated, as would their neighbors to the north in Massachusetts Bay, that they were to be "a

9. See Bradford and Council to the Dutch Governor, New Plymouth, March 19, 1627, printed in Bradford, *History, 2,* p. 25.
10. Cotton Mather, *Magnalia Christi Americana* (2 vols. Hartford, 1855), *1,* p. 111.

beacon of hope" for other men. Nonetheless, for some of them the opportunity to set forth as soldiers of the Kingdom of Christ was at least one more reason for going. The decision to seek a home in the New World was not made without consideration of the difficulties involved, nor without bitter opposition from some.

> It was answered, that all great, and honourable, actions, are accompanied with great difficulties; and must be, both en-terprised, and overcome with answerable courages. It was granted the dangers were great, but not desperate; the diffi-culties were many, but not invincible. For though their were many of them likely, yet they were not certaine; it might be sundrie of the things feared, might never befale; others by providente care and the use of good means, might in a great measure be prevented; and all of them (through the help of God) by fortitude, and patience, might either be borne, or overcome. True it was, that shuch attempts were not to be made and undertaken without good ground, and reason; not rashly, or lightly as many have done for curiositie, or hope of gaine, etc. But their condition was not ordinarie; their ends were good and honourable; their calling lawfull, and urgente; and therfore they might expecte the blessing of God in their proceding.[11]

The decision to leave Holland for America having been made, the Pilgrims had to decide where to go and how to raise the money to get there. Resolution of the first was comparatively easy. Although the fertility and tropical climate of Guiana were tempting, the majority agreed to settle in English North Amer-ica. The Pilgrims knew that under a charter granted by James I in 1606, two trading companies, one centered in London, the other in Plymouth, controlled title to all the land on the North American continent between thirty-four and forty-five degrees north latitude. They also knew that the Virginia Company of London, whose right to settle extended up to forty-one degrees, had already planted a successful colony at Jamestown. To solicit a patent from this company, two agents were sent to London from Leyden in 1617.

While they awaited a decision on their petition for a patent, the Pilgrims looked for friends to underwrite the cost of re-

11. Bradford, *History, I,* p. 60.

moval to the New World. This was the most difficult problem they encountered, for it was perfectly clear that they required outside help. After efforts during 1619 to obtain backing from the London Company failed, they began to look for new sources of financing. At this point, the Dutch made them a proposition about settling in New Netherland, and Thomas Weston, a London ironmonger, also offered support. Weston headed a company of merchant adventurers that had existed for about ten years and was searching for investment opportunities.[12] Because the Dutch offer was uncertain, and because Weston had helped them before, the Pilgrims rejected the Dutch overture and instructed their agents in London, John Carver and Robert Cushman, to make the necessary arrangements with Weston's company.

Early in February 1620, probably through the efforts of Weston, the Pilgrims received a patent to settle in the Virginia grant. Meanwhile talks between the Pilgrim agents and Weston continued. Since Weston and his company were looking primarily for profits, agreement between the adventurers (the men who invested only their money) and the planters (the men going out to settle) proved difficult. The adventurers drove a harder bargain than the Pilgrims had anticipated, and when Carver and Cushman accepted new conditions without consulting the people back in Leyden, angry words passed between Leyden and London.

The Pilgrims had earlier agreed that the planters and adventurers should constitute themselves a joint-stock company for seven years and that all profits and benefits should be held in common during this time. But they had not agreed that houses and improved land, and in particular gardens, should also be common property; they had expected that these would belong from the beginning to the individual planter. Furthermore, they expected that two days in the week would be set aside for each man to work for himself. When news reached Leyden that Cushman and Carver had assented to joint ownership of everything for seven years, a letter was dispatched to the agents ordering them not to exceed the bounds of their commission. Cushman sent back an angry reply, suggesting that, if the Pilgrims wanted to go to America, they had no alternative but to agree to Weston's terms.

With this matter still undecided, those leaving for America

12. Ibid., pp. 99–100; see also Ruth A. McIntyre, *Debts Hopeful and Desperate: Financing the Plymouth Colony* (Plimoth Plantation, 1963), pp. 14–16, 33–34.

boarded the *Speedwell* on July 22, 1620, at Delftshaven, for the voyage to England. Some left their families, all left their friends of a generation; and because a majority of the Church remained, their beloved John Robinson stayed in Leyden. On the deck of the ship, Robinson led them for the last time in prayer and commended them to the protection of the Lord. Then, tears coursing down his cheeks, he stepped ashore, and on a falling tide the Pilgrims sailed for Southampton.

Troubles awaited them there. Fortunately, preparations to fit out the *Mayflower,* which they had chartered to carry them to America, were well under way, and persons recruited by their agents, Carver and Cushman, to join the expedition were already aboard. Some of them, at least, were old friends, and Bradford later remembered the "joyfull wellcome, and mutuall congratulations," when the *Speedwell* arrived.[13] But, in spite of this progress in readying the expedition to sail, the problem of coming to terms with the adventurers remained unresolved. Carver and Cushman had disregarded their instructions and agreed to the alteration of conditions proposed by Weston. But when Weston arrived from London, the Pilgrims insisted that they would not be bound by this agreement, and argued that Weston had no right to alter the conditions which he had first offered. Weston, in turn, promptly stopped all further payments toward their departure for America.

Forced by Weston's intransigence to find £100 to clear the port, the Pilgrims sold some of their provisions and, writing a letter to the adventurers to explain why they refused to sign the agreement, put to sea. Almost at once they had a new disappointment. The *Speedwell,* which they purchased in Holland, leaked so much that her captain refused to continue, and both ships returned to Dartmouth where the *Speedwell* was put on the ways and recaulked. Again they set sail. One hundred leagues from Land's End, leaks in the *Speedwell* forced them to return to Plymouth. Their departure for America had now been delayed nearly a month, and if they were to settle before winter came, they could not risk further postponement. Transferring the provisions and some of the passengers from the *Speedwell* to the *Mayflower,* the company parted, some heading east in the *Speedwell* for London, the rest sailing west for the New World.

13. Bradford, *History, 1,* p. 126.

Plagued by difficulties and disappointments, the Pilgrims persevered. Although they sailed without assurance of continued financial backing from England, faith in themselves and in their God had given them the strength to endure. This resolution would be severely tested in the months ahead.

2

"A Place of Habitation"

WHEN the *Mayflower* dropped anchor in Provincetown Harbor on November 11th, the prospects for successful settlement seemed grim. From the ship the Pilgrims looked upon a wilderness that reached to the edge of the sea. Uncertain as to who or what prowled through its gloom, they knew that the nearest English settlement was hundreds of miles to the south, that no one could help them in the forthcoming struggle to survive. They had no homes to live in, no fort to defend them, no docking facilities to receive them. Moreover, although only one passenger had died on the voyage, confinement for eleven weeks in crowded living conditions, the meager shipboard diet, and an inability to stay dry had already undermined their health. Many of them were now coughing, and in the five weeks the *Mayflower* lay at Provincetown, four perished, including William Bradford's wife, Dorothy. Bradford laconically wrote that she accidentally fell overboard, but he was away from the ship at the time.[1] If Dorothy took her own life, she would not be the last of those facing the desolation of the frontier to do so.

For the first several days as the ship lay at Provincetown, the Pilgrims went ashore to stretch their cramped muscles and to try to regain their strength. Some of the men cut firewood and, despite the absence of fresh water, the women turned to the washing of clothes. The primary concern, however, was to find a place to establish a permanent settlement. The shallop, a small boat

1. C. Mather, *Magnalia, I,* p. 111.

stowed below decks during the crossing and used for sleeping, needed repairs, and rather than wait for their completion, sixteen men, carrying muskets and wearing armor, waded ashore from the longboat on November 15th and set off to investigate an opening (the Pamet River) that could be seen from the ship. Miles Standish commanded this expedition, which proved inconclusive in its efforts at exploration but discovered several baskets filled with corn and buried in the ground by Indians. Standish and his men took some of the corn, and in the spring of the following year the kernels were used for seed. The crop harvested from the seed later saved the plantation from starvation.

A second expedition left to explore the Pamet River after Standish's return. It reported that the place did not offer a satisfactory anchorage for large ships, and on December 6th, after discussion and rejection of the proposal to settle there, ten men sailed in the shallop to search farther west. On December 7th, they investigated Wellfleet Bay and the next morning coasted along the shores of the Cape. That afternoon the sea increased and rain and snow blew in. As conditions worsened, the pilot, Coppin, who had sailed into Cape Cod Bay on an earlier voyage, thought he recognized a harbor opening ahead and steered the shallop for it. The little boat was pounding hard in the heavy seas, and before it could reach the opening the rudder tore loose and the mast shattered and carried away. His eyes straining through the mist for familiar landmarks, Coppin saw breakers ahead and ordered the shallop beached through the surf. The seaman who was attempting to steer with what was left of the rudder had steadier nerves. Ordering the men at the oars to row for the opening, he encouraged them to believe that they would find safety beyond. A few moments later the shallop was riding in the lee of Saquish Head, inside Plymouth Bay, and the terrors of the wild night outside were behind.[2]

The following day the shallop's crew found that the opening through which they had rowed in the night formed the entrance into a bay protected by two arms of land. Reaching southwesterly from the mainland, a barrier of high land separated the bay from the ocean, and off the southern terminus of this barrier (the Gurnet) a short promontory (Saquish Head) projected

2. Bradford, *History, 1,* pp. 173–74; for Samuel Eliot Morison's interpretation of the approach to Plymouth on the night of December 8th, see Bradford, *Of Plymouth Plantation,* S. E. Morison, ed. (New York, 1959), footnote 3, p. 71.

southeast. From the south, a low spit of land, covered with scrub pine, thrust northeasterly off Manomet Bluff. Between the spit and Saquish Head lay the opening to the bay. To the west across a mile and a half of open water, the shallop's crew could see the land rise unevenly from the shore. They were not the first Englishmen to visit Plymouth. John Smith had stopped there in 1614 on his voyage to New England, and in 1619, only a year before the Pilgrims sailed for America, Captain Thomas Dermer anchored in Plymouth Bay. Dermer wrote in his journal that the place would be excellent for a plantation, provided there were at least fifty persons, a necessary number, he believed, for protection against the Indians.[3]

To men who had already spent a month looking for a place to settle, Plymouth also seemed satisfactory. On Saturday, December 9, the crew of the shallop rested on Clark's Island and prepared to observe the Sabbath. On Monday they landed at Plymouth and found fresh water and cleared ground, but they saw no Indians. By December 16th the *Mayflower* swung at anchor in Plymouth Bay.

In the weeks that followed the Pilgrims struggled to survive. Most of them probably continued to live aboard ship, for Captain Jones decided to winter in Plymouth Bay. Nonetheless, weakened by scurvy, chilled by the dampness and cold of winter which penetrated lodging and clothing, men and women sickened and died, and before summer came, nearly half the *Mayflower*'s 102 passengers were dead. Those who kept their health took care of the sick, and when the weather permitted worked ashore; those who died were buried ashore in unmarked graves to prevent the Indians from discovering the weakness of the settlement. In January, fire destroyed the thatched roof of the common storehouse, and with it some of the supplies. Bitterly disappointed— but grateful that the persons asleep in the building had escaped with their lives—they continued their efforts to establish a settlement.

During those grim winter months a few men tried to oppose the elected civil government. Because the patent obtained from the Virginia Company was useless and because some men had threatened disobedience while the *Mayflower* was still at sea, the Pilgrims on November 11th had drawn up and signed the May-

3. Bradford, *History, I,* pp. 206–07.

flower Compact at Provincetown. Forty-one men, including all the free adult males who were passengers, promised to "covenant and combine our selves togeather into a civill body politick . . . and by vertue hearof to enacte, constitute, and frame shuch just and equall laws, ordinances, acts, constitutions, and offices, from time to time, as shall be thought most meete and convenient for the generall good of the Colonie, unto which we promise all due submission and obedience."[4] But a few ignored their promise, and when the existence of the plantation seemed to hang in the balance, they challenged the authority of the elected governor, John Carver. Jamestown experienced the same trouble; authority had temporarily disintegrated there in 1608, and only the assumption of dictatorial power by Captain John Smith had saved the colony from disaster.[5] At Plymouth a majority rallied to the support of the governor, and through Carver's exercise of wisdom and patience, unrest and opposition subsided. Carver survived only long enough to guide Plymouth through this early crisis. He died shortly thereafter and was succeeded as governor by William Bradford.

Early in March, the first signs of spring appeared and, encouraged by nature's promise that winter was ending, the colonists began to prepare their fields for planting. Spring also brought the first Indian visitor to the plantation. On March 16th, Samoset walked out of the forest and spoke to the Pilgrims in their own language. Samoset, whose home was in Maine, had learned to speak English through contact with sailors fishing off the Maine coast. He remained at Plymouth only briefly, but a few days later he returned to prepare for the coming of Massassoit, chief of the Wampanoag people, whose territory extended from Narragansett Bay eastward to the sea. Shortly thereafter Massassoit visited Plymouth where he was received with all the pomp and circumstance the little settlement could muster. Squanto, who had been taken from New England in 1614 by an English sea captain and who had jumped ship four years later to return home, accompanied Massassoit and stayed when Massassoit departed for home. The only known survivor of the Patuxet Indians who, before pestilence had wiped them out in 1617, lived

4. Bradford, *History, 1*, p. 191.
5. John Smith, *A True Relation of Occurrences and Accidents in Virginia* (London, 1608), printed in *Travels and Works of Captain John Smith*, Edward Arber, ed. (Edinburgh, 1910), p. 97.

near Plymouth and whose cleared fields the Pilgrims were using, Squanto showed the Pilgrims how and when to plant and when and where to fish, and until he died in 1622 lived with them as their friend and guide. Bradford called him "a spetiall instrument sent of God for their good beyond their expectations." [6]

When the *Mayflower* sailed for England in April 1621 those who watched from shore must have felt a tug at their hearts as the ship turned down the Bay toward the open sea. Captain Jones had done what he could to help the Pilgrims in that first bleak winter. He waited a month while they decided where to settle. In December, when his men were still healthy, he had allowed his passengers to live aboard while buildings were set up ashore to receive them and their possessions. In spite of the misery they endured and continued to endure, none of the Pilgrims returned to England in the *Mayflower*. They were confident that living conditions were going to improve, and they were not disappointed.

The first summer in New England the Pilgrims fished and hunted and worked on their homes, and in the autumn, after the harvest was in, they celebrated their first thanksgiving. Massasoit, accompanied by some of his warriors, attended and contributed five deer to the festivities. The prospects for the winter, in contrast to those of the previous year, were excellent. Food was plentiful and sufficient to see the plantation through until the following summer. The sickness of the early months had run its course, and all of the settlers were healthy. Seven dwelling houses were completed and preparations for others made. The most powerful Indian chieftain in southeastern New England was their ally. Edward Winslow, writing home to England in the fall of 1621, could assure his readers: "I never in my life remember a more seasonable year than we have here enjoyed; and if we have once but kine, horses and sheep, I make no question, but men might live as contented here as in any part of the world." [7] But Winslow's enthusiasm was premature, as he himself later recognized.

In November 1621 the *Fortune* arrived from England bring-

6. Bradford, *History, I*, p. 202.

7. Edward Winslow, "Letter Sent from New England," Plymouth, December 11, 1621, printed in *Mourt's Relation or Journal of the Plantation of Plymouth* (London, 1622), reprinted in Alexander Young, *Chronicles of the Pilgrim Fathers* (2d ed. Boston, 1844), p. 233.

ing a patent and thirty-six new settlers. The patent was particularly welcome for it gave the Pilgrims the assurance that their settlement was legal. When the *Mayflower* had returned to England in May, Captain Jones carried word that the Pilgrims had settled north of the Virginia grant. Weston and the other adventurers had at once begun efforts to obtain a patent from the Council for New England, a group of noblemen to whom James I in November 1620 had granted all the land in North America between forty and forty-eight degrees. These efforts were successful, and by June 1, 1621, the adventurers had secured a patent made out (as was the patent granted by the Virginia Company) to John Peirce and his associates. Written to promote the settlement of a new plantation and to attract capital, the Peirce patent favored the financial investor rather than the planter. For every person transported to America, it granted 100 acres to Peirce and his associates; to men who came to the plantation at their own expense, it also gave 100 acres; and to each of the adventurers went a direct grant of an additional 1500 acres. For the planters, it held out the promise that after seven years, if the settlement succeeded, the Council would issue a new patent more suited to the needs of an established plantation.

Enthusiasm for the thirty-six settlers arriving on the *Fortune* was more restrained. While the new arrivals were welcome as an addition to the strength of the plantation, they were utterly destitute, and the burden of their support was thrown upon those already settled. The community promptly went on half rations, and Governor Bradford warned the adventurers in England that the coming of the *Fortune* with its indigent passengers would bring famine upon the settlement.

By the spring of 1622 Bradford's mournful prophecy had come true. Instead of the expected supplies, seven more immigrants came late in May with letters from Thomas Weston requesting that the settlers lend the newcomers seed corn and promising further arrivals. Knowing that something must be done to obtain additional food, Bradford sent Edward Winslow early in June to the Maine coast to buy provisions from fishing ships. Winslow's efforts were partly successful, and, while the ship captains had little to spare, they received him kindly, giving him what they could. Late in June the promised arrivals came, and during the months of July and August 1622, Plymouth provided quarters for a company of sixty "lusty men" sent by Weston to begin a new plantation.[8] Weston had not exaggerated when he had warned that many of the newcomers were rude fellows. They came without their families and no one seemed capable of maintaining civil order among them. When they departed in September for Wessagusset (Weymouth), the Pilgrims hoped they had seen the last of them.

A more welcome visitor also stopped at Plymouth in the summer of 1622. John Pory, Secretary of the Virginia Colony, arrived by ship on his way home to England. Arriving after the harvest was in, Pory wrote enthusiastically about the plenty he found at Plymouth. He noted the abundance of waterfowl, eels, lobsters, fruits, turkeys, and fish, and testified to the excellence of the bluefish, reporting that it was the best fish he had ever tasted and required "noe addition of sauce." He thought the harbor "pleasant for aire and prospect," but he did not like the climate, for it was too cold in summer and in an easterly wind a wet fog drifted in from the North Atlantic. Yet he found all the inhabitants healthy. The town itself, he noted, was built on the side of a hill. A great broad street stretched up the hill running from east to west, and on either side were houses constructed of hewn planks. The whole settlement was surrounded by a 2700-foot palisade, and at the time of Pory's visit the settlers were building a fort on the top of the hill. News from Virginia in June 1622 of the dreadful Indian massacre in that colony had reminded them that they must maintain a watchful readiness for trouble. Pory reported that while Plymouth's relations with the Indians had generally been good, "stand they day and night preciselie upon their guarde." [9]

More settlers arrived at Plymouth in 1623 aboard the *Anne* and *Little James*. Alice Southworth, now a widow, was among them; she and her husband had once been members of John Robinson's Leyden Church. Governor Bradford, a widower since 1620, was expecting Mrs. Southworth; he had successfully courted her by mail, and shortly after her arrival they were married. Massassoit, a black wolf's skin thrown over his shoulder and a black blanket girdling his waist, attended with four "kings" and 120 men—who at the groom's request left their bows and arrows at the governor's house. White settler and Indian feasted

8. Bradford, *History, I*, p. 271.

9. John Pory, *John Pory's Lost Description of Plymouth*, Champlain Burrage, ed. (Boston, 1918), p. 43.

on venison provided by the guests and, after eating, the Indians danced for their English friends.[10]

Some of the passengers aboard the *Anne* and *Little James* were not as welcome as Alice Southworth. They were people whose transportation costs to America were not financed by the stock company but who had paid their own way and who were called "particulars" because they had come "on their particular." Their presence introduced a new and dynamic element and required an attempt to integrate into the life of the colony men who did not share its economic burden. After their arrival, the coincidence of political objectives and economic commitment, which had brought at least a measure of stability and harmony to Plymouth, was broken.

The most immediate problem was to decide upon what terms the newcomers should be received. Directed by the adventurers to give these people land and to permit them to work for themselves, Governor Bradford and the company planters assigned home lots to them on the condition that they consent to the laws of the plantation and pay an annual tax. Because they had paid their own way to America, they were free to work for themselves. They were not, however, admitted to political citizenship, and they were also barred from the Indian trade.[11] The basis for discrimination against them is not difficult to understand. Bradford surely reasoned that Plymouth, as a company settlement in which the colonists were engaged in trying to pay off the debts contracted in settlement and to earn a return on the investment, should not allow outsiders to share in the Indian trade, the one substantial source of income then available. Similarly, citizenship depended upon a commitment to these economic goals; those who did not have this commitment should not be given a part in the government of the plantation, since they did not share in its obligations. However reasonable these arguments may have seemed to the company planters, to at least some of "the particulars" they were less compelling. Shortly after their ar-

10. Emanuel Altham to his brother, Sir Edward Altham. Letter #1 undated and not superscribed, endorsed in a later ink, 1622 New England (the date is inaccurate, for Altham did not arrive until the summer of 1623); the letter was in fact written in September 1623. Typescript copies of these letters are in the Historical Manuscript Room of Yale University Library. The letters are now published in *Three Visitors to Early Plymouth*, Sidney James, ed. (Plimoth Plantation, 1963). Quotations are from typescript copies.

11. Bradford, *History*, *I*, pp. 326–27, 393.

rival, disappointed by the rigors of life in America and by their reception at Plymouth, they began to complain.

In March 1624, John Lyford, an ordained minister of the Anglican Church, landed at Plymouth, and although not himself a particular, became the spokesman for their complaints. More than three years had passed since first settlement and the continuing absence of a clergyman had become the cause of growing concern among the adventurers in England. Robert Cushman, Plymouth's agent in London, had written Bradford that he and Edward Winslow, who was temporarily in England on plantation business, had reservations about Lyford's coming, but they had given way to conciliate some of the adventurers. In spite of their lack of enthusiasm, neither Cushman nor Winslow thought any harm would come from it.[12]

According to Bradford, when Lyford arrived, "he saluted them with that reverence and humilitie as is seldome to be seen." [13] He joined the Plymouth Church, and in his confession renounced all national and diocesan churches, thus cutting his ties with the Anglican Church. Plymouth welcomed him at first. The Church allowed him to do some teaching and the Pilgrim leaders gave him special consideration befitting a man of God. They consulted him on important business and granted him a larger amount of food than went to others.

But the Plymouth Church still hoped that John Robinson would come to the New World and refused to ordain Lyford minister. Perhaps disappointed in this expectation, perhaps for other reasons, Lyford became the center of mounting opposition to Bradford's leadership, and wrote letters back to England charging Bradford and the Plymouth Church with discrimination, waste, and poor management. After Lyford posted the letters in a ship about to depart for England, Bradford, who had learned of Lyford's actions, rowed out to the ship, opened the letters, and made copies of them. He then returned to the shore and for a time said nothing; but when at a subsequent date Lyford and some others set up a second church at Plymouth, Bradford summoned Lyford to appear before the men of the plantation. Before this body, called a general court, Bradford produced the letters and asked Lyford for an explanation; Lyford stated that he had merely written the charges given him

12. Ibid., pp. 357–58.
13. Ibid., p. 380.

by others, but when he sought corroboration for this testimony, no one came to his support. Deserted by his erstwhile companions, Lyford then confessed to his perfidy and pleaded for forgiveness. In spite of his confession and forgiveness, he soon was again writing to England repeating his previous charges and, in particular, criticizing religious separatism at Plymouth. This could not be forgiven, and in the spring of 1625 the General Court sentenced Lyford to banishment.

John Lyford's conduct and treatment at Plymouth have been points of controversy ever since. Critics of the Pilgrims have defended Lyford and argued that his Anglican practices were unpalatable to the Pilgrims, who hounded the man out of the plantation. William Hubbard, a seventeenth-century Massachusetts clergyman and historian, first rallied to Lyford's defense, noting that the beginning of the quarrel between Lyford and the Pilgrims came over the baptizing of a man who had not joined the Plymouth Church.[14] Bradford's history is the single contemporary account. If the Plymouth governor's narrative is accurate, Lyford's banishment was justifiable, for he was guilty of treachery. In his letters to England, Lyford appealed to the adventurers to send over a sufficient number of people to overthrow Bradford's leadership, and he attacked the principles of Congregational worship for which the Pilgrims had themselves left England. It hardly was to be expected that he would escape the wrath of the colony's leaders. Nor could the plantation yet tolerate factionalism; it was too new, its survival still dependent upon the preservation of internal unity.

Lyford's difficulties and his charge that "diuers poor souls" did not enjoy the means to salvation are sometimes cited to show that the significant division at Plymouth in 1624 was between church members and non-church members and that the plantation was a small Bible commonwealth where the "saints," a minority, dictated to the "strangers." A careful reading of Bradford does not support this contention; the division seems rather to have come between the company planters and the men who paid their own transportation costs to Plymouth. The basis for dissension, which Lyford tried to exploit, was, in other words, economic, not religious. Lyford charged the Pilgrims with religious irregularities and discrimination, but Lyford was trying to win the sympa-

14. William Hubbard, *A General History of New England* (Cambridge, 1815), pp. 93–94.

thies of the adventurers in England. Accusations of religious error at a time when dissenters were encountering increasing persecution in England were the one means of accomplishing his purpose.

Lyford's reports that the church members would allow none but themselves to live at Plymouth is absurd, and is refuted by his own complaint that the church was but a small minority of the plantation. An accusation that the Pilgrims discriminated against men who were not separatists is equally nonsense. Before the *Mayflower* sailed, Robinson had begun to lead his church back from a position of rigid separation from other churches, and for the Pilgrims to discriminate against nonseparatists, when many of the people of the plantation were probably nonseparatists, would have been sheer folly. Lyford's charge that some were denied the means of salvation was in one sense true, for unlike the Anglican Church, which did not attempt to distinguish between the elect and the damned, the Plymouth Church allowed only men and women who seemed to show evidence of regeneration to become members. Yet anyone who convinced the church that he or she was one of the elect could join. Moreover, to convince the church that one was a saint was apparently not too difficult, and, after Lyford departed, at least some of his supporters became members.[15] Neither did discrimination in the enjoyment of the sacraments against those who were not saints then exist at Plymouth. With no minister ordained to the church, there could be no enjoyment of the sacraments. Members and nonmembers alike were required to attend the services conducted by Elder Brewster, so no one could argue that he or she was denied a chance to participate in the organized worship of God. The fact that everyone was required to worship according to Congregational principles undoubtedly irked some, but the Pilgrims had not come to America to establish freedom of religion; they had come instead to live and worship in the way they believed God required of men.

Of the settlers who arrived aboard the *Anne* and *Little James*, and from whom Lyford apparently drew his support, some were not only destitute of food and clothing, but were also wholly unsuited for life in America. Robert Cushman wrote from England that it worried him to see "so weake a company" sail for the

15. Bradford, *History, I*, p. 406.

plantation.[16] A number of the people who came on the two ships were known to the Pilgrims and were welcomed as old friends; but for those who came on their own, hoping to find a better life in America, Plymouth was a bitter disappointment. Before they had lived in the colony for three months, they had begun to complain. Governor Bradford wrote to the adventurers in September 1623: "Touching those which came unto us in ther pertikular, we have received them in as kindly maner as we could, according to our abilitie and offered them as favorable termes as we could . . . yett they are sundrie of them discouraged I know not whether by the countrie (of which they have no triall) or rather for want of those varietis which England affords." [17] Some indeed were so discouraged that they left Plymouth, but others remained and forwarded their complaints to England. They objected to the diversity of religion at the plantation, to the "neglect of family duties on the Lord's Day," to the want of sacraments, to the inadequate provision for the secular education and catechizing of children. They charged the Pilgrims with negligence in enforcing equal payment of taxes and they complained about the location of Plymouth. The water was "not wholsome," the ground was "barren and doth bear no grasse," the fish did "not take salt to keepe sweete," the country was "anoyed with foxes and woules," the Dutch were too close, the people too thievish, the mosquitoes unbearable.[18] Some had come to America expecting to find a land of milk and honey. They had not found it, and, unwilling to blame themselves for their misfortunes, they had shifted the blame to the country and on those already there. John Lyford was a natural leader for their discontent.

Like other early settlements in America, Plymouth was plagued by those who came expecting to find ease and happiness and found only hard work and discomfort. In 1624, to discourage further such arrivals, Edward Winslow warned that Plymouth was not Elysium: "Some there be that thinking altogether of their present wants they enjoy there [England], and not dreaming of any there [America], through indiscretion plunge themselves into a deeper sea of misery." Winslow added:

16. Ibid., p. 318.

17. William Bradford and Isaac Allerton, Plymouth, Sept. 8, 1623; no address given, but context shows that it was sent to the adventurers in London, printed in *American Historical Review, 8* (1902/3), p. 301.

18. Bradford, *History, I,* pp. 363–66.

I write not these things to dissuade any that shall seriously, upon due examination, set themselves to further the glory of God, and the honor of our country, in so worthy an enterprise, but rather to discourage such as with too great lightness undertake such courses; who peradventure strain themselves and their friends for their passage thither, and are no sooner there, then seeing their foolish imagination made void, are at their wits' end, and would give ten times so much for their return, if they could procure it; and out of such discontented passions and humors, spare not to lay that imputation upon the country, and others, which themselves deserve.[19]

The passions generated by the Lyford incident tend to obscure and confuse its historical significance. Whether Governor Bradford dealt unjustly with Lyford is not ultimately as important as the fact that he successfully weathered this challenge to his leadership, a crisis that could have split the plantation and brought disaster and failure to the colony. Although the Leyden Pilgrims were by 1624 a minority of the plantation, the Governor retained the support of the majority of the settlers in his struggle with Lyford. He retained their support because he had realized the need in America to attract and hold the loyalty of the colonists.

For more than a decade Bradford, Brewster, and the others who came from Leyden had lived as exiles, as people apart from the society around them. Forced by their separation to draw strength from each other, they knew that factionalism could not be tolerated. Moreover, they also knew that in a group cut adrift from the rest of society, while the need for strong leadership was critical, confidence in that leadership was essential. Before the Pilgrims sailed from Southampton, John Robinson had warned: "And as men are carfull not to have a new home shaken with any violence before it be well settled and the parts firmly knite, so be you, I besheech you, brethren, much more carfull, that the house of God which you are and are to be, be not shaken with unnecessarie novelties or other oppositions at the first setling therof."[20]

Governor Bradford undoubtedly remembered Robinson's ad-

19. Edward Winslow, *Good Newes from New England* (London, 1624), printed in Alexander Young, *Chronicles of the Pilgrim Fathers* (Boston, 1844), p. 373.
20. Bradford, *History, I*, p. 134.

vice. He believed in the vigorous exercise of leadership and, in consultation with the men whom he trusted, he made the decisions at Plymouth. But Bradford also did not forget that, in the absence of police power, he needed the confidence of the men who settled the plantation. Had he forgotten this, Plymouth could well have destroyed itself, and the landing of the Pilgrim Fathers have been only one more in a series of dreary failures to establish permanent settlement in America. As it was, Emanuel Altham, captain of the *Little James,* was not very sanguine about the future of the settlement. He thought that what hindered the plantation most was the type and character of the people settled there. Over half the people were women and children, and "diuers of the rest are very vnwillinge, soe that only the burden lieth one the shoulders of some few whoe are both honest wise and Carefull, and if it were not for them few the plantation would fall and come to no thing." [21] That this did not happen was in no small part due to the political acumen of its governor.

Five years after the settlement of Plymouth the Pilgrims could look with pride upon their accomplishments. They had somehow summoned the strength and courage to survive during the first terrible winter. In the months that followed, they had built their plantation and there was no longer any doubt that theirs was a permanent settlement, the first in America north of Jamestown. They had thwarted an attempt to overthrow their political and religious control of the colony, an attempt which, had it succeeded, would have nullified the very purpose of their exile. In surviving these first years they had successfully met the greatest challenge of their lives. Their continuing presence on the New England coast was proof.

21. Emanuel Altham to Sir Edward Altham. Letter #2 undated and not superscribed, endorsed in a later ink, 1621 New England; written from Plymouth probably in March 1624.

3

"This Way is No More"

Jоhn Lyford's letters charging religious irregularities had serious repercussions among the adventurers in England and led directly to the break-up of the stock company which had financed settlement. Expecting a return on their investment, the adventurers were disappointed by the consistent failure of the plantation to return a profit. More disturbing yet, instead of the anticipated flow of wealth from America to England, they continued to underwrite the shipment of goods to Plymouth in order to keep the colony going. Some saw Lyford's complaints as justifiable reasons for refusing Plymouth further support.

The Pilgrims had for some time been aware of the discontent in England. The settlement was scarcely a year old when the adventurers began to complain, and in July 1621, Thomas Weston expressed his displeasure that the *Mayflower* had returned to England empty. Anxious to reassure Weston and the other investors, the Pilgrims worked feverishly that summer and autumn, and in December, the *Fortune* sailed for England carrying clapboards, two hogsheads of beaver, otter skins, and a signed copy of the financial agreement rejected at Southampton a year earlier. Letters from Leyden pointing up a continuing dependence upon the adventurers for transportation to America, and an understanding of their own need for further support had finally brought the Pilgrims to accept Weston's terms. The *Fortune* was not well-named. Somewhere in the North Atlantic a French warship captured the ship and escorted her into the Ile de

Dieu, where the French seized the cargo valued at £400. It was more than two years before another ship laden with furs and clapboards arrived safely in England.

In the intervening months, factionalism disrupted the company of adventurers. In 1622, Thomas Weston relinquished his interest in the business and advised the Pilgrims to dissolve their ties with the company. Weston warned that opposition had already developed to helping the plantation further or to transporting the people still in Holland who wanted to come to America. The same year, another one of the adventurers, John Peirce, managed to have the patent which had been granted to the colony in June 1621 canceled. Obtaining a new patent made out to himself, he sailed for New England, where he intended to establish himself as lord proprietor of Plymouth Plantation. A storm, however, drove Peirce's ship back to England, and upon his return, the other adventurers, who had by now discovered what Peirce was up to, forced him to assign the new patent to them.

Even after Weston left the company and Peirce's plans were frustrated, troubles among the adventurers continued. John Robinson wrote from Leyden in 1623 warning of the division in the company. A few, he thought, "are absolutely bent for us," and a few "are our bitter profesed adversaries"; the rest, he wrote, had no strong convictions either way.[1] One year later, burdened by the cost of keeping the plantation supplied with manufactured goods, disappointed by the failure of a fishing vessel sent to Plymouth in 1623 and from whose operation great profits were expected, and angered by the reports contained in Lyford's letters, the majority of adventurers agreed to withhold further support from the plantation.[2]

The reasons given for abandoning Plymouth were religious. Charging the colonists with separatism, they piously stated that "they should sinne against God in building up shuch a people." They agreed to reunite only if the Plymouth Church renounced separatism and if the planters allowed them equal voice in governing the settlement.[3] Several of the adventurers, however, stood by the original agreement, and one, James Sherley, a London goldsmith, thought there were other reasons many of his

1. Bradford, *History, I*, p. 370.
2. Ibid., p. 419.
3. Ibid., p. 423.

former associates had quit: "First and mainly, the many losses and crosses at sea; and abuses of seamen, which have caused us to rune into so much charge, debts and ingagementes as our estates and means were not able to goe on without impovrishing ourselves." Sherley added that the factionalism which had rent the company for the past two years had broken wide open and destroyed any hope for further cooperation.[4]

To unravel the threat of religion from that of financial loss is now impossible. A few of those who abandoned the settlement may have been staunch Anglicans disenchanted by the Plymouth Church's refusal to ordain Lyford as minister and by his reports of separatism. Others who were Puritans may have decided that for reasons of conscience they too could not continue their backing of a separatist plantation. But probably in the balance, as Sherley himself believed, economic considerations were paramount to the religious for most investors. Of the three adventurers who continued to play major roles as creditors of the plantation after 1627, two, James Sherley and Richard Andrews, are known to have been Puritans.[5]

Although the colony still needed help from England, Governor Bradford, arguing that many of the settlers had refused to work for the company, utilized the split among the adventurers to press for a full division of assets. This proposal was unacceptable to the adventurers who had not withdrawn from the company in 1624 and Bradford's efforts to cut the economic ties between the planters and remaining adventurers failed at first. Miles Standish, whom Bradford sent to England to urge the distribution of assets, arrived in the middle of an outbreak of the plague and was able to accomplish little. Sherley and the others, even if Puritan sympathies had affected their decision to stand by the plantation, were interested in the realization of profits and did not want a liquidation. When Sherley informed Bradford that a majority of the adventurers had deserted the enterprise, he advised that "all shuch things as ther [these] appertaine to the generall be kept and preserved togeather," and warned that "it must rest in you to make all good again." The colony's debt, Sherley believed, was about £1400. Nonetheless, convinced that

4. Ibid., pp. 426–33.
5. James Sherley to William Bradford, London, December 27, 1627, *Governor William Bradford's Letter Book,* reprinted from the *Mayflower Descendant* (Boston, 1906), p. 28.

the existing relationship was unsatisfactory, Governor Bradford continued to urge a final dissolution of the company, and in 1627 Sherley and his associates finally agreed. For £1800 they sold all their interest in the plantation to the settlers. Bradford thought the agreement fair, although he was not sure where Plymouth was going to find £200 to meet the annual installment payments.[6]

Liquidation of the joint-stock company in 1627 did not alter existing economic patterns at Plymouth; this change came four years earlier. Until 1623 the Pilgrims had attempted to live in a communal relationship of economic equality; individuals worked not for themselves but for the company and all assets were divided equally. But in 1623 the planters asked Bradford to permit men to work for themselves and pay a tax to the plantation. After consultation with Brewster and others the Governor agreed and assigned each family a plot of land for present use; the extent depended upon the size of the family. All assets, however, continued to be held in common and land could not be conveyed by inheritance.

Bradford believed that the incentive of property was important. Communal ownership of property, he later wrote, had produced confusion and discontent and had not given the stimulus necessary for the physical improvement of the colony. At Plymouth some men had not exerted themselves because tangible evidence was lacking that their efforts in any way contributed directly to their personal well-being: "The experience that was had in the commone course, . . . may well evince they [the] vanitie of that conceite of Platos and other ancients, applauded by some of later times: that the taking away of propertie and bringing in communitie into a comonewealth, would make them happy and florishing; as if they were wiser than God." Bradford continued: "For the yong men that were most able and fitte for labour and service did repine that they should spend their time and streingth to worke for other mens wives and children with out any recompence." A system which permitted each man to work for himself, the Governor believed, proved more satisfactory for the individual and for the plantation; "for it made all hands very industrious, so as much more corne was planted than

6. Bradford, *History, I*, p. 428. The Pilgrims also assumed £600 of the £1400 owed in 1624. See McIntyre, *Debts Hopeful and Desperate*, p. 32.

other waise would have bene by any means the Gov[erno]r or any other could use and saved him a great deall of trouble and gave farr better content." [7]

Bradford wrote long before anyone was interested in defending the free enterprise system. Moreover, "communism" in early Plymouth was not communism at all, but an extreme form of exploitive capitalism in which all the fruits of men's labor were shipped across the seas and from which there seemed little tangible benefit. In the sense that communal economic patterns had existed at Plymouth, Governor Bradford thought they had not been a success.

Although dissolution of the company did not change the pattern of economic life, it did considerably alter the economic structure. In 1627 the common possession of all assets ended and the planters were at last free from joint ownership with those shadowy figures across the Atlantic.

The problems the plantation confronted were two: to whom and in what proportion should the company properties be divided, and what plan should be adopted to pay off the debt? Governor Bradford called the company planters into general court and made the following proposals: he proposed that all adult men who "were either heads of families, or single young men, that were of ability and free" should share in the division of property, even if they were not former members of the joint-stock company. Bradford explained why:

> First, they considered that they had need of men and strength both for defense and carrying on of bussinesses. 2ly most of them had borne their parts in former miseries and wants with them, and therfore (in some sort) but equall to partake in a better condition, if the Lord be pleased to give it. But cheefly they saw not how peace would be preserved without so doing, but danger and great disturbance might grow to their great hurte and prejudice other wise.[8]

Bradford further proposed that a single man be given one share in the company properties and a head of family one share for each member of the household. Ownership of a share or shares would then entitle a person to a certain amount of property (de-

7. Bradford, *History, 1,* pp. 300–02.
8. Bradford, *History, 2,* p. 8.

pendent upon the number of shares held) when the assets were divided. Each man owning a share or shares would, in turn, be liable proportionate to the number of shares held, toward the debt owed to the English adventurers. Fifty-eight men shared in the division of assets in 1627 and were subsequently known as "The Purchasers" or "Old Comers." [9]

First, the plantation divided the livestock. The settlers were grouped in twelve companies totaling 156 people and including slightly less than forty families; each company received a cow and two goats. In January 1628 came an allotment or division of land. To forestall complaints, division was by lottery, and all acreage surveyed and considered adequate before distribution began. Since meadow was in short supply, all meadowland continued to be held in common. Fishing, fowling, and access to water remained free to all men. In the division of housing, the governor and four or five others were allowed to keep their homes; the rest of the dwellings were valued, and the man who lived in a better home paid an equalizing fee to the man who lived in a poorer one. Although such a property division could have sparked explosive dissension, Bradford handled the matter well. The decision to include persons who were not former members of the company and the attempt to divide equally undercut any basis for discontent. According to the Governor: "This distribution gave generally good contente and setled mens minds." [10]

Bradford, however, was worried. He feared that dividing the responsibility for the plantation's debts among so many would make it difficult if not impossible to meet the annual sum of £200 promised to the English creditors, and he was afraid that the settlers would be unwilling to raise the money to finance further emigration from Leyden. He therefore decided that, to liquidate the debt and bring over the people still in Holland, he and a few of the other principal men would have to assume personal responsibility for the financial obligations of the plantation. He summoned the colonists and offered his terms. He and eleven associates, who would be known as "the undertakers," would contract to pay the full purchase price of £1800 and any other debts the settlement owed at the time. In return the colonists

---

9. Ibid., pp. 8–9. *Records of the Colony of New Plymouth,* Nathaniel Shurtleff and Daniel Pulsifer, eds. (12 vols. Boston, 1856–61), *2,* 177, hereafter cited as *Ply. Col. Rec.*

10. Bradford, *History, 2,* 8–12; *Ply Col. Rec., 12,* pp. 9–13.

would grant Bradford and his associates a monopoly of the Indian trade for six years and would pay an annual tax of three bushels of corn or six pounds of tobacco. (This tax was in fact never paid.) Fearing opposition at the time, Bradford did not communicate his plan to bring the Leyden group over. The colonists agreed to accept this arrangement, and the Plymouth Undertakers, Bradford, Standish, Allerton, Winslow, Brewster, John Howland, John Alden, and Thomas Prince, and the four associates in England, James Sherley, John Beauchamp, Richard Andrews, and Timothy Hatherly, became responsible for the financial obligations of the plantation.[11]

The plan to transport the Leyden families was satisfactorily completed. In August 1629 thirty-five persons arrived at Salem on the ships that carried John Endecott and the advance party to found the Massachusetts colony, and in May 1630 a second group from Leyden landed at Salem. Efforts to secure a new patent from the Council for New England also were successful. William Bradford and his associates replaced John Peirce as grantee and colony boundaries were established superseding the provision granting 100 acres for each settler.

But while the undertakers were able to bring over the Leyden families and obtain a new patent, the hopes of liquidating Plymouth's debt did not have such a happy conclusion. By 1631 it had mushroomed to nearly £6000. Some of this, of course, the undertakers had knowingly incurred. The cost of transporting the people from Leyden was more than £500 and the cost of procuring the patent saddled Plymouth with further expense.[12] Part of the debt, however, came as the result of an unsuccessful fishing and trading expedition to which Isaac Allerton, Plymouth's agent in England, committed the undertakers without their knowledge. Bradford suspected that some of these ventures were begun with the expectation that if they proved successful, the Plymouth undertakers need not share in the profits; however, when the ventures failed, they were to share the losses. Allerton had begun, probably in 1627, to trade on his own, and by 1630 was using undertaker credit to finance his own enterprises. When early evidence reached Bradford of Allerton's personal profit, the governor chose to ignore it and earnestly hoped the agent would be more circumspect in the future. But by 1630 Allerton was no

11. Bradford, *History, 2,* pp. 29–30; *Bradford's Letter Book,* p. 40.
12. Bradford, *History, 2,* pp. 67, 130.

longer content with doing business on a small scale. He hired a ship and charged the cost to the undertakers. This was too much and Allerton was fired; but not before serious damage was done.

During the following six years, James Sherley handled the plantation's financial affairs in England. Sherley may not have cheated the undertakers, but when in 1636 Richard Andrews and John Beauchamp wrote from London and requested that Plymouth begin to pay its debts, Bradford and his associates were astonished. Between 1631 and 1636, according to Bradford's reckoning, they had shipped more than £10,000 in beaver and otter skins to England; yet here were two of the London partners complaining that they had not received payment. Sherley, to whom the beaver and otter had been consigned, was discharged from his position as factor, and the next year Andrews initiated action against him in Chancery Court.[13]

By the mid-1630s Plymouth's need for a business connection in England had lessened. The colony had expanded and had begun to prosper. To the north, settlement of Massachusetts Bay and burgeoning commercial activity at Boston meant the existence of a market forty rather than 3000 miles away. After they discharged Sherley, the Plymouth undertakers decided to make an end to the business once and for all, and began efforts to achieve a settlement with their English creditors. The negotiations dragged on for six years until finally in 1642, with the help of Massachusetts intermediaries—who took the opportunity to have a major part of Plymouth's debt assigned as a gift to the Bay Colony—a sum was agreed upon and eventually paid. To pay this debt, Bradford and several others were ultimately forced to sell portions of their real estate holdings.[14]

Thus ended a business in which the colonists were certainly the financial losers. That they paid their debts and did not repudiate them is to their credit. Yet Plymouth had a real obligation to the men in England who had financed the plantation; at least some of them had been good friends to the little settlement. Sherley may have profited at Plymouth's expense, but without him the plantation would have faced perilous and uncertain times after

13. Bradford himself admitted that part of the trouble stemmed from poorly kept accounts. See ibid., pp. 229–30; Massachusetts Historical Society *Proceedings*, Ser. II, *45* (Boston, 1912), pp. 611–23.

14. Bradford, *History, 2*, pp. 260, 288–300; *Winthrop Papers, 1645–1649*, Massachusetts Historical Society, *5* (Boston, 1947), pp. 2–4.

the majority of the adventurers quit in 1625. Plymouth remembered the adventurers gratefully. In 1660 the colony General Court ordered £20 sent to Mr. Ling, "one of the Marchant Venterors att our first beginings, being fallen to decay and haueing felt great extremity and poverty." [15]

By 1627 people had lived at Plymouth for seven years and the plantation was beginning to take on a look of permanence. Isaac DeRasieres, Secretary of the Dutch settlement at New Netherland, visited Plymouth that autumn. He wrote that a crossroad, running north to a little brook and south toward the plantation fields, bisected the great street leading up the hill to the fort, and where the two intersected, the colonists had built a square enclosure upon which they mounted four small cannon to sweep along the streets of the town. Eight-foot pales still enclosed the whole settlement. The houses were built of hewn planks and behind the homes were gardens fenced at the side and back with planks to keep the animals out. Many of the houses had thatch roofs, although shortly after DeRasieres' visit, the settlers voted to lessen the danger of a general conflagration by prohibiting its future use. The overall impression was one of neatness and DeRasieres thought the houses and courtyards aligned in good order.[16]

While DeRasieres was at Plymouth he attended public worship. The meeting was held on the ground floor of the fort upon the hill, and the plantation assembled to the beating of a drum. The men, each wearing a cloak and carrying a musket, fell into line three abreast before Captain Standish's door and, led by a sergeant, the column marched to the fort. Behind tramped Governor Bradford dressed in a long robe; to his right was Brewster, to his left Standish, sidearms buckled to his waist and carrying a cane. Each man at meeting placed his arms near him, for, DeRasieres noted with interest, the colonists apparently never relaxed their guard.

Both DeRasieres and an earlier visitor, John Pory, Secretary of the Virginia Colony, took care to comment on the caliber of the people they encountered at Plymouth. Although Bradford re-

15. *Ply. Col. Rec., 3*, p. 191.

16. Isaac DeRasieres to Samuel Bloomaert, 1628, in *Narratives of New Netherland. 1609–1664*, J. Franklin Jameson, ed. (New York, 1909), pp. 111–12; *Ply. Col. Rec., 12*, p. 8.

peatedly complained about the type of people who came to Plymouth between 1621 and 1623, Pory, visiting in 1622, thought the people of a higher quality than those he knew in Virginia. DeRasieres believed that the Indians in the neighborhood of Plymouth conducted themselves better than the Indians at home, apparently because the English set a better example.[17]

Visitors to Plymouth showed less enthusiasm for the colony's economic prospects. Basic to the existence of a settled family plantation in the New World was a soil sufficient for the raising of crops. The soil at Plymouth was not good. John Pory, accustomed to the black loam of Virginia, complained that he found the ground at Plymouth rocky; and even in comparison to the land a little further west in New England, it was poor.[18] In fact, so disheartened did some become with farming at Plymouth that between 1631 and 1645 people were continually leaving the town to settle elsewhere in the colony. Yet the soil at Plymouth raised sufficient produce to keep the settlement going. When a few of the inhabitants moved in 1644 from Plymouth to Eastham, one who stayed behind noted that people left not because of want but because they sought better lands.[19] Plymouth after 1623 grew its own food and had some corn left over to trade with the Indians. Nonetheless, the export of agricultural products could not alone provide the basis for substantial prosperity.

In the first years of settlement, Plymouth expected great profits from fishing. There were plenty of fish in New England waters as practically every visitor to the country could testify. Emanuel Altham, who came over on the *Little James* in 1623, wrote home: "And first to speake of the fishinge that is in this country, inded it is beyond beleefe. . . ."[20] Recognition of the profits to be made fishing the banks of the western North Atlantic had existed in Europe before 1600, and annually a large fishing fleet sailed for North America. But Plymouth never found fishing profitable. Bradford too had high expectations for fishing but he was quickly disillusioned. In 1625 he advised Plymouth's agent in England not to promote fishing ventures for they drew

17. *Narratives of New Netherland*, pp. 112–13; Pory, *Description*, p. 42.
18. Pory, *Description*, p. 49; A Short Account of the Present State of New England, 1690, Miscellaneous Bound Manuscripts, Massachusetts Historical Society, Boston.
19. *Plymouth Church Records 1620–1859* (2 vols. New York, 1920), *I*, p. 84.
20. Emanuel Altham to Sir Edward Altham, September, 1623.

men and money from more beneficial employments.[21] Perhaps because of bad luck in the early years, probably because the plantation (after the liquidation of the joint-stock company in 1627) lacked the capital to build the ships and to sustain losses, perhaps because most of the settlers at Plymouth were not sailors and did not want to make their livelihood from the sea, the plantation did not become a major fishing port. Plymouth also tried exporting clapboards, and attempts were made to manufacture salt, but neither was an economic success. The important sources of revenue were beaver skins shipped to England and, after 1630, the sale of livestock to Massachusetts settlers.

The beaver trade began not long after first settlement. In the early autumn of 1621 the plantation shallop sailed into Massachusetts Bay to explore and traffic with the natives. Without goods to barter (apparently none of the Pilgrims had foreseen much potential in the Indian trade), the shallop's crew dug into their pockets and were able to return to the plantation with a few beaver pelts. Thereafter, for fifteen years Plymouth traders were active from Long Island to Maine. Permanent trading posts were built on the Penobscot and Kennebec Rivers in Maine, at Manomet south and west of Cape Cod in the present town of Bourne, and on the Connecticut River north of Hartford. From these posts, factors operated the year round, bargaining and haggling with the Indians, trading tools and cloth for fur. So successful were the colony's activities that Governor John Winthrop of Massachusetts indignantly protested in 1634 that Plymouth exercised control over all the important fur regions in New England. Bradford's own statement that between 1631 and 1636 more than £10,000 in beaver and otter skins were shipped to England indicates that the trading enterprises prospered.[22]

By 1636, however, the days of great profits in the fur trade were already ending for Plymouth. In 1634 the French captured the trading post at Penobscot; efforts to retake it verged on comic opera and ended in fiasco. Two years later, settlement along the Connecticut River meant the eventual abandonment of the trade there. Even Kennebec profits declined and in 1638 some favored closing that post. Part of the sentiment favoring retirement from Kennebec can be attributed to a new source of

---

21. *Bradford's Letter Book*, p. 13.
22. *Winthrop Papers, 1631–1637, 3* (Boston, 1943), p. 167; Bradford, *History*, 2, pp. 229–30.

profit, the sale of livestock, a market even more lucrative than the Indian trade.

The year 1629 marked the arrival of the Massachusetts Bay Company Puritans, and Plymouth, which had been the largest settlement in New England, became a place of secondary importance. The colonization of Massachusetts, however, gave Plymouth a strong economic boost. Plymouth settlers had owned livestock since 1624, but in the absence of an external market, the animals could not provide a source of money income. The settlement of comparatively wealthy immigrants in the Massachusetts Bay area, meant that for the first time Plymouth enjoyed a nearby market. And with a continuous influx of newcomers into Massachusetts between 1630 and 1640, the raising of livestock became very profitable. By 1638 a farmer was asking and getting £20, and even more, for a cow; the price of a milk-goat was £3, and some sold for £4; even corn was at 6 shillings a bushel.[23] From the sale of its agricultural produce Plymouth prospered, and as men prospered, their need for additional land increased.

23. Bradford, *History, 2,* pp. 269–71.

4

"Liberty to Go and Seek Out a Convenient Place or Two or Three"

Until the settlement of Massachusetts opened up new markets and brought prosperity to Plymouth, the amount of acreage in use in the colony remained small. When the colonists met to liquidate the joint-stock company in 1627, they agreed to allow each adult male (servants were not included) to share in the distribution of land. The number of shares which an individual received was determined by the number of persons, excluding servants, who were resident in the household; each share entitled the owner to twenty acres of land. With marketing opportunities virtually nonexistent, however, there was little immediate pressure to take up land and place it in cultivation. For the purpose of keeping settlement intact, the planters therefore agreed that those men whose lots lay closest to the town would share their land with those whose lots were farther away.[1] After 1630 the opening of new markets thirty miles to the north in the Massachusetts Bay Colony caused mounting opposition to a continuance of this policy. The settlers at Plymouth wanted more and better land, and they became anxious to take up the full acreage divided among them in 1627. Some of the lots granted in 1627 lay across Plymouth Bay and to farm them would require permanent settlement there.

1. Bradford, *History*, 2, p. 11.

Governor Bradford and others watched the beginning of a plantation across the Bay at Duxbury with decided misgivings and tried to restrain the exodus from Plymouth. The Plymouth Church continued to expect men who farmed at Duxbury to return to the village on the Sabbath. People who lived across the Bay found it difficult to return weekly, especially in the winter, and the expectation that servants might work the lands at Duxbury while the owners remained at Plymouth was not practical. In 1632 the church reluctantly bowed before the inevitable and dismissed the families settled in Duxbury. The emigration from Plymouth, however, continued, and in 1633 the General Court, concerned over the declining number of inhabitants, required all non-residents to relinquish claims to one acre lots in Plymouth.[2] The Court hoped this action would make the town more attractive to people arriving in the Massachusetts Colony in search of a place to settle.

The systematic maintenance of land records at Plymouth began in 1635, and during the four years that followed, more than five companies of settlers and 130 individuals received land. Of the five companies, four consisted of families who left the Massachusetts Colony to settle Scituate, Sandwich, Taunton, and Yarmouth; the fifth included a number of Scituate people who, unhappy with prospects there and anxious to move to the Cape, eventually settled at Barnstable. Of the individuals who received land, some were newcomers to the colony, anxious to set up housekeeping in one of the established towns; others were men who had settled earlier but now felt the need for additional acreage. About half were termed freemen, a word used to designate political citizenship, including the right to vote and to hold colony office.[3] The size of grants to individuals varied, ranging from a few acres to several hundred. But except for one large grant to four adventurers, no one appears to have received more

2. *Ply. Col. Rec., I*, p. 17.
3. Ibid., pp. 42–116. Because of occasional lack of first name, of possible confusion between fathers and sons with the same names, I have generally refrained from using exact figures, since they could imply an accuracy that I believe is not warranted. In this particular instance, of 138 men who were granted land, sixty-six were freemen. Failure to become a freeman, therefore, did not seem to limit a person's chances for land. On the other hand, the average size of grants made to freemen, when this information could be obtained, suggests that the size of their grants was larger than the size of those made to nonfreemen.

than 300 acres at one time; most grants were considerably smaller.[4]

Until 1639 the governor and seven assistants, elected annually by the freemen and sitting as the Court of Assistants, exercised control over distribution of the colony's lands. This court was the executive instrument of the government and conducted the business of the colony when the General Court of Freemen was not in session, but it was not in this role that the Court of Assistants acted when it exercised jurisdiction over Plymouth's lands.

The colony patent of 1629 conferred title to all land within its limits upon William Bradford and his "associates." Just who the "associates" included is no longer entirely clear: the term could have referred to the "undertakers" who actually paid the costs of securing the new patent. It probably meant the people who bought out the joint-stock company in 1627 and were thereafter known as the Purchasers.[5] Between 1633, when the colony began keeping a permanent record of election results, and 1640, a majority of the persons elected in each year to sit on the Court of Assistants were Purchasers. Bradford himself, either as governor or as one of the assistants, was annually elected to the Court.[6] When the Court distributed Plymouth's lands it apparently acted on behalf of the Purchasers of 1627. The terms of the settlement by which Bradford and the Court of Assistants subsequently surrendered jurisdiction over Plymouth's lands to the colony freemen tend to bear this out.

No evidence exists to suggest that before 1636 the Court of Assistants' right to distribute land was forcefully challenged. In 1636 the October session of the General Court of Freemen acknowledged the Court of Assistants' control of colony lands and ordered people who wanted grants to take their requests to this court. But some opposition to a continuance of this policy was forming, and the same session of the General Court (which directed men in want of land to take their requests to the governor and assistants) also appointed the governor, the seven assistants, and eight freemen a committee to revise all the laws of the colony. In committee, the governor and assistants were asked to

4. Ibid. Because some of the grants do not specify the amount of acreage, it is not possible to state categorically that no one received a grant in excess of 300 acres.

5. See Chapter 3, pp. 30, 31.

6. *Ply. Col. Rec., I,* passim.

surrender control of the land.[7] Confronted with a situation that, were it ignored, could have produced serious consequences, the governor and assistants effected a compromise. They obtained the General Court's consent to allow them to seek out and reserve certain lands for the Purchasers. In turn, they agreed that once the Purchasers had their lands, the colony freemen through the General Court would exercise control over all further land grants.[8]

The governor and assistants were, however, in no hurry to implement this agreement, and during the three years which followed, the Court of Assistants continued to grant land to individuals. By March 1639 the freemen's patience was exhausted, and the colony grand jury angrily demanded to know under what authority the governor and assistants continued to dispose of land to persons or to townships, and what lands they had reserved for the Purchasers.[9]

In light of this renewed pressure, the Court of Assistants ceased to make further grants, and in 1640 the Purchasers came to a final settlement with the freemen who promised to underwrite to a limit of £300 expenses incurred in securing the Bradford Patent. Before December 1640 the Purchasers were to choose two or three tracts of land and until then the General Court agreed not to authorize any new settlements. Then, after the Purchasers had selected their lands, all ungranted land in the colony would belong to the freemen, and all land within existing townships would become the property of the freemen and persons there resident to whom the colony had given a grant to settle. As agreed, the Purchasers in December 1640 announced their choice of places, and Bradford indicated that he was ready to turn over the patent. That took place the following March, whereupon the freemen promptly handed the patent back to him for safekeeping.[10]

Thus, control over Plymouth Colony's undistributed lands passed from the Court of Assistants to the freemen. This transfer undoubtedly occurred because of a growing unwillingness on the part of some to continue entrusting control of the undistributed land in the colony to a few men. In 1634, two years

7. Ibid., p. 43; *II*, pp. 11, 16; Bradford, *History, 2,* p. 282.
8. *Ply. Col. Rec., II,* p. 16.
9. Ibid., *1,* p. 119.
10. Ibid., *2,* pp. 10–11. For the list of Purchasers see Ibid., p. 177.

before the Court of Assistants was asked to surrender the patent, the freemen in Massachusetts curtailed Governor Winthrop's power, including the right of the governor and assistants to dispose of land; knowledge of that event may have given some at Plymouth similar thoughts.[11] Clarification of title to the land was becoming necessary, for an increasing number of men who had not settled in Plymouth until after 1630 were becoming freemen. They were perhaps less willing to acquiesce in executive control of land distribution than were those who had lived at Plymouth for a decade and were the friends and neighbors of the men who sat on the court. But at least part of the motivation behind the effort to wrest control from the magistrates may have developed from a dissatisfaction with the court's policy of making small grants, a policy that may have been oriented to the granting of land on the basis of present need.

Because no sources are extant, no one knows who precipitated the question of giving the freemen exclusive control. But the procrastination of the Court of Assistants suggests that the majority of magistrates, although they were also freemen, had little enthusiasm for the idea. Such a step meant a diminution of their own power; more important, they may have believed that it signified the end of an effective policy of restraint in land distribution. Bradford had this consideration very much on his mind ten years earlier, and wrote that he thought it necessary "to keep shuch a mean in distribution of lands, and other courses, as should not hinder their growth in others coming to them." [12] There was no reason that his thinking on the matter should have changed.

In the years when the Court of Assistants controlled Plymouth's land, only once had the court made a large grant for purposes other than settlement. This grant, which extended three miles inland from the high water mark at Scituate, was made in 1633 to Timothy Hatherly, Richard Andrews, James Sherley, and John Beauchamp. All four were English creditors of the plantation. Bradford and the assistants apparently made the grant in the expectation of the grantees realizing a cash profit, for it was simply too much land for four men to use for planting. Hatherly was the only one of the four to settle later in the

11. John Winthrop, *The History of New England,* James Savage, ed. (2 vols. Boston, 1859), *I,* p. 129.
12. Bradford, *History, 2,* p. 8.

colony, and by 1650 Hatherly bought out the other three and organized the Conehasset Company to administer the land and offer
shares.[13] Before 1640 the court made no other grants to proprietary groups except to persons actually wanting to settle a new
town.[14]

But as a consequence of Governor Bradford's surrender of the
patent, this policy changed; Bradford and the other Purchasers
of 1627 were the first to receive dividend grants of land. Under
the terms of the agreement negotiated with the freemen, the
Purchasers were allowed to reserve three large blocks of virgin
land. One tract lay on Cape Cod and, stretching across the Cape
from "sea to sea," extended from the eastern boundary of the
town of Yarmouth, settled only a year earlier, three miles to the
east of the Indian village at Nemskaket. A second was situated
southwest of Plymouth and reached eight miles into the country
from the shores of Buzzards Bay. The third lay on the western
edge of the colony between the Pawtucket and Sowamsett Rivers, and extended from the limits of Narragansett Bay eight
miles into the interior. Towns later settled on the three tracts
included: South Orleans, the greater parts of Harwich and
Brewster, Dartmouth, Fairhaven, New Bedford, Little Compton, Swansea, Rehoboth, Seekonk, and Attleboro, Massachusetts; East Providence, Cumberland, Bristol, and part of Pawtucket, Rhode Island.[15]

The Purchasers, in asking for the three large tracts, and the
General Court, in granting them, apparently did not intend that
the Purchasers thereby acquire exclusive title to all the land included in these limits. Sale by the Indians to extinguish their title, a
policy which Plymouth Colony tried scrupulously to observe before Governor Bradford's death, had to occur before any of the
lands were opened to settlement. Moreover, Indian villages were
located in all three areas, and no evidence exists to suggest that
in 1640 the Purchasers expected to displace these people from
their homes. The boundaries of the tract lying on the western
edge of the colony were, in fact, specifically written to include
Causumpsit Neck, "the cheef habitaçon" of Massassoit and the

13. Conehasset Proprietor Records, Plymouth County Court House, Plymouth,
Massachusetts, *1;* Ply. Col. Rec., *12,* pp. 158–60; see also Samuel Deane, *History of
Scituate* (Boston, 1831), pp. 4–6.

14. See supra, p. 39.

15. *Ply. Col. Rec., 2,* pp. 10–11. Bradford, *History,* (Morison, ed.), footnote 8,
p. 429.

Wampanoag Tribe; undoubtedly this was done to insure the Wampanoags from future incursions by the General Court. The intention of the Purchasers and the Court in 1640 seems rather to have been to reserve blocks of land in which the Purchasers, many of whom before 1640 believed they had received "smale proporčons of land and many of them meane," could, when the time seemed propitious, choose lands which were attractive to them.[16]

Fifty-eight people shared in this land dividend: six were English creditors; twenty had come on the *Mayflower* and included every signer of the Mayflower Compact, servants as well as heads of families, who had survived and remained in the colony; fifteen had come on the *Fortune* in 1621, twelve on the *Anne* and *Little James* two years later; five, excluding the six English creditors, may not have come on any of the four ships. All of the above except the adventurers were residents of Plymouth in 1627.[17]

Settlement of the Cape Cod tract began within five years, but the Purchasers made no immediate effort to take up their lands to the south on Buzzards Bay or in the western part of the colony. In 1640 they had little use for land thirty miles from Plymouth and exposed to attack if the Indians began to make trouble. Nor did the freemen who now controlled the ungranted lands in the colony begin at once to start distributing it to themselves. Between 1640 and 1653, the General Court made only about half the number of grants to individuals that the Court of Assistants had made in the three years preceding Bradford's surrender of the patent.[18] Perhaps the restraint of the freemen who knew their claims were now secure and recognized the need of subduing land already granted them was partially responsible. Probably more important was the temporary but significant lessening of the demand for land.

For ten years commencing in 1630, thousands of Puritans, fleeing the persecutions of Charles I and Archbishop William Laud, departed for New England. By 1640 there were ten thousand people living in the New England colonies, where before 1630 the settled inhabitants had numbered less than 500; but by

16. *Ply. Col. Rec., 2*, pp. 10–11; *11*, p. 16.

17. Ibid., *2*, p. 177; *12*, pp. 3–6; Bradford, *History, 2*, pp. 399–411.

18. The colony records show grants of land from 1633 to 1691; for grants between 1640 and 1653, see *Ply. Col. Rec., 1, 2*, and *3*, passim.

1640, the great migration to New England was over.[19] Civil war broke out in Scotland in 1638 and spread within ten years to England thus checking the tide. Puritans rallied to their cause at home and for a few years the number of departures from New England exceeded the number of arrivals.[20]

Termination of the Puritan immigration from England dealt a death blow to the inflationary pressures which had been building in New England for a decade. The value of a cow slipped from £20 to £5; the prices of other kinds of livestock fell proportionately.[21] While men had settled seven towns in Plymouth Colony between 1630 and 1640, only two new towns were established in the next ten years. In addition, this was a time when friction with the Narragansett Indians was increasing, when alarms were frequent, and the risks of war seemed great. A significant decrease in the number of land grants in Plymouth Colony and little apparent interest on the part of the freemen to give themselves land dividends is not difficult to understand.

After 1650, expansion and the push for land resumed, probably because after an interim of consolidation men were again becoming restless, and because an increasing number of young men and women were coming of age. In 1652 the Purchasers reached agreement with the Wampanoag Indians for the sale of the Acoakset lands southwest of Plymouth, one of the tracts reserved in 1640. In the same year, the General Court voted to distribute land to freemen, now called the "old freemen," who were residents of the colony in 1640. By 1670 the General Court had given land to the old freemen of Plymouth, Marshfield, Scituate, Duxbury, Barnstable, Taunton, and Sandwich.[22]

For nonfreemen anxious for land, date of arrival in the colony

19. Estimates of the population in New England in 1640 range from ten to forty thousand. See Evarts B. Greene and Virginia D. Harrington, *American Population before the Federal Census of 1790* (New York, 1932), pp. 8–9, 13.

20. William L. Sachse, "The Migration of New Englanders to England, 1640–1660," *American Historical Review, 53* (1948), p. 251.

21. Bradford, *History, 2* pp. 291–92.

22. *Old Dartmouth Historical Sketches,* 64 (New Bedford, 1954), p. 516; *Ply. Col. Rec., 11,* p. 60; Plymouth Colony Deeds, vol. *3,* pt. I, p. 83; vol. *2,* pt. I, p. 181; Thomas Weston, *History of the Town of Middleboro* (Cambridge, 1906), pp. 585–86; Little Compton Proprietor Records, *1;* Major's Purchase Proprietor Records, *1;* Dartmouth Proprietor Records, *1,* p. 2; Bridgewater Proprietor Records, *2,* pp. 1–2. Copies of originals of these manuscripts are kept at the Plymouth County Court House, Plymouth, Massachusetts, except for the Little Compton Proprietor Records, which are in the town offices of Little Compton, R.I.

also seemed to be important. The General Court had voted in 1636 that children born in New Plymouth (and after them, children brought up there) should receive land before anyone who came from England or from another colony. In 1661 the Court carried out this promise and gave children born to the first settlers permission to purchase land from the Indians. The Court also agreed that men who were once servants and who had land due them by covenant could buy a tract along the Sakonnet River. They were called the old servants and were without exception persons resident in the colony before 1640.[23]

Colony land policy from 1640 until 1670 clearly favored the men who settled early, although persons not among the early arrivals continued to receive grants. The Court also followed a liberal policy in giving additional land to existing townships and left to the townships the basis upon which these lands were to be distributed. But if a person wanted land for profit, his opportunity to share in lands distributed by the colony seemed to increase in proportion to the length of his settlement.

The trend in Plymouth Colony after 1640 to favor persons who settled early can be viewed sympathetically. No one, I think, can begrudge the Purchasers of 1627 their land dividends. Most of them, perhaps all except the six English adventurers, had come to Plymouth before 1624. They had endured desperate privation and at times their survival had seemed doubtful. They had invested their lives and their resources in the effort to build homes for themselves in America. They were entitled to believe that they deserved preferential treatment in the distribution of land in the colony they had begun. That others would follow in their footsteps in trying to obtain land dividends was inevitable.

In spite of liberal dividends to Purchasers, old freemen, firstborn children, and old servants, no one could become very wealthy by owning and selling land in seventeenth-century Plymouth. Even at Freetown (Freetown was a dividend given to the old freemen), where each of the twenty-six proprietors received one-half square mile of land for £11–10–0, and where within thirty years the value of one share (one twenty-sixth of the grant) appreciated 900 per cent, the grantee's profit was less than £100.[24] To minimize a £100 profit in a society which paid unskilled labor

23. *Ply. Col. Rec., II*, p. 16; *3*, pp. 215–16.
24. Richard L. Bowen, *Early Rehoboth* (4 vols. Rehoboth, 1945–50), *I*, pp. 80, 85.

a daily wage of two shillings six pence would be unwise; yet relative to the commercial opportunities which existed in the Massachusetts Bay Colony, a profit of £100 realized over a period of thirty years was not very startling. After 1700, land values in southeastern New England began to rise dramatically; Josiah Tomson, grandson of a *Mayflower* passenger, left real estate in 1726 at Middleboro valued at £4,568.[25] But it was the grandsons who enjoyed the opportunity to make substantial profits from the sale of land if their fathers and grandfathers had retained possession.

In fact, the original grantees often sold. At Dartmouth, only five of the fifty-six men owning shares in the township lands in 1694 had a surname identical to that of the original proprietors who had first met in 1652.[26] Moreover, because land became valuable only after settlement, usually the original owners sold to men who intended to settle and not to speculators. Of twenty-one shares in the Sakonnet lands, by 1695 fourteen were held by men who were either residents or had sons resident in the town.[27] Further indication that a majority of town proprietors were residents of the towns comes from the place of proprietary meetings. Once people moved onto the land of a new township and began to settle, proprietor meetings generally seem to have been held in the town. Bridgewater's town and proprietor meetings during the early years of settlement appear in the same book.[28] Yet Bridgewater was one of the towns settled as a result of a dividend grant.

There was, of course, some speculation. Dartmouth's proprietor records show that several men from Portsmouth, Rhode Island bought and sold shares in the township.[29] One man in particular, Edward Grey, who lived in the town of Plymouth, traded extensively in lands belonging to the town; by 1670, Grey owned eight shares in Plymouth's lands at Punckatesset.[30] But Grey's speculative ventures were apparently the exception rather

25. *Mayflower Descendant, 24* (Boston, 1922), p. 168.
26. Dartmouth Proprietor Records, *1*, p. 2; Bristol County Deeds, *1*, pp. 326–27, printed in Bowen, *Rehoboth, 2*, pp. 48, 49.
27. Petitions from the residents of Little Compton to Sir William Phipps, Governor of Massachusetts, Feb. 27, 1692, printed in Bowen, *Rehoboth, 1*, pp. 8–9.
28. Bridgewater Town Records, Bridgewater, Massachusetts, *1*. In 1674 the town began to keep a separate book for land.
29. Dartmouth Proprietor Records, *1*, p. 3.
30. *Mayflower Descendant, 27* (Boston, 1915), pp. 171–72.

than the rule in the colony. Because speculation was exceptional rather than usual, and because ownership of a town was spread among a number of people, a majority of whom were inhabitants of the town, hostility between absentee proprietor and settler did not develop in seventeenth-century New Plymouth.

Furthermore, due to the General Court's intention that new towns prosper, colony policy before 1675 favored the settler at the expense of the absentee proprietor. In 1663, to spur the development of new plantations, the Court ordered men who owned land and would not live upon it, and refused to sell or lease, be taxed toward the support of the township in which their unused land was located. A statute passed in 1665 ordering the township of residence be the taxing township apparently did not alter the law, for three years later Bridgewater demanded a rate from proprietors who were not inhabitants.[31] In no other instance did the colony even recognize the existence of absentee proprietors before 1675. Once settlement had begun, a policy of granting liberal land dividends to early settlers was not allowed to hinder the development of a town.

For a man anxious to settle in Plymouth Colony, the colony government was not the only source to which application could be made for a land grant: the prospective settler could petition in a particular township for a grant from the town itself. If his application was favorably received, if he settled in the town before further grants to the town from the General Court ceased or before the provisions closed for entry with equal rights in the common lands of the township, the settler could become not only a land owner but a proprietor in the town's undivided lands as well. In particular he might find this possible if he settled in one of the towns established before 1650.

Before the General Court began to distribute dividend lands, the establishment of a town in New Plymouth, as was the practice in Massachusetts and Connecticut, began with a court grant to a number of families petitioning for a place to settle. This was the pattern followed in the settlement of Taunton. In 1637, forty-six families, some of whom were living in Dorchester, Massachusetts, met and decided to leave their homes and settle a new town. It is difficult to determine why these particular people

31. *Ply. Col. Rec., II,* p. 141.

wanted to move, but their experience was not unique. Other families were moving from their homes to begin new settlements in eastern New England and in the Connecticut River Valley. Probably many of them were looking for more and better land.

Soon after the decision to move, the Dorchester people began efforts to secure title to a tract of land about forty miles west of Plymouth and thirty miles south of Dorchester. As the land lay within Plymouth Colony the men hoping to settle petitioned for a grant and were successful. The colony government granted them land with the customary requirement of first gaining legal title from the Indian owner (in this instance Massassoit), and in 1638 the settlement of Taunton began.[32]

Control of the land sold by Massassoit did not pass to all or even to a majority of the settlers of Taunton. Seven of the first settlers appointed by the colony government controlled distribution of the land and admitted men to residence in the town. (No one, of course, simply moved into a seventeenth century New England town; in order to keep out troublemakers and paupers, towns allowed none to settle without permission.) These men, called "committees" (commissioners), administered the land in trust for all settlers, and their actions in dividing and granting land were subject to review by the General Court.[33]

To each of the settlers who moved to Taunton the commissioners gave a lot of six acres upon which to build a home. But in the subsequent division of planting lands, allotments were not equal, for the settlers agreed to make the division according to the tax that a person paid in a colony levy and the number of persons in a family. The size of land grants distributed under this formula varied considerably: from six acres for a single man who paid a tax of two shillings to ninety-four acres for the head of a family of six who paid a tax of £2 and three pence.[34]

The colony government had early established the policy of unequal division in the assigning of town lands and the procedure followed at Taunton was not unusual. In 1638 a warrant, drawn up by the General Court, directed town commissioners to determine the extent of a grant according to the "seüall estates, rankes,

32. Samuel H. Emery, *History of Taunton, Massachusetts* (Syracuse, 1893), pp. 28–29, 94; *Ply. Col. Rec., 1*, pp. 142–43.

33. Taunton Proprietor Records, Old Colony Historical Society, Taunton, Massachusetts, *1*, p. 37.

34. Ibid., *2*, p. 6; list printed in Emery, *History of Taunton*, pp. 129–30.

and quallities" of a person. When Yarmouth was settled in 1638–39, the Court explicitly directed "an equall diuision" of the planting lands "to eich man according to his estate and quallitie." [35] Like Taunton, Barnstable in 1643 divided land according to estate and to the number of persons resident in each household. Rehoboth's settlers, even before they began settlement, submitted a record of the value of their estates, and the value determined the size of each inhabitant's grant. [36]

Much of the land granted to Taunton's early settlers remained undivided for some years. Called common land or "the commons" because it belonged to all who settled the town, it was not taxable, but it was available for cutting firewood and grazing cattle. Moreover, when the settlers wanted additional land for planting, acreage could be withdrawn from the commons and divided among individuals. All colony towns had common lands and all endeavored to maintain a strict control over them. Nonresidents were prohibited from using the commons.

The pattern of settlement at Taunton was also followed in other New Plymouth towns. But while such a policy worked well in the settlement of Taunton, in some towns it was less successful. In 1637, the same year plans were begun for the move to Taunton, ten men from the Massachusetts village of Saugus asked for and received permission to look for a site within Plymouth Colony. The following year they received a grant and began settlement of Sandwich. A few families, however, were already living in this area, and meeting as a church with William Leverich, who had moved from Duxbury, as their minister. Leverich and several others looked upon the General Court's grant to the Saugus men with decided misgivings. [37]

Leverich questioned the Court as to the extent of power conferred by its grant. Leverich asked whether the Massachusetts men, whom he called "undertakers," held full grant of the land or whether the grant was conditional upon the settling of a number of families "that may be vsefull for the common wealth and cheifly fitt for church fellowship." The Court assured Leverich that the Sandwich grant was conditional and that the "commit-

35. *Ply. Col. Rec., I*, pp. 114, 117.

36. Barnstable Town Records, MSS, Barnstable County Court House, Hyannis, Massachusetts, *I*, p. 5; Leonard Bliss, Jr., *The History of Rehoboth* (Boston, 1836), pp. 25–6.

37. *Ply. Col. Rec., I*, pp. 57, 88–89.

tees," a name the Court thought more appropriate than undertakers, had an obligation to settle other families in the town.
Leverich also asked if the Saugus men who shared in the grant
but remained in Massachusetts had any right to land in Sandwich. The Court replied that they did not. Leverich further
wanted to know if the commissioners could substitute other men
for those who had not come, and if they abused their power,
what course of redress was available. The Court responded that
the commissioners, indeed, had the power to substitute one who
settled for one who had not. If they abused their power, the
aggrieved party could appeal to the General Court. Leverich and
the people he represented suggested the creation of two townships, one for Massachusetts arrivals and one for people already
there, but the Court rejected the idea.[38]

The colony government, however, kept its promise to accept
responsibility for a fair settlement and in 1639 intervened in
Sandwich. The division of meadow had provoked outraged protests from some and the Court believed that the protests were
warranted. It ordered the meadow divided anew and, to ensure a
more equal distribution, ordered other settlers representing the
rest of the town to join the commissioners in making a new division.[39]

The Sandwich commissioners were soon in further difficulty
with the government. The General Court heard a complaint,
probably from Leverich, that they were receiving persons unfit
for church membership and that much of the land had already
gone to such unpromising people. It immediately ordered the
commissioners to come to Plymouth and not to dispose of any
more land for the time being. Appearing before the Court they
were directed not to receive any new settlers without the consent
of Mr. Leverich and the Sandwich Church. To forestall further
trouble the Court appointed a colony assistant to oversee future
land divisions.[40]

Developed to meet the needs for establishing some kind of local control during the early stages of settlement, the system of
court-appointed commissioners was in most instances a temporary expedient. By 1675, in a majority of the towns settled be-

38. Ibid.
39. Ibid., p. 117.
40. Ibid., p. 134. Similar troubles in Yarmouth, also settled by Massachusetts
families, led to intervention by the General Court. Ibid., p. 142; *2*, pp. 121, 128, 130.

fore 1640, the adult male residents who were accepted inhabitants controlled the distribution of town lands. In 1642, four years after the first settlement of Taunton, forty-six men paid a twelve shilling tax to pay off the debt arising from the Indian purchase, and thereafter the forty-six, known as "the purchasers of Taunton," controlled the town's lands.[41] In the town of Plymouth until 1639, the Court of Assistants granted land, and in March 1640, when Governor Bradford surrendered the patent, the General Court agreed that the governor and assistants should continue to distribute the town's lands. This was unacceptable to the inhabitants of Plymouth and within a year they had persuaded the Court of Assistants to surrender control to the town. Similarly, in Duxbury, Marshfield, Scituate, Sandwich, and Barnstable, the inhabitants gained control of the town lands.[42]

Moreover, in most of the towns settled before 1650, the opportunity to share in the town's undivided lands, to become, in other words, a proprietor of the town, was at first extended to later settlers. Six years after the first settlement of Taunton, the town voted to allow new settlers who agreed to pay the twelve-shilling fee a right in all future divisions of township lands.[43] Of ninety-seven heads of families listed as being in Taunton in 1675, fifty-eight owned a purchase right in the town; seventeen bore the same surname as a proprietor; eight others were proprietors in another grant in the township. Not counting persons having a probable relationship to a proprietor, thirteen heads of families (about thirteen per cent of the total) were without a proprietary share in one of the three major grants in the township; even if

41. Taunton Proprietor Records, *2*, p. 6. The records do not state explicitly when the transfer of control took place. In 1649, the "Purchasers" authorized the selectmen to distribute small parcels of land to needy persons. This would indicate that by then the forty-six Purchasers were deciding upon the allocation of land. Presumably the change of control occurred as a consequence of the twelve-shilling payment seven years earlier.

42. *Ply. Col. Rec., 11*, p. 35; *Records of the Town of Plymouth, 1* (Plymouth, 1889), p. 6, hereafter cited as *Plymouth Town Records; Copy of the Old Records of the Town of Duxbury, Massachusetts, 1642–1770*, George Etheridge, ed. (Plymouth, 1893), p. 14; Marshfield Town Records, Marshfield, Massachusetts, *1*, pp. 1–2; Scituate Town Records, Scituate, Massachusetts, *1*, p. 38; *Library of Cape Cod History and Genealogy, #104, Sandwich and Bourne Town Records* (Yarmouthport, 1910), p. 5; Barnstable Town Records, MSS., p. 2.

43. Emery, *History of Taunton*, p. 85.

they are included, the figure climbs to only twenty-one per cent.[44] Barnstable, like Taunton, tried to assure later settlers an opportunity to share in the town's undivided land. Barnstable voted in 1643 that the common land in the town be for the use of the present inhabitants and their sons and successors by purchase. But in 1670 the town voted to share the commons among the *present* inhabitants and those "whom the town shall think fit." [45]

In towns settled before the General Court began to grant "dividend lands" to early settlers, a pattern of land distribution therefore evolved in a form somewhat different from that often followed in towns established after 1650. The government would make a grant to a group of persons who wanted to settle. Unlike the policy adopted in towns which were settled as a consequence of dividend grants, men who did not actually settle forfeited a right to their grant. At first a small number of men appointed by the General Court distributed land and admitted inhabitants. In time, however, the inhabitants of the town gained control of the undistributed land, and in some towns at least, later settlers were allowed to become equal proprietors in these lands. In contrast, in towns settled on dividend lands, once the initial grant was made, a proprietary right could be acquired only by purchase from a grantee. By 1670 the pattern which emerged in townships established before 1650 already showed signs of change. This occurred partly because control of the town lands passed into the hands of the inhabitants and because of the growing scarcity of undistributed land in the colony.

One change was in the policy of determining the size of a person's grant according to his wealth and the number of people in his household. In 1653, Taunton agreed to divide land by heads and the value of estate. Nine years later the town voted "that the former act of dividing by head and estate should be of no force for the future," and that thereafter land should be divided according to whether and how much a man had paid towards securing the land from the Indian owner. Some of the Taunton settlers opposed the new policy and complained to the General Court but the Court did not intervene. When Taunton divided a

44. Ibid., pp. 85, 100, 120, 133–35. List of the heads of households in 1675 is printed in ibid., p. 93. Original is at the Old Colony Historical Society in Taunton.
45. *Library of Cape Cod History and Genealogy*, #105, *Barnstable Records* (Yarmouthport, 1910), pp. 1, 8.

tract of upland in 1674, the town voted to divide as equally in quantity and quality as possible. And so anxious were the settlers to ensure a fair division that the surveyors were allowed to vary the acreage in each lot to make up in quantity what was lacking in quality.[46]

There were other changes too. Efforts were made in some townships, that once had been generous in giving later settlers rights in the undivided lands, to restrict further increases in the number of proprietary shares in the township. Taunton, by 1678, had closed its twelve-shilling list.[47] In the town of Scituate, a bitter fight over distribution of the undivided lands required intervention by the General Court. The Scituate freemen and purchasers, who under a grant made in 1635 held title to the township, had surrendered their title in 1647 to the inhabitants of the town. Since no one could have compelled the freemen and Purchasers to give up control, the surrender must have been made willingly; yet twenty-three years after this surrender, some of the freemen and purchasers, or their successors, repudiated the act as illegal and petitioned the General Court to restore control to the rightful owners. The Court heard the petition, and after failing to effect a compromise locally, appointed a committee to lay out land to persons who had settled in Scituate before 1647. Opposition to this plan, however, was so determined that it was dropped, and bitter disputation over the township's lands continued. Finally, in 1683, the town agreed that the surrender of 1647 was legal and that the freemen and purchasers and the householders, together with their male children, would have joint proprietary control.[48] Scituate thus fought off an attempt to return permanent control over its lands to people who had settled before 1647. Twelve years after the agreement in Scituate, Barnstable divided a portion of meadowland. The division went to men who were inhabitants in 1670, their heirs or successors by purchase; the town also voted to give one acre to any male born in the township, twenty-four years old or married, and a present inhabitant.[49]

46. Taunton Proprietor Records, *2*, p. 14; *Ply. Col. Rec., 3*, p. 122; Taunton North Purchase Proprietor Records, Old Colony Historical Society, Taunton, Massachusetts, *1*, p. 2.

47. Emery, *History of Taunton*, pp. 85, 91, 132–35.

48. Davis Papers, Massachusetts Historical Society, Boston, 68; *Ply. Col. Rec., 5*, pp. 69–70; Scituate Town Records, *2*, pt. II, pp. 22–23a.

49. Barnstable Town Records, MSS., *1*, pp. 90–91.

Both Barnstable and Scituate thus showed some awareness of the decreasing opportunity to gain a share in the township lands, and it is important that both towns tried to do something about it: Scituate by admitting the male children of householders as equal proprietors in the town's undivided lands; Barnstable by giving an acre of meadowland to any adult male born in the township and a resident. But it is also important that while attempting to keep open an opportunity to share in township lands Barnstable and Scituate discriminated against persons who were not the children of parents already resident in the township.

The consequence of granting generous land dividends and of decreasing opportunities to share in the undivided acres of established townships was certain: eventually the supply of available land would be exhausted, and by 1675 this had, in fact, happened. Although the population of the colony at this time was probably less than 7,500, and although the colony extended over more than 1,600 square miles, most of the land was reserved for the Indians or in the possession of individuals or proprietary groups.[50] Recognizing the problem as early as 1667, the General Court made conditional a grant establishing the town of Swansea by requiring that colony residents desiring to settle have priority: some of them, the Court noted, were in want of land. Seven years later the Court gave Samuel Sabury a grant contingent upon his finding a place not already allocated to someone else. That was the difficulty; not that all of the arable land was in use.[51] In 1689 persons holding shares in the four tracts belonging to the township of Taunton numbered seventy-four; the number of square miles they owned about 115. Taunton's North Pur-

50. In 1680 Governor Josias Winslow reported to England that Plymouth Colony counted 1200 "listed men" from sixteen to sixty. Winslow meant by "listed men" militiamen; although by 1680 a few men were excused from militia service, the number 1200 would have included almost all of the adult males in the colony. In the eighteenth century Thomas Jefferson estimated that the number of males above and below sixteen were about equal. Jefferson also estimated the total number of males and females to be equal. Thomas Jefferson, *Notes on Virginia*, 2nd ed. (Philadelphia, 1794), pp. 126–28. Using eighteenth century estimates as the basis for determining population in the seventeenth century has clear limitations. But I think it could be argued that, given Winslow's figure of 1200, Plymouth Colony's population in 1675 was less than 7500. Winslow's estimate is printed in *Calendar of State Papers, Colonial Series, America and West Indies, 1574–1696*, Sainsbury and Fortescue, eds. (9 vols., London, 1860–1903), 1677–1680, #1349, hereafter referred to as *Cal. of State Papers, Col. Ser.*

51. *Ply. Col. Rec., 5*, pp. 24, 150–51.

chase Tract, granted in 1668, did not have even a first division until 1696, and the proprietors of Rochester were still dividing their lands in 1806.[52] But for men like Samuel Sabury, the problem of finding land remained, and except for Indian lands opened up after King Philip's War and sold to meet the expenses of the war, the ownership of land after 1675 usually depended upon the ability to buy from a previous white owner.

The result was the narrowing of economic opportunity, for most white owners were not content to sell their land for a few coats and hoes. Taunton had been more fortunate than most other towns in securing the approval of the General Court in purchasing two large tracts from the Wampanoag Indians in 1668 and 1672, when land was already scarce. But even at Taunton the increasing exclusiveness of a proprietary interest in the town's lands was apparent. The percentage of heads of families listed as proprietors in one of the four major grants belonging to the town dropped from nearly eighty per cent in 1675 to less than fifty per cent by 1689.[53]

The narrowing of economic opportunity must not be exaggerated to suppose the creation of a large landless class. Persons dissatisfied with existing possibilities could presumably move to one of the other New England colonies. In addition, the colony and the towns were sensitive to the need of preventing the formation of a landless group. Scituate and Barnstable tried to make provision for young men reaching maturity; so, for example, did Bridgewater, which in 1682 voted to distribute land among the men in the town who were twenty-one and older and had no interest in any other lands. Duxbury in 1686 granted thirty acres of land to each of three persons provided they settled

52. Francis Baylies, *An Historical Memoir of the Colony of New Plymouth* (2 vols. Boston, 1866), *2*, pt. II, p. 81; Emery, *History of Taunton*, p. 128; Taunton North Purchase Proprietor Records, *1*, p. 9; Rochester Proprietor Records, Plymouth County Court House, Plymouth, Massachusetts, *1*, p. 181.

53. Seventy-four persons, including "sons of Aaron Knapp deceased," owned shares in Taunton lands in 1689. Baylies, *Historical Memoir*, p. 81. The number of heads of families listed as resident in Taunton "where Mr. Danforth settled" (1687) is 128. Sixty-two of the 128 are among the seventy-four proprietors. The other twelve are either nonresident proprietors or younger sons. Of the sixty-six heads of household who are not proprietors, twenty-eight have the same surname as a proprietor; fourteen others have the same surname, and in some cases the same given name, as someone who was earlier listed as a proprietor. Twenty-four were neither proprietors nor have the same surname as a present (1689) or former proprietor. The list of heads of families is available at the Old Colony Historical Society in Taunton.

upon it.[54] Still, by 1675, the days when a person without capital resources could obtain a proprietary interest in the undivided lands of a township were, for the most part, over. This was of some consequence in a society in which the economic status of almost everyone depended upon ownership of land.

Seven years after the settlement of Plymouth, Governor Bradford had anticipated the possible consequences of allowing popular control of the colony's lands. As a member of the Court of Assistants he had consistently followed a policy of giving only limited grants, apparently conditioned to some extent by a person's capacity to use the land in the foreseeable future; and when he and the assistants gave up the patent in 1640, they had evidently done so with some reluctance. What would have happened had the Court of Assistants continued to dispose of Plymouth Colony's land? Would the court have tried to continue to restrict a' grant to men who intended to settle it and to limit the size? No one knows.

54. See footnotes 17, 18 supra; Bridgewater Town Records, Bridgewater, Massachusetts, *1*, p. 80; Duxbury Town Records, Duxbury, Massachusetts, Miscellaneous Records, 1642–1745, Land, *1*, p. 4.

5

"A Due Course for the Suppressing of Error"

IF LAND policy in Plymouth Colony developed in response to conditions imposed by settlement in America, the relationship which existed between the churches and the state continued to be influenced by ideas brought over from Europe. The Pilgrims had come to Plymouth resolved to build a society structured and governed according to the will of God: to achieve this goal and to sustain their society they knew that their civil government must support and nourish religion.

They knew this because no one in their experience had questioned the state's responsibility to do otherwise. Like other early seventeenth-century Englishmen, they believed God required man to love Him and that this was the first and great commandment. But the Pilgrims also believed God instructed man to use certain procedures in obeying this commandment. Although they well knew that men seemed unable to agree upon procedures, they, no more than those who persecuted them, questioned the assumption that the primary duty of the state was to cherish, support, and preserve the worship of God and the purity of religious doctrine. Civil government, of course, also existed to order human experience in the world; but in 1620 that this in itself could constitute a legitimate objective of government would have been thought nonsense. Belief in the separation of church and state and the willingness to tolerate dissent did not arrive aboard the *Mayflower* in 1620. Instead, the Pilgrims brought with them knowledge of the civil government's responsibility to support religion and to choke off dissent.

Governor Bradford understood and recognized this responsibility. Writing in the flyleaf of one of his books, Bradford asked the question: "Was it lawful for a magistrate to meddle in religion?" To answer the question, he cited the writings of the sixteenth-century Protestant divine, Peter Martyr. God, Martyr stated, commanded that "the prince should have the book of law and that both the tables were committed to the magistrate's power." Martyr insisted that even the heathen Aristotle knew "that there was no greater virtue than religion," and that the duty of the magistrate was to require that people "live well and virtuously." John Robinson, Bradford noted, agreed: the magistrate was the preserver of both tables and could punish breaches of both. He should not only "provoke" his subjects into hearing the word of God "but may inflict the same," and he must use the civil power to insure "that wicked and flagitious persons be neither taken into nor baptized into the church." [1]

In spite of Bradford's acceptance of his responsibility to support religion, the linkage between church and state in Plymouth was considerably looser before 1650 than in the Massachusetts Colony. For one thing, it was the practice in Massachusetts for the government to turn to the clergy for advice: confusion sometimes occurred as to the nature of God's will. The clergy were the local experts in understanding and interpreting the Bible, through which the Puritans believed God made his will known.[2] Although Plymouth's government was also anxious to find God's will, there is little evidence to indicate that a similar utilization of clerical advice ever developed significantly in Plymouth Colony. Bradford consulted William Brewster "in all weighty affairs." Brewster, of course, was an old friend and lay elder of the Plymouth Church. Bradford also consulted John Lyford in the early weeks of Lyford's sojourn at Plymouth. Once, Governor Richard Bellingham of Massachusetts wrote to Bradford for an opinion on what constituted rape and asked him to send the question along to the Plymouth Colony clergy. Bradford did so; but on no other occasion is there any evidence to suggest that he or

---

1. Bradford copied these sentences from Martire Vermigli Pietro (Peter Martyr), work unknown, and John Robinson, *A Justification of Separation from the Church of England* (Amsterdam?, 1910), in the back flyleaf of his personal copy of Robinson's *Justification*. The book is at Pilgrim Memorial Hall in Plymouth, Massachusetts.

2. Winthrop, *History of New England, I,* p. 163.

his successors, Edward Winslow and Thomas Prence, formally requested an opinion from the colony clergy.[3]

Lack of evidence does not prove the clergy were less influential than clergy in the Massachusetts colony, but this seems to have been the case. Clergy of the stature of Massachusetts' great divines simply were not available for consultation in New Plymouth: there was no John Cotton, no John Wilson, no Richard Mather settled in or near the town of Plymouth. Moreover, for the first nine years, with the exception of Lyford's brief residence, the Plymouth Church had no minister for Bradford to consult had he wished to do so. And neither Ralph Smith nor John Reyner, who successively filled Plymouth's pulpit from 1629 until 1654, apparently exercised much influence. The church was glad to see Smith resign in 1636, and it forced Reyner out in 1654. Two more eminent clergymen, Roger Williams and John Wilson, lived at Plymouth briefly, but both departed; and while Charles Chauncy, who became president of Harvard in 1654, settled at Plymouth in 1638, two years later he left for Scituate. With no trained clergyman available for most of the first decade of settlement, and with men of only secondary stature present thereafter, Bradford, although a devout Puritan, and one who attempted to rule according to the will of God, had to rely upon himself and other laymen for decisions.

The absence of distinguished clergymen may suggest and explain why the clergy were less influential in New Plymouth, but it does not explain the failure of the government before 1650 to enact legislation supporting the churches in the colony. In 1638 Massachusetts moved to ensure that men worshipped and maintained their churches, and before 1650 the Bay Colony enacted laws compelling attendance at worship and punishing men judged guilty of "Contempt of the Word." Every inhabitant, under penalty of assessment or distress, was required to contribute to the maintenance of the church and deviation from the Congregational form of worship was not permitted.[4]

Plymouth's government, however, continued to avoid legislation and preferred its traditional policy of acting only in individ-

3. Bradford, *History*, *1*, p. 381; *2*, pp. 310–28.
4. Samuel S. Green, "The Use of the Voluntary System in the Maintenance of Ministers," Historical portion of the *Report of The Council of the American Antiquarian Society, April 28, 1886* (Worcester, 1886), pp. 23–24; *Records of the Government and Company of Massachusetts Bay* (5 vols. in 6, Boston, 1853–1854), *1*, pp. 240–41.

ual cases. Thus, in 1637 the Court of Assistants heard a petition from Ralph Partrich, Duxbury's minister, "in the behalf of the church and neighborhood of that side, wherein they shewed the danger of the dissolution of their church estate" unless the court granted them control of the lands between the North and South rivers in Duxbury. Partrich stated that since the Plymouth Church had called its members home, and since much of the land in Duxbury had already been granted to "servants and other yeong men, from whom they could expect little help," the church probably would break up unless it were given lands to offer prospective settlers. Bradford and the assistants listened sympathetically and ordered that none of the lands lying between the two rivers be granted without the approval of Partrich and three others. Two years later the General Court similarly directed the men responsible for settling the town of Sandwich not to admit further inhabitants without consent of the Sandwich Church.[5]

The government also tried men for committing religious offenses. Mark Mendlowe appeared before the General Court in 1641, charged with drawing his eel pots on Sunday. Proving he did so because "of necessytie," he was not punished. The next year George Willerd went before the Court accused of announcing that men who contributed to the minister's rate were "fooles, and knaues and gulls" and that the refusal of baptism to children was "a deuelish practice." Willerd was bound over to appear before the next Court but the court records show no further disposition of the case.[6]

Why did the government prefer to act only in specific instances and fail before 1650 to pass general legislation? Perhaps Governor Bradford and others in the Plymouth government preferred to deal with each situation on an ad hoc basis. Perhaps while they accepted and approved the duty of the state to defend the churches and to enforce uniformity, they may sometimes have experienced doubts about how rigorous they should be. Bradford probably remembered John Robinson's parting advice to the Pilgrims: that if God should reveal new ways—and Robinson thought God would—they must not hesitate to accept them.[7]

5. *Ply. Col. Rec., 1*, pp. 84, 134.

6. Ibid., *2*, pp. 4, 17.

7. Edward Winslow, *Hypocrisie Unmasked* (London, 1646), reprinted from the original (Providence, 1916), p. 97; see also John Robinson, *Works,* Robert Ashton, ed. (3 vols. Boston, 1851), *3*, p. 103.

The question was perplexing: how much could the magistrate tolerate in allowing new ways and still fulfill his responsibility to God? Furthermore, in spite of their intellectual heritage, the people who came from Leyden and who had worshipped for more than a decade without positive state support for their church may have experienced some reluctance in departing from a pattern of voluntarism in America. The church had prospered in Holland without active state intervention; could it not do so in America? Was it not better to do so, and when possible avoid recourse to the authority of law? If this kind of thinking existed (and there is no proof that it did), it may explain why Plymouth moved so slowly and hesitantly to use the authority of the state to support its churches. Whatever their thinking, Plymouth's leaders were at first willing to allow more deviation than was permitted in Massachusetts, and before 1645 seemed reluctant to crush minor divergencies from orthodoxy.

Charles Chauncy was a case in point. In 1638, Chauncy arrived at Plymouth to assist John Reyner minister to the needs of the church. Chauncy's credentials were impressive: he had once held the professorship of Greek at Trinity College, Cambridge; Plymouth considered itself indeed fortunate to have the services of such a distinguished clergyman.[8] But Chauncy's stay at Plymouth was short-lived, for he soon aroused the church by insisting that baptism could be administered only through total immersion. While the church agreed that immersion was acceptable, it protested that "in this cold country not so convenient." The church assured Chauncy that he could immerse anyone desiring that form of baptism but insisted that the more customary, and less chilly, baptizing by sprinkling be permitted. Chauncy, however, stated that sprinkling was unacceptable. As a result of the argument Chauncy moved to Scituate, but the colony government allowed him to pursue his irregular baptismal practices there.[9] When Chauncy later became president of Harvard, the Corporation required he abandon immersion before electing him to office.[10]

Chauncy was not an easy man to deal with, and soon after his removal to Scituate a number of persons in the Scituate Church,

8. Bradford, *History, 2,* p. 302.
9. Winslow, *Hypocrisie,* p. 101.
10. Samuel E. Morison, *Harvard College in the Seventeenth Century,* pt. I (Cambridge, 1936), p. 323.

led by William Vassall, withdrew and established a second church. Chauncy promptly accused Vassall and his dissidents of irregularities, including a liberal policy in receiving church members. Vassall replied that the Second Church was ready at any time to hear complaints about the fitness of its members, but admitted to "some difference" in the use of the sacraments. Vassall acknowledged: "we hold the practise that particular church fellowship is an Apostolic ordinance, which should be entered into by all that can attain unto it, and that the best entrance thereunto is to manifest our graces by covenanting one with another; but in case that God denies any the means of particular Church fellowship, then the Churches upon the manifestation of their grace should recieve them to communion." [11] Vassall apparently meant that the Second Church would admit godly persons to communion who were not in covenant with (the members of) a particular church. This was a departure from usual Congregational practice. Three New Plymouth ministers rallied to Chauncy's support and attacked Vassall's church; but there is no evidence that the colony government attempted to interfere with the Scituate Second Church.[12]

Certain actions, of course, the government would not tolerate. Samuel Gorton, who defied the authority of the General Court and established a rump church, was expelled in 1638. But Gorton, in spite of his subsequent apologists, was notoriously difficult to live with; even Roger Williams found him impossible and wrote that Gorton was "bewitching and bemadding poor Providence." Williams eventually forced Gorton to depart from Warwick. Two years before Plymouth banished Gorton, the colony had asked Williams himself to leave. After his expulsion from Massachusetts, Williams had settled in the uninhabited western reaches of Plymouth Colony. In 1636, according to Williams, Governor Edward Winslow of Plymouth had written communicating "his oune and others love and respect to me, yet lovingly advising me since I was fallen into the edge of their bounds and they were loath to displease the Bay to remove but to the other

---

11. Many of the letters written during this controversy are printed in Deane, *Scituate,* pp. 61–84; originals are in Norwell First Church Records, Norwell, Massachusetts.

12. Vassall later found himself in trouble with the Massachusetts General Court over a petition to establish religious freedom. He eventually returned to England and later emigrated to the West Indies. See Winthrop, *History of New England,* pp. 260–61 and ibid., footnote 2, p. 260.

side of the water." Winslow gave Mrs. Williams some money to help with their removal, and Williams seems to have remained on friendly terms with Bradford and Winslow.[13]

The presence of people like Gorton, the splitting of the Scituate Church, and the manifest evidences of declining piety all troubled and distressed Governor Bradford and others and produced a stiffening attitude toward religious adventurism. This stiffening occurred partially because of pressure brought to bear by the Massachusetts Colony; given the commitment to maintain the churches it was probably inevitable. Immigration into Plymouth Colony during the 1630's and the proliferation of settlement seemed to have broken down the unity which once existed. Among the newcomers were some who, like Gorton, rejected the Congregational way of worship; and there were others who seemed to show little capacity even to order their private lives. As early as 1642, Governor Bradford was alarmed by the increasing number of offences against the moral code, and in June that year, revulsion and horror swept the colony when Thomas Graunger of Duxbury was indicted for bestiality "with a mare, a cowe, two goates, diuers sheepe, two calues and a turkey." [14] The General Court found Graunger guilty and sentenced him to die, the only man ever executed in Plymouth Colony for a crime other than murder. Bradford thought Graunger's offense symptomatic of a general moral letdown and tried to explain this in a society where wickedness "was so much witnesed against and so narrowly looked unto, and severely punished when it was knowne." [15]

He postulated several reasons for the moral decline: "One reason may be that the Devil may carry a greater spite against the churches of Christ and the gospel here, by how much the more they endeavour to preserve holiness and purity amongst them." Or perhaps due to the continuous watch maintained,

---

13. For Gorton's side of the story, see *Copy of Samuel Gorton's Letter to Nathaniel Morton,* Warwick, June 30, 1669, printed without a title page, p. 9. The letter is also found in Peter Force, *Tracts* (4 vols. Washington, 1843–1846), *4, #7.* For Plymouth's version of why Morton was expelled, see Winslow, *Hypocrisie,* p. 67. The statement of Roger Williams is taken from Howard M. Chapin's introduction to the 1916 reprint of *Hypocrisie Unmasked,* p. viii; for Williams' account of his own expulsion from Plymouth see Williams to Major Mason, Providence, June 22, 1670, Massachusetts Historical Society, *Collections,* Ser. I, *1* (Boston, 1806), pp. 276–77.

14. *Ply. Col. Rec., 2,* p. 44.

15. Bradford, *History, 2,* p. 308.

moral offences were more frequently discovered in Plymouth than in other places. Such thoughts, however, did not satisfy the Governor, and he advanced another reason. He explained that, along with the godly men who had come to New England had come a few of the ungodly. Some were servants brought by the settlers; some had been sent by English merchants who transported for profit and cared little about the character of their passengers. Bradford mournfully concluded: "thus, by one means or other, in 20 years' time it is a question, whether the greater part be not grown the worser." [16]

Three years after Graunger's execution the question of degree of variance in religion to be allowed in New Plymouth confronted the General Court. Someone, probably William Vassall, presented a petition to the October session of the Court proposing: "To allow and maintaine full and free tollerance of religion to all men that would preserue the Civill peace." The petition produced a crisis. Bradford, Winslow, and Thomas Prence stood unalterably opposed, and argued with all their forensic skill in support of orthodoxy. The majority of deputies were equally determined to establish toleration. But Bradford would not yield, and when his arguments failed, he used his authority as governor to prevent the petition from coming to a vote. On this issue there could be no compromise. Once full and free religious toleration was accepted, the direction and guidance which the church was supposed to give the individual and society would be of little value. [17]

After 1645 the government of New Plymouth became more rigorous and systematic in its efforts to suppress religious deviationists. An attempt to establish a Baptist Church at Rehoboth in 1649/50 failed because the colony government intervened. Obadiah Holmes, a Baptist, had moved to Rehoboth from Massachusetts, and in 1649 he and ten others withdrew from the Rehoboth Church and organized as Baptists. This action provoked cries of protest and four petitions were presented to the General Court; one of the petitions came from the Massachusetts government expressing surprise and concern at the failure of the General Court to restrain the Baptists. Massachusetts had heard reports of anabaptistry in New Plymouth but had hoped

16. *Ibid.*, pp. 316–17, 322.
17. The only account of this appears in a letter written by Edward Winslow to John Winthrop, November 24, 1645, printed in *Winthrop Papers, 5*, pp. 55–56.

that God, "by the endeavo^{r}s of yourselves and the faithfull elders," might have cured this unwelcome infection. "But now to our great greife, wee are credibly informed that your patient bearing wth such men hath produced another effect, namely, the multiplying and encreasing of the same errors; and wee feare maybe of other errors also, if timely care be not taken to suppress the same." Plymouth's General Court promptly issued an order to desist and directed Holmes to file a bond of £10.[18] Massachusetts later showed what it would do with Holmes when he was caught rebaptizing in the colony and ordered whipped. Massachusetts accused Holmes not only of illegal baptism but of baptizing Goodwife Bowdish in the nude, a charge Holmes stoutly denied.[19]

More disturbing to the tranquillity of the Puritan churches in Plymouth Colony than Reverend Holmes and his baptismal practices was a sectarianism (anticipatory of the "New Lights" movement of the eighteenth century) that was gaining converts on Cape Cod. Restiveness on the Cape was unhappily familiar: because undesirable persons were admitted to residence by the local authorities, the colony government had judged it necessary to intervene in 1639 at both Yarmouth and Sandwich to control further immigration.[20] Massachusetts families had settled both towns and it is possible that impatience with orthodox Puritanism may have contributed to their decision to move to the Cape.

At Sandwich in particular, religious agitation was causing the colony government increasing concern. In 1651 the minister of Sandwich, William Leverich, complained to Reverend John Wilson of Boston about sectarianism among the people in the town: "divers of them transported with their (though not singular) Fancies, to the rejecting of all Churches and Ordinances, by a new cunning, and I perswade my selfe one of the last but most pernicious plot of the Devill to undermine all Religion and introduce all Atheisme and profaneness." Leverich informed Wilson that he had contemplated leaving Sandwich but was "disswaded by divers our honoured Freinds . . . at least for the present." Troubled and discouraged by the hostility from some in the

---

18. *Ply. Col. Rec.*, *2*, pp. 147, 156, 162; *Records of Massachusetts Bay*, *3*, p. 174.
19. Obadiah Holmes to the Governor of Massachusetts, September 12, 1651, printed in John Clark, *Ill Newes from New England*, Massachusetts Historical Society, *Collections*, Ser. IV, *2* (Boston, 1854), pp. 53–55.
20. *Ply. Col. Rec.*, *1*, pp. 134–42.

town, Leverich found some comfort teaching Christianity to the Indians among whom, a contemporary noted, "he meets with an abundant blessing upon his endeavours."[21]

As the signs of sectarian difficulties increased, the colony government began to act. In June 1650 the General Court passed legislation punishing people who slandered a church or minister and ordered a fine of ten shillings or a whipping for persons profaning the Sabbath. The following year the Court voted to require people to attend church.[22] The new laws, however, seemed to give little check to the decline of religion. In 1653, Leverich carried out his earlier intention and left Sandwich for Long Island. Not long after his departure, John Mayo, minister of the Eastham Church, moved to Boston. Rehoboth petitioned asking a way be found, as in other colonies, to compel recalcitrants to contribute to the support of the ministry. Dissension broke out in the Bárnstable Church; even the Plymouth Church experienced trouble. In 1654, Plymouth asked John Reyner, minister to the church since 1636, to resign.

For Bradford, now past sixty and reaching the end of a life in which religion had been so important, such goings on were too much to endure. Bradford informed the General Court convening in June 1655 that unless it took "some speedy course" to halt the deteriorating state of religion in New Plymouth he would resign as governor. He specifically wanted action taken to remedy the neglect of competent maintenance for the ministry and the failure to take measures for the suppression of error.[23]

Bradford's prestige carried the Court. It ordered persons who denied the Scriptures as "a rule of life" to suffer corporal punishment at the discretion of a magistrate although such punishment might not extend to life or limb. And limited steps were taken to compel men to support the ministry.[24] A decade earlier the commissioners of the New England Confederation, a league linking Massachusetts, Connecticut, New Haven, and Plymouth, had recommended the four colonies bring the civil power of the state to bear upon those who would not contribute to the ministry. Re-

21. William Leverich to John Wilson, Sandwich, September 22, 1651, in Henry Whitford, *Strength out of Weakness* (London, 1652), Massachusetts Historical Society, *Collections,* Ser. III, *4* (Cambridge, 1883), pp. 180–83.
22. *Ply. Col. Rec., 11,* pp. 57–58.
23. Ibid., *3,* p. 80.
24. Ibid., p. 81; *11,* p. 64.

questing further time to consider the recommendation, one of the two Plymouth commissioners had refused to sign and nothing came of the proposal in Plymouth Colony.[25] But in 1655, under the pressure of Bradford's ultimatum, the Court agreed to act. The new legislation still placed the primary reliance for support of the ministry upon voluntary contributions. Under the new law, no clergyman of any congregation could leave his church until he had complained to the magistrates and they had heard both sides. If the magistrates upon hearing a complaint believed the congregation was not properly supporting the minister, they should make every effort to persuade the congregation to do so. But if persuasion failed and "plaine Obstinacye against an Ordinance of God" continued, then the magistrates were "to vse such other meanes as may put them vpon theire duty."[26]

In spite of Bradford's outburst and the legislation which followed, religion in some of the towns continued to languish and sectarianism to spread. The decline of unity in religious life was aided and abetted by the arrival of Quaker missionaries whose effective proselyting and very presence was a test of the resolution of the colony to defend its churches.

25. Ibid., *9*, p. 20.
26. Ibid., *11*, p. 64.

6

"Signes of Gods Despleasure"

Militant, determined to convert men to their beliefs, and willing to risk martyrdom to do it, the first Quakers came to Boston in 1655. Massachusetts fought them savagely, and in 1656 proposed the New England Confederation prohibit Quakers from entering the four Puritan colonies. The following year, probably at the Bay Colony's request, the commissioners wrote to Rhode Island and asked that colony to prevent further arrivals and to force the removal of Quakers already there.[1] The fury with which Massachusetts herself tried to stamp them out is familiar: when repeated warnings and whippings had little effect, Massachusetts warned that Quakers banished from the colony would be executed if and when they returned. Following through on this warning, Massachusetts grimly hanged four persons including a woman. New Plymouth sent none to the gallows, but the colony tried practically every other method of repression. Steadfast in his commitment to the need for a learned ministry, certain that the magistrate ruled as the steward of God and must govern in accordance with His ways, the Puritan could not meet with equanimity what seemed to him the Quakers' subversion of religious and civil authority. He seemed not to recognize that the institutionalizing of worship had lessened for some the sense of communion with their creator and established the need for a more immediate experience.[2] His harassment and punishment of

1. *Ply. Col. Rec., 10*, pp. 156, 180–81.
2. *Records of Massachusetts Bay, 4*, pt. I, pp. 383–90, 419 and passim.

the Quakers were desperate attempts to choke out something which seemed to imperil the very meaning of life itself.

Trouble from the Quakers first came in Plymouth Colony at Sandwich, which since 1653 had been without a settled minister. In 1656 the General Court heard a complaint that some people were meeting at a private house in Sandwich on the Lord's day and verbally attacking the colony magistrates and ministers. Disturbance of the Sabbath had occurred before at Sandwich, but the complaint made in 1656 accused one Nicholas Upsiall of complicity. Upsiall, who was not a resident of the colony, was a Quaker.[3] Brought to court in Plymouth, he was found guilty of disturbing public worship and of slander; but the Court which sentenced Upsiall acted with restraint and chose not to punish him severely. It allowed him to remain in Sandwich until the worst of winter was past and then directed he leave the colony and not return. The Court also heard a complaint that two women, residents of Sandwich, had abused the speaker during the Sunday service. One of the women, who had been convicted of the same offense earlier, was sentenced to a whipping; the other woman's sentence of a whipping was suspended upon her promise not to offend again.[4]

The Court sentencing Upsiall was the last one attended by Governor Bradford. Although in his sixty-eighth year, he continued to govern the colony until just before his death in early May 1657. In his last years Bradford had known bitter disappointment. His hopes for a community knit together in the worship of God were not realized. Around him he saw the decline of piety and the spread of the cancer of sectarianism. He recalled better days when the Pilgrims first lived at Plymouth and had tried to walk in God's ways, when men had not argued angrily about what those ways were. In December 1617, William Brewster and John Robinson had written to the Virginia Company: "We are knite togeather as a body in a most stricte and sacred bond and covenante of the Lord." Bradford had copied the letter into his manuscript history of Plymouth Plantation, and on the blank page opposite he later wrote:

> O sacred bond, whilst inviollably preserved . . . O that
> these anciente members had not dyed or been dissipated, (if

3. *Ply. Col. Rec., 3,* p. 111.
4. Ibid., p. 112.

it had been the will of God) or els that this holy care and constante Faithfullness had still lived, and remained with those that survived. . . . I have been happy, in my first times, to see, and with much comforte to injoye, the blessed fruits of this sweete communion, but it is now a parte of my miserie in old age, to find and feele the decay and wante thereof (in a great measure), and with greefe and sorrow of hart to lamente and bewaile the same.[5]

The sadness in his heart which bursts forth in these sentences is an unhappy postscript to a splendid life.

The question of whether New Plymouth would have pursued a policy of moderation toward the Quakers if Bradford had lived is one of the "ifs" of history for which there can be no answer. Before he died, colony efforts to check them were not as repressive as they later became. Nonetheless, Bradford's opposition to toleration in 1645 and his ultimatum delivered to the General Court in 1655 indicate that he would not have allowed the subversion of organized religion, and that was exactly what the Quakers intended.

Thomas Prence succeeded Bradford as governor of the colony in June 1657. Born in 1600, Prence arrived at Plymouth in 1621 on the *Fortune*. Although he apparently lacked much formal schooling—his handwriting is unbelievably bad—his family background, and perhaps some wealth, early established him as an important man in the settlement and by 1653 the freemen were annually electing him an assistant. In 1634 he became governor of the colony for a year, probably because neither Bradford nor Edward Winslow, his immediate predecessor, wanted the job, and in 1638 he was again elected to that office. Between 1633 and 1657, he served as an assistant except for two years spent as governor. Prence was a staunch defender of the New England way. He supported Bradford in the row over toleration in 1645, and as a commissioner of the Confederated Colonies, voted with the majority favoring the compulsory support of a minister by all the inhabitants in a town. Tactless, perhaps even humorless, possessing a stern countenance, Prence was, so one of his contempo-

---

5. Bradford, *History, I,* p. 123. I have not seen the passage but S. E. Morison states that it is written in an "aged hand." See Bradford, *History* Morison ed., footnote 6, p. 33.

raries thought, "a Terrour to evill doers." [6] He was surely a terror to the Quakers, who bitterly hated him.

At the first General Court over which he presided following the death of Bradford, Prence asked for and was given legislation to repress Quaker activity in New Plymouth. To compel the support of the ministry in some towns infected by the Quaker virus, the Court passed legislation spelling out with more precision the requirement that all inhabitants of a town support the settled minister. The wording of the law enacted two years earlier (after Bradford's ultimatum) was vague and simply directed the magistrates, if adequate support was not forthcoming, "to vse such other meanes as may put them vpon theire duty." [7] The new legislation ordered that in every township four men be chosen by the inhabitants, or in case of their refusal, by the magistrates, to assess the inhabitants for the maintenance of the minister. The Court added that if any town agreed to pay its minister in some other way, it was at liberty to do so, provided it furnished him proper support. [8]

Other legislation attempted to curtail Quaker proselytizing. The Court ordered anyone bringing a Quaker into Plymouth by boat to pay a fine of twenty shillings a week as long as the Quaker remained. Any Quaker entering the colony was ordered apprehended and "comitted to Goale there to be kept Close prisoners with such victualls onely as the Court aloweth vntill hee or they shall defray the charge both of theire Imprisonment and theire Transportation away." Moreover, to discourage colony residents from accepting Quaker doctrines, the Court directed that anyone refusing the oath of fidelity to the government—and a Quaker, because he believed any oath was a sin, refused— must pay a fine of five pounds. All meetings without court approval were prohibited under penalty of a forty-shilling fine for the speaker, a forty-shilling fine for the owner of the place where the meeting was held, and a ten-shilling fine for every hearer that was a head of family. [9] The legislation accomplished little, for the Quakers kept right on coming.

Within a year the severe punishment of the Quakers commenced. Banishment had proved ineffective for there was no way to prevent a banished missionary from returning, and Prence's

6. *Plymouth Church Records, I*, p. 147.
7. See Chapter 5, p. 68.
8. *Ply. Col. Rec., II*, p. 67.
9. Ibid., pp. 67–68, 100–01.

patience wore thin. In February 1658 the Court of Assistants instructed two Quakers to depart the colony within forty-eight hours or suffer a whipping. When both men appeared at Plymouth six days later, the sentence was carried out. A few weeks later, four men from Sandwich appeared before the General Court charged with "tumultuose carriage" at a Quaker meeting. Cleared of this charge, they were fined twenty shillings each for not removing their hats while in court. The harassment of colony residents who had become Quaker converts continued during the summer. Fourteen Sandwich men accused of failure to take the oath of fidelity were fined five pounds each.[10]

As a further step in its efforts to reduce the Quaker infection, the General Court appointed George Barlow as special marshal to enforce the law at Sandwich where the Quakers were especially active. Barlow carried out his duties of persecution with such enthusiasm that the men who appointed him later acknowledged that he was a disgrace to the government he served, and eventually Barlow found himself in difficulty with the Court for overstepping his authority. He was unable to keep peace within his own family: one of his stepdaughters appeared before the bench charged with "choping of him in the backe," and he and his wife on another occasion were reproved by the Court "for theire most vngodly liueing in contension one with the other." [11] Barlow's appointment is the single instance in seventy years of the colony superimposing a law-enforcement officer upon a town. He was undoubtedly more effective in winning sympathy for the Quakers than in subduing heresy.

In June 1658, Humphrey Norton, banished the previous October, reappeared before the Court and, not the least chastened to be back so soon, asked the Court's permission to read a prepared statement denouncing Governor Prence. Prence, answering for the Court, refused unless Norton would first allow him to see the statement. Norton rejected the Governor's demand and began a verbal tirade calling Prence a liar and a malicious man; Thomas Prence's reaction to this outburst defies imagination. The Court ordered Norton and another Quaker whipped and thrown into jail for refusing to take the oath of allegiance to England.[12]

10. Ibid., *3*, pp. 124, 127, 130.
11. Ibid., pp. 190, 206; *4*, pp. 7, 10.
12. Ibid., *3*, pp. 139–40. A short article on Norton by Frederick B. Tolles, "A Quaker's Cause—Humphrey Norton to John Endecott 1658," is in the Huntington Library *Quarterly, 14* (1950), pp. 415–21.

Norton's defiance was symptomatic of a distressing year. The weather and incidence of sickness were worse than usual and the Quaker missionaries seemed to be making substantial progress in gaining converts. In October the General Court anxiously took cognizance of God's anger against Plymouth and ordered a day of humiliation; but the Court continued to act.[13]

To expedite the removal of Quakers who were poor, the General Court in 1659 offered to finance departure; but other laws passed by the Court that year were less generous. To cut off the circulation of Quaker literature, the Court ordered town constables to confiscate outright any that was found, and in Sandwich, George Barlow was directed to search several homes. Any inhabitant could now apprehend a foreign Quaker, and to take care of an increasing number of occupants, the house of correction was enlarged. It became a crime to entertain a Quaker or to furnish one a horse; it was even illegal for a Quaker to ride. Joshua Coxall of Rhode Island forfeited his horse for committing that offense. But in spite of Plymouth's vigorous efforts the Quakers continued to make trouble. They ignored the fulminations of the government and went right on holding their monthly meetings. Even the General Court apparently recognized that it was powerless to prevent them, for it appointed four men, "or any two of them," to attend "Quaker meetings to endeauor to reduce them from the error of theire wayes." [14]

The government also acted swiftly to curtail criticism of its policies. James Cudworth, captain of the Scituate militia company, lost both his freeman's status and his command for opposing the policy of repression. Denied the right to take his seat as a Scituate representative to the General Court in 1659, Cudworth the next year appeared before the Court for writing a letter home to England deploring the colony's persecution of the Quakers. Although Cudworth himself never became a Quaker, he did not again command the Scituate company until after Governor Prence's death: when the company elected him captain in 1666, the Court informed the militiamen that their choice was unadvised. Other Plymouth men were brought into court for entertaining Quakers and for refusing to assist colony officers enforce the law.[15]

Although Plymouth's policy of repression failed, no doubt

13. Ibid., p. 151.
14. Ibid., *3*, p. 204; *II*, pp. 121, 124, 126.
15. Ibid., *3*, pp. 130, 162, 183, 188–89, 198–99; *4*, p. 126.

exists that the Quakers themselves suffered miserably. Some endured the humiliation and agony of public whipping; others imprisonment. Some were sentenced to both.[16] James Cudworth wrote to England in December 1658 that the lot of Quakers confined in the Plymouth jail was wretched. Given only coarse bread and water, they were allowed no communication with the outside world. Quaker converts also endured considerable distress. For Sandwich residents who became Quakers, Cudworth charged that persecution was leading to impoverishment. Although many at Sandwich were in desperate financial straits, a Quaker could do business out of the town only at his peril, for warrants (which in Sandwich the colony was apparently powerless to serve) awaited him in other towns. Rhode Island merchants who attempted to trade in Sandwich and relieve worsening economic conditions were not allowed to do so. Moreover, the government continuèd to fine Sandwich Quakers for refusing to take the oath of fidelity, for attending Quaker meetings, for permitting Quaker meetings in their homes, for threatening speeches, even for killing their cattle so that the colony could not confiscate the livestock in payment of fines.[17]

The suffering of the Quakers earned them the sympathy of posterity, and in the first half of the twentieth century a generation excoriated the Puritans for their bigotry, "puritan" becoming a nasty word. Perhaps while we share in that indignation we can also be more realistic toward the fury of the Puritan attack. Plymouth tried patience and forbearance, but they did not work, for when banished, the Quakers returned to continue their harassment of the established churches. Faced with the alternatives of allowing them to roam at will through the colony or to fight them with repression the colony chose the second course. New Plymouth was neither the best, nor the worst, of the four Puritan colonies in its treatment of the Quakers. Massachusetts whipped, fined, mutilated, and finally executed. New Haven sentenced Quakers to mutilation. Connecticut was the most lenient, for John Winthrop Jr. insisted upon a policy of moderation, but Quakers were not welcome there.[18]

With the exception of persons who disturbed public worship

16. Ibid., *3*, pp. 173, 185, 191.
17. Cudworth's letter was printed in George Bishop, *New England Judged Not by Man's But by the Spirit of the Lord* (London, 1661), pp. 128–37.
18. Ibid., pp. 154–56; *Records of Massachusetts Bay, 4*, pt. I, pp. 407, 419; *The Public Records of the Colony of Connecticut, 1* (Hartford, 1850), pp. 283, 303, 308, 324.

and were charged with breach of the peace, physical harassment of the Quakers ceased in Plymouth Colony in 1661. The hangings in Massachusetts caused some to speculate as to the wisdom of a policy of repression. Moreover, evidence of sentiment favoring a relaxation of policy in New Plymouth had been apparent for some time. Captain Cudworth wrote that many felt sympathy for the people in Sandwich, and Cudworth remembered the anger which greeted the court order depriving him of the Scituate captaincy because he opposed the colony's policy of repression. He recalled: "Had not I been present, and made a speech to them I fear there had been such Actings as would have been of sad Consequence." [19]

The persecution of the Quakers in New England ceased, however, not because of mounting internal resentment, but because of pressure from England. In 1660 the Interregnum ended and Charles II became King of England. The following year he ordered the New England colonies to cease further punishment of Quakers and in the future to send these people home for trial.[20] Plymouth sent no Quakers home to England but the colony seemed anxious to avoid trouble with the crown: after the summer of 1661 no one was molested simply for holding Quaker beliefs, and the colony treasurer wrote off nearly £300 due in fines from the wretched men and women who had become Quaker converts.[21] Two years later the General Court passed legislation directing that if persons coming into New Plymouth could, under the laws of England, be accounted vagabonds, they were to be whipped and ordered to depart.[22] While the law omitted specific mention of the Quakers and required conviction under the laws of England, it was otherwise similar to legislation enacted in 1661 to keep their missionaries out of the colony. But either it was not enforced or vagabonds were scarce, for no one was convicted in the decade that followed. In any case, once the opposition to their proselytizing ceased, the missionaries themselves gradually lost interest in visiting Plymouth, and whether any were active in the colony after 1664 is doubtful. By then there is some evidence that a group of Quakers was meeting regularly at Sandwich.[23]

19. Bishop, *Judged Not*, p. 128.
20. *Cal. of State Papers, Col. Ser.*, 1661–1668, #168.
21. *Ply. Col. Rec.*, 8, p. 105.
22. Ibid., *11*, pp. 206.
23. Frederick Freeman, *The History of Cape Cod* (2 vols. Boston, 1862), *2*,

Governor Prence gave additional support to the Puritan churches in the years which followed easing of the Quaker attack. The law passed in 1657 requiring the choosing in each town of four men to make an equal and proportionate rate upon all the inhabitants for the support of the minister had not been wholly satisfactory, and in 1670 the General Court ordered the burden of collection shifted from the minister to men appointed by the town. The Court further warned that if the towns failed to appoint these men, the Court would appoint them. Conduct of persons on the Sabbath was also more strictly regulated. The Court passed laws banning travel on Sunday, prohibiting "violent riding," punishing sleeping and playing during worship, and the smoking of tobacco within two miles of the meeting house. Efforts were undertaken to ensure a closer supervision of religion in new settlements, and legislation enacted prohibiting the settlement of a town without the presence of what the Court judged to be a competent number of people to carry on the worship of God. While such a consideration undoubtedly had earlier affected the establishment of a town, it had not hitherto been stated in law. The Court, in addition, cautioned newly begun settlements that should they prove remiss in settling a minister, the Court would tax the town and use the money to encourage prospective candidates.[24]

The significance of this legislation lies not so much in the enactment of the laws themselves as in the extent to which by 1670 Plymouth was legally committed to a defense of organized religion. The efforts to envelop the churches in a protective shroud of legislation reflected increasing pressure from Massachusetts to act in support of Puritan orthodoxy. Primarily it indicated the declining state of religion, a decline which by 1650, even without a little pushing from the Bay Colony, was painfully apparent, and could no longer have been safely ignored. The scattering of settlement, the loss of cohesiveness, the faltering in commitment, all seemed to demand an institutionalization and formalization of religion which earlier had not been necessary. Arrival of the Quakers in the middle 1650s only exacerbated an existing situa-

---

footnote, p. 61, points out that the Monthly Meeting of Friends shows a meeting was established in Sandwich before 1660. The minutes of the Sandwich Meeting (now in the safe of the Moses Brown School, Providence, Rhode Island), however, date from 1672.

24. *Ply. Col. Rec., II,* pp. 100, 140-41, 214, 224-25.

tion and intensified a need. Legislation written during and after their attack upon Plymouth Colony's churches was the logical extension of a policy initiated before their arrival. Whether or not this legislation rekindled the languishing fire in Puritan hearts, it contributed to and assured the continuing maintenance of the colony churches. To ensure that the civil power in turn sustained organized religion, the government also tightened requirements for participation in political life.

7

"A Civil Body Politic"

U NTIL the invasion of Quaker missionaries and the succession of Thomas Prence as governor, a majority of the free adult males in New Plymouth enjoyed at least a limited opportunity to participate in the colony's political life. In the years immediately following establishment of the plantation this opportunity existed because the men who settled were sufficiently realistic to know that they faced substantial difficulties in preserving domestic tranquillity; and if the plantation were to survive, discontent must be held to a minimum.

One means of limiting the development of political unrest was to obtain and hold a consensus of support for an established civil authority. Moreover, organization of the plantation as an economic unit had encouraged a democratic base for politics. All the adult males, excluding servants under contract to individuals, were stockholders of the joint-stock company which financed the settlement of Plymouth. As stockholders they had shared, in partnership with the English adventurers, ownership of the plantation and its assets; as stockholders, they had participated in its government. By 1623 such alarming reports of democracy at Plymouth had circulated across the Atlantic as to cause concern among the adventurers, and in September Governor Bradford had written a reassuring letter stating that it really was not true that women and children could vote at Plymouth.[1] Bradford, of

1. William Bradford and Isaac Allerton, Plymouth, Sept. 8, 1623, printed in *American Historical Review, 8* (1902–03), 299.

course, would have denied that the Mayflower Compact instituted democracy at Plymouth. Bradford believed that men elected to office were elected to govern and that decisions were not
subject to popular review. Thus for most men the opportunity to
participate in politics was probably limited to casting a ballot.
But at least this opportunity had existed and had given men the
feeling that they had some control over their destinies.[2]

After the dissolution of the joint-stock company and the economic reorganization of the plantation, the Purchasers may have
refused to extend voting rights to men who were not Purchasers.
If this occurred, and there is no evidence that it did, the number
of people excluded was small. Most adult males who were not
personal servants had been offered the opportunity to share in
the purchase arrangements.[3] And if, indeed, the tie between economic commitment and the right to vote continued after 1627, it
was not for long. The settlement of the Massachusetts Colony
and the immigration into Plymouth which flowed from it eliminated economic obligation as a prerequisite to voting. Too many
people were coming into the colony, men and women who had no
stake in economic arrangements worked out before their arrival.
Confronted with the problem of converting the government of a
single settlement into an institution capable of administering a
number of towns, Plymouth's leaders had to decide who was
going to run the colony. Some arrangements had to be made for
establishing citizenship, some criteria found to differentiate between those who would be allowed to participate and those who
would not.

Massachusetts had quickly found its answer to this problem.
Less than a year after settlement began at Boston the colony's
General Court voted that only church members—persons who
had given evidence that they were among God's elect—could
vote in colony elections and hold colony office. Massachusetts
Puritans believed that they had good reason to restrict the franchise to the elect. Convinced that they stood in a special relationship to God, consecrated to the end of building a society which
would shine as a beacon to other men, they had no intention of
surrendering control of the colony to the unregenerate. No one

2. My argument that most men could vote in early Plymouth is spelled out in
greater detail in "The Franchise and Political Democracy in Plymouth Colony,"
William and Mary Quarterly, 20 (October, 1963), pp. 513–26.
  3. Ibid.

had to settle in Massachusetts, but once settled, an individual gave implicit consent to its political structure.[4] Governor John Winthrop undoubtedly hoped that the saints would outnumber the sinners, but whether they did, would not alter one whit the control of Massachusetts by the elect.

Like Massachusetts, Plymouth began to use the word freeman to designate citizenship, including the right to vote for the governor and assistants and to hold colony office. But unlike the Bay Colony, Plymouth did not at first attempt to spell out statutory requirements for freemanship. Before 1656 no legislative statement of qualifications existed; and even thereafter candidates were required only to secure the approval of the freemen in their towns before presenting their names to the General Court. Additional legislation passed in 1658 excluded "opposers of the good and who[l]some lawes of this Collonie or manifest opposers of the true worship of God or such as refuse to doe the Countrey seruice." [5] These conditions represent the extent of legislative disfranchisement until 1672.

Plymouth also differed from Massachusetts in not requiring proof of regeneracy for admission to the status of freeman. Peregrine White of Marshfield became a freeman in 1652, but White (born during the Atlantic crossing in 1620) did not join the Marshfield Church until 1698, a few years before he died.[6] Plymouth even allowed some men to be freemen who did not worship as Congregationalists. In March 1665 the royal commissioners, sent by Charles II to visit New England, proposed to Plymouth's General Court "that all men of competent estates and civell conversation, though of different judgments, may bee admitted to bee freemen, and have libertie to choose and bee chosen officers both civell and milletary." The Court cheerfully replied that its practice always was to allow men "though of different judgments, yett being otherwise orthodox" to become freemen.[7] Plymouth had never admitted to citizenship Quakers or others who rejected the need for a trained ministry, and in

4. *The Book of the General Lawes and Libertyes Concerning the Inhabitants of Massachusetts* (Cambridge, 1649), preface. I have used the facsimile edition (Cambridge, 1929).
5. *Ply. Col. Rec., II,* pp. 65, 101.
6. Ibid., *3,* p. 7. Marshfield Church Records transcribed from the original records by George E. Bowman and printed in *The Mayflower Descendant, II* (1909), p. 38.
7. *Ply. Col. Rec., 4,* pp. 85–86.

fact the colony promptly disfranchised any persons who showed sympathy for the Quaker religion. But the assurance given the royal commissioners was not a mere empty statement, for Plymouth's list of freemen in 1670 included several members of the Swansea Baptist Church.[8]

Moreover, the criteria used in the process of selection were evidently not rigorous. A 1633 tax list compiled for Plymouth and Duxbury, then the only settled towns in the colony, numbered eighty-nine taxpayers, three of whom were women. Of the eighty-six men, fifty-four were freemen in 1633 and fourteen more were later admitted. Of the remaining eighteen who never made it, only ten are known to have been residents of the colony ten years later.[9]

A rate list is unfortunately not a complete index to the adult male population. In Plymouth Colony, where no poll tax existed, it did not include men who rented or who were servants. But with better land available elsewhere there were probably few tenants living in the two towns in 1633. No information exists to indicate the number of people who were servants. Seventeen males had come on the *Mayflower* as personal servants, but by 1633 those who were not dead had fulfilled the conditions of their indentures, and of the four who survived in 1633 and were living in the colony, three were freemen.[10] How many others came as servants after 1620 no one knows; my own guess is that they were not many. The problems in negotiating from the New World to bring over a servant from England, the opportunities for indentured service in the Massachusetts Colony after 1630, and the general lack of wealth in Plymouth suggest that most people probably managed without them.

8. List of the Swansea Baptist Church members copied by Ezra Stiles: List of the Pastors in New England, Ezra Stiles Papers, Yale University Library, New Haven; *Ply. Col. Rec., 5,* pp. 274–79.

9. *Ply. Col. Rec., 1,* pp. 9–11; the following lists of colony freemen are available from which I have compiled a single master list: for 1633, ibid., pp. 3–4; 1636/37, ibid., pp. 52–53; 1646, ibid., *8,* pp. 173–77; 1658, ibid., pp. 197–202; 1670, ibid., *5,* pp. 274–79; 1675, Colonial Society of Massachusetts, *Publications, 24* (Boston, 1923), pp. 149–55. There are also scattered through the first four volumes of *Ply. Col. Rec.,* the names of the men who became freemen in individual years. A breakdown of the eighteen "taxpayers" who did not become freemen shows that two of the eighteen were entered on the tax list as "Hatherly's two men," and "Mr. Collier's men"; for two others, only last names were entered; of the remaining fourteen, the names of two do not thereafter appear in the colony records. Two others died in 1633, and ten were definitely residents of the colony in 1643. See a militia list for that year printed in *Ply. Col. Rec. 8,* pp. 187–96.

10. Bradford, *History, 2,* pp. 399–411, 441–48; *Ply. Col. Rec., 1,* pp. 3–4.

Ten years after the tax list of 1633 was taken, Plymouth Colony, acting on instructions received from the recently organized New England Confederation, counted its militia. The colony considered as eligible for military service all able-bodied men between the ages of sixteen and sixty, including magistrates, ministers, and servants. This militia roll of 1643, therefore, provides an almost complete count of the adult males resident in the colony. Of the men whose names appeared on the militia roll and were at least twenty-one, between twenty-five and thirty per cent were freemen.[11]

The proportion is not so low as it first might seem. If, as is probable, men were not thought eligible to become freemen until they had left their paternal homes or were themselves the heads of families, unmarried men past twenty-one who continued to live under a parental roof were excluded from consideration. That the age of twenty-one was not in fact necessarily a symbol of adult status is borne out by the policy followed in the town of Barnstable of using the age of twenty-four or marriage to determine whether a person would share in a division of town lands.[12]

---

11. To arrive at these estimates, I have compared the militia roll with a list of freemen kept from 1633 to 1646. The militia roll listed 625 men between ages 16 and 60. Thomas Jefferson later estimated that in eighteenth-century Virginia, one-quarter of the males over 16 were between 16 and 21. (See Thomas Jefferson, *Notes on the State of Virginia*, 2d. ed. [Philadelphia, 1794], pp. 126–28.) Some of the men on the Plymouth militia list who were between 16 and 21 in 1643 had reached age 21 by 1646. I have estimated this number to be one-half of the number who were not 21 in 1643. Thus, the number of men on the militia list of 1643 who were 21 or older by 1646 was about seven-eighths of the total list or approximately 560 men. Some confusion exists because of different spellings of names, but approximately 150 of the 560 were freeman. Of course, I am not oblivious to the possibilities of errors in my calculations. For one thing, there is no way of knowing how many men on the lists in 1643 were dead or had moved to another colony by 1646. For another, Jefferson's estimate of one-quarter of the male population over 16 being between 16 and 21 was for a settled society in which population was increasing much faster than in seventeenth-century Plymouth. Finally, the list of freemen, which on the basis of names appearing on it seems to be a list of all men who were or became freemen from 1633 through 1646, includes a number of names which do not appear on the militia roll taken three years earlier. Some of these people were former freemen who were deceased by 1643, and some were freemen who by 1643 had moved to another colony; others may have come to Plymouth between 1643 and 1646. Still, on the freemen list appear a few names unaccountably missing from the militia count of 1643. This may indicate that the list of 1643 is not as complete as I have suggested, but if this is in fact so, what categories of persons were left off the militia roll is puzzling. The governor of the colony and several ministers are included, and if they were not excused from military obligation it is difficult to imagine who was.

12. *Barnstable Records*, p. 15.

Furthermore, although less than thirty per cent of the men listed as militiamen in 1643 were freemen in 1646, nearly fifty per cent of them had become freemen by 1670.[13] Some of the persons carried on the militia roll of 1643 must have died while they were still young men; others probably left the colony. The fact that, even so, one of every two militiamen became a freeman indicates that opportunity for full political citizenship was extended to a majority of the adult males in the colony.

Doubt exists that the opportunity for citizenship was always welcomed and exploited. Robert Carr, one of the Royal Commissioners visiting Plymouth in 1665, wrote home to Whitehall that he had been told that men sometimes did not want to become freemen, that the government in fact had to compel them.[14] Although proof for Carr's assertion is lacking, there is evidence that people were occasionally laggard in exercising their political rights and fulfilling their political responsibilities. The colony government once or twice had to prod towns to send representatives to the General Court. Even persuading men to attend, and remain at, town meetings, where issues affecting their own immediate interests were at stake, caused difficulties; to enforce attendance, the towns usually found it necessary to assess fines upon absentees.[15]

Some men may have taken little interest in becoming freemen because they already enjoyed certain rights. In 1636 a committee chosen by the General Court and instructed to prepare a codification of the laws of the colony reported back:

> And finding that as freeborne subjects of the State of Engl.
> we hither came indewed with all and singular the privi-

13. A comparison of the militia list and the master freemen list (see n. 9 above) indicates that about 298 of the 625 militiamen, or 48 per cent, eventually became freemen.

14. Robert Carr to the Secretary of State, the Earl of Arlington, Gay Transcripts, *1*, p. 22, Massachusetts Historical Society, Boston. The date of the communication as given in the Transcripts, which were copied from papers in the British Record Office, is 1655. Since Carr was one of the four commissioners visiting New England a decade later, and had not, so far as I can ascertain, been in America earlier, I suppose the copyist read the numeral six and thought it five. Carr's statement that it was difficult to persuade men to become freemen echoes Edward Winslow's comment that Massachusetts had similar difficulty. See Edward Winslow, *New Englands Salamander, Discovered* . . . (London, 1647), printed in Massachusetts Historical Society, *Collections,* Ser. III, *2* (Cambridge, Mass., 1830), p. 139.

15. *Ply. Col. Rec., 6,* p. 265. For example, see *Records of the Town of Plymouth, 1* (Plymouth, 1889), p. 20.

ledges belon͠g to such. . . . That according to the . . . due priviledge of the subject aforesaid no imposicon law or ordnance be made or imposed . . . but such as shall be made [or] imposed by consent according to the free liberties [of the] State and Kingdome of Engl. and no otherwise.[16]

The "we" in this declaration, of course, referred only to the freemen of the colony. Whether or not in 1636 the committee expected the freemen would include most of the free adult males, it did recognize that some men were not and probably would not become freemen. To protect the rights of these nonfreemen, the committee suggested that although the freemen alone should have the power to make laws, in levying taxes the rate must be equal for freemen and nonfreemen alike. And it also recommended that a man who was not a freeman should have the right to present his complaints to the General Court. The committee's proposals were accepted and enacted into law.[17] The fact that these rights were granted to those who were not freemen may have induced some men not to seek freeman's status with the burden it imposed.

While becoming a freeman conferred the opportunity of voting in the General Court and of holding colony office, it also carried the obligation to assemble at sessions of the Court. Failure to attend court called for the payment of a heavy fine. Until 1638 this requirement extended to all the sessions of the Court, but as the colony expanded, it became clear that it was unreasonable to ask people from towns on the Cape and to the west to convene at Plymouth three or four times a year. In 1638 the freemen who had assembled for the March Court voted to elect representatives or deputies to join with the governor and assistants to make and enact all legislation.

Even after the principle of representation was adopted in 1638, however, there remained the requirement that all freemen attend the election court in June. Recognizing the hardship this requirement placed on some, the General Court eventually agreed that freemen from Rehoboth, forty miles west of Plymouth, could vote by proxy, and in 1652 this privilege was extended to all the freemen in the colony. Subsequent efforts by the

16. *Ply. Col. Rec., II*, p. 6; *3*, p. 162.
17. Ibid., *II*, p. 11.

General Court to reenact the earlier requirement of attending the June election court were overwhelmingly rejected by the freemen. Marshfield's freemen stated that they thought it a burden to appear personally—Marshfield was twelve miles from Plymouth. The Court backed down but thought it necessary to impose a ten shilling fine on freemen who failed to vote at all. Some of the freemen obviously looked upon political responsibilities as a burden rather than a privilege and opportunity.[18]

When the freemen established representative government in 1638, they agreed that since the General Court was the taxing instrument, any man, freeman or not, who had taken the oath of fidelity to the colony and was the head of a family and a settled resident, could vote in the election of deputies. This decision was a far-reaching one. Only freemen could be elected as deputies to represent the different towns. The law was explicit on this point and was enforced.[19] Only freemen were eligible to hold colony office and freemen alone continued to vote in the June court for the election of governor and magistrates. But the fact remains that the right of representation was granted to the great majority of male taxpayers, while in Massachusetts only freemen could vote in the election of deputies.

Plymouth Colony at this time had no property qualification for voting. While only residents could vote, legislation passed in 1643 defined a resident as any person "that liueth and is quietly settled in any Towneship and not excepted against within the compasse of three months after his comeing, in this case shalbe reputed an Inhabiᵗ of that place."[20] And in 1644 the General Court specifically noted that the law was passed to make sure that poor people could become residents. The Court went on to explain that the law was not intended to include people who refused to take the oath of allegiance to the government.[21] Taking the oath, however, meant only that an individual had to swear his loyalty to the colony, and while the oath requirement discriminated against Quakers, the law predated their arrival in Plymouth and was not written to keep them from voting.

For a majority of the adult males in early Plymouth, there seems to have existed at least a limited opportunity to participate

18. Ibid., pp. 55, 59; *3*, p. 115; *11*, p. 84.
19. A deputy elected by Marshfield in 1644 was not allowed to sit because he was not a freeman. Marshfield Town Records, *1*, p. 73.
20. *Ply. Col. Rec.*, *11*, p. 40.
21. Ibid., p. 44.

in the colony's political life. Bradford and other leaders of the plantation were not crusaders for democracy, but they knew that in America the restraints of tradition were an inadequate base upon which to build a civil order, that they needed the support of the people who had settled Plymouth. Moreover, the economic organization of the plantation dictated the establishment of a pattern which extended the right to vote to a majority of the free adult males. This pattern, established for pragmatic reasons, persisted after the immediate reasons for it had disappeared. Thus in 1633 four of every five male taxpayers in the towns of Plymouth and Duxbury were or would become freemen. Of all the adult males present in the colony a decade later, one of every two eventually achieved freeman's status. After 1638 all the males who had taken the oath of allegiance and were heads of families and settled residents could vote in the election of representatives to the General Court. Finally, no one was excluded either from becoming a freeman or from voting for deputies by a property qualification.

To argue that only a small minority of men could participate in the political affairs of the colony is nonsense. Some men were barred from citizenship: persons who were not members of the joint-stock company could justly complain that they had no voice in the government of the plantation; and in the 1630s and 1640s other men presented themselves to the General Court as candidates aspiring to freeman's status, and, for reasons unknown, were not accepted. Furthermore, the opportunities to become a freeman were apparently greater if a man was a resident of Plymouth, Duxbury, or Marshfield, towns settled by Plymouth families, than if he lived in towns like Taunton or Scituate, which were established by Massachusetts settlers.[22] But while such inequities existed, and while not all who aspired to it did become freemen, a majority of the adult males in the colony (until after the arrival of the Quaker missionaries) apparently enjoyed at least a limited right to participate in the political life of the colony.

The deterioration of organized religion in the 1650s, intensified by the arrival of the Quakers, apparently caused some rethinking about who could be trusted with a voice in the govern-

22. In 1643 the number of militiamen in the town of Plymouth was 148, the number who were or became freemen about 90. Of 104 militiamen in Scituate, only about 40 ever became freemen. Ibid., *8*, pp. 187–92.

ment. After the death of Bradford, Thomas Prence became governor, and the qualifications for participation in political life were tightened.

In 1658, Prence's first year in office, the General Court ordered that in the future a man desirous of becoming a freeman must wait a year from the time his name was presented to the Court before he could be admitted. The practice was observed earlier, but it had not been required by law. The Court also directed that no Quaker should be admitted a freeman, and that anyone already a freeman who became a Quaker would be disfranchised. Even sympathy for the Quakers could lead to loss of freeman's status, and did for two persons; one was James Cudworth, the other a town deputy to the General Court.[23] Since 1638 the General Court had possessed the authority to reject deputies "insufficient or troublesome." Additional legislation was written in 1658 to ensure that representatives elected by the towns were in agreement with the policy of suppressing Quakers. The Court, in writing this law, for the first time gave explicit recognition to the possibility that men who were not freemen could not be trusted in the election of deputies. The statute began: "It is enacted by the Court and the authoritie thereof That wheras the Number of freemen in many places is but smale and the Inhabitants of the towneships many more whoe haue equall voqtes with the freemen in choise of Deputies . . . [that] it hath or may come to passe that very vnfitt and vnworthy persons may be chosen." Prence's government clearly hoped to prevent infiltration of the General Court by subversive influences. Acting in accordance with this policy the General Court refused to seat a deputy from Sandwich.[24]

A decade later, after the Quakers had won at least tacit permission to live in the colony (although they continued to be deprived of any political rights), the General Court revised the qualifications necessary to vote for representatives to the Court. The franchise was closed to all who were not "ffreemen or ffreeholders of twenty pound ratable estate and of good conversation haueing taken the oath of fidelitie." And in 1672 the Court extended the legal minimum requirement of £20 ratable estate to men wishing to become freemen.[25] The two laws marked a

23. *Ply. Col. Rec., 11,* pp. 79, 101; Cudworth, of course, was not allowed to take his seat as a deputy from Scituate. Ibid., *3,* pp. 162, 189. See also Chapter 6, p. 74.
24. Ibid., *11,* pp. 91–92.
25. Ibid., p. 223; *The Book of the General Laws of the Inhabitants of the Jurisdiction of New-Plimoth* (Cambridge, 1672), p. 16. In 1685 the requirement to

distinct break with the past, for the right to vote now became dependent upon the possession of a required amount of property.

Documentary evidence showing the extent of disfranchisement has not survived the ravages of three hundred years. In eighteenth-century Massachusetts, about one-quarter of the adult males could not meet the requirement of £20 ratable estate to vote in town meetings.[26] But differences between the taxing systems of the two colonies and between the value of property in the seventeenth and eighteenth centuries suggest that more than twenty-five per cent were prevented from voting in Plymouth Colony. Plymouth taxed only livestock, land, and vessels and goods used in trade. Massachusetts taxed these, and buildings as well, thus adding significantly to a man's ratable estate.[27] Also land values were low in seventeenth-century Plymouth. In 1669 Taunton valued an acre of improved land at fifteen shillings, meadow and pasture at ten shillings, and dormant land at one shilling an acre. The town of Plymouth's valuation of property in 1670 was a little higher: an acre of improved land carried an assessment of twenty shillings.[28] Ownership of livestock, of course, added to a man's taxable estate. The assessed value of a pair of oxen in the town of Plymouth was £7; a cow, £2-5-0; sheep, six shillings; swine, five shillings. Weavers whose looms were constantly employed were assessed at £30; tailors and fishermen at £20.[29] Fourteen acres of land and two cows thus would fulfill the property requirement in the town of Plymouth; so would four acres, a pair of oxen, and three cows. But not everyone who farmed owned this much property. If the law requiring a minimum of £20 of ratable estate was enforced—and

---

vote for deputies was further tightened. Persons who were not freemen or freeholders needed £30 ratable estate to vote. Men wishing to become freemen were to be 21 or older, have the testimony of a majority of the freemen in their town that were of sober conversation and orthodox in the fundamentals of religion, be freeholders, or have £20 ratable estate, or be "generally known and approved by the Court." The latter clause, by removing the absolute property requirement imposed in 1672, was a return to earlier policy. See *The Book of the General Laws of New-Plimouth* (Boston, 1685), pp. 17, 18, 59.

26. Robert E. Brown, *Middle-Class Democracy and the Revolution in Massachusetts, 1691-1780* (Ithaca, 1955), p. 95. Brown suggests that in practice almost any adult male could vote.

27. Ibid., pp. 81, 90. Massachusetts, however, did not tax dormant land; ibid., p. 89; *Ply. Col. Rec., 6*, p. 221.

28. Taunton Proprietor Records, *1*, chap. 4, Old Colony Historical Society, Taunton, Mass.; *Plymouth Town Records, 1*, p. 116.

29. *Plymouth Town Records, 1*, pp. 116-17.

that is a big if, for I suspect that in spite of court fulminations, individual towns often did as they liked—some men were kept from voting.

In the town of Plymouth, two years before the General Court passed the minimum property requirement, the town initiated action to restrict the number of men eligible to vote in town meetings. A list of ninety-eight men who voted in recent town meetings was drawn up and a committee appointed, which included Governor Prence, to consider who should be accounted townsmen and therefore eligible to vote. The committee recommended eligibility only for men who were inhabitants and freeholders when Plymouth became a township in 1640, for their heirs, and for others "as are housekeepers of honest life and are like to approve themselves soe as they may be benificiall to the commonwealth according to theire capasitie and abilities." This recommendation was accepted and sixty-seven men were found to meet the committee's criteria.[30]

The town, acting before the General Court set the £20 property requirement, did not, at least explicitly, tie voting to a minimum of wealth. But Thomas Prence, as one of the committee submitting the recommendation to the town and as governor of the colony when the town acted, may well have influenced both the town and General Court's actions to stiffen the requirements for voting. It would be unwise to assume that disfranchisement in the town of Plymouth is an accurate measure of the proportion of men in Plymouth and throughout the colony later disfranchised by the £20 taxable estate requirement. However, even if the two are wholly unrelated, which seems unlikely, the town of Plymouth's action in denying the right to vote in town meetings to nearly one-third of the men who had earlier exercised it, underscores the trend away from a more inclusive democracy.

Opportunity to vote in the election of civil officers is only one measure of political democracy; another is the making of policy and the actual exercise of power. Measured by this criterion, the

30. Ibid., pp. 90–91, 100–02, 107–09. *1.* Thirty-two names on the first list are left off the second list. Two names are illegible on the first list. Several names which do not appear on the first list are included on the second list. Of the thirty-two left off the second list, seventeen were later included on what I presume to be a voting list taken in 1676. See pp. 148–49.

trend in seventeenth-century Plymouth was toward a wider participation in policy decisions. In the early years of settlement when disturbing reports about democracy in the plantation circulated across the Atlantic, and when men could have readily assembled to discuss policy, the decision-making power was exercised by Governor Bradford. Bradford himself did not pretend that it was otherwise. In his letter to calm the adventurers' apprehensions in 1623, the Governor stated he seldom submitted matters to the voters for decision. While this letter was written to reassure the stockholders that Plymouth's government was not democratic, and Bradford's statement may have been more positive than practice warranted, there is no reason to doubt its essential truth.

A majority of the early settlers apparently agreed that responsibility for governing the plantation rested with the governor. In 1623 when Bradford asked the General Court for a decision on policy toward the Massachusetts Indians the Court in turn referred the question back to the Governor and his advisers.[31] That was not so extraordinary. In the seventeenth century most Englishmen believed that the government should govern. Had not John Robinson counseled those departing for the New World to be obedient to their rulers; and was not Robinson in turn echoing John Calvin's insistence upon the supremacy of the civil governor?[32] The Pilgrims knew that if they were dissatisfied they could vote the magistrates out of office at the next elections; but they also knew that until then, the magistrate ruled.

So long as Plymouth remained a small and isolated plantation, most men probably were content to let Bradford govern without curtailing his power. Lyford and John Oldham tried to stir up a rebellion in 1625, but failed when the majority supported the Governor. No evidence exists of a further challenge to Bradford's authority before the middle of the next decade. Plymouth knew its governor and trusted him. When men could stop and exchange pleasantries with him, when they could look up from their planting and see him working in the adjacent field, it seemed foolish to worry over the extent of his power. However, as settlement began elsewhere in the colony and people came to whom Bradford was unfamiliar, some men did begin to worry.

In October 1636 the freemen called in General Court for a read-

31. Winslow, *Good Newes*, p. 331.
32. Bradford, *History, I*, p. 134; Perry Miller, *Orthodoxy*, p. 6.

ing of the colony laws. Finding "divers . . . worthy the re-
forming, others the rejecting and others fitt to be instituted and
made," the Court ordered a committee of eight freemen and
eight magistrates to prepare a revision. The committee met in
November, and in their sessions the magistrates and freemen
agreed to limit the power of governor and assistants. Henceforth, the freemen were to choose a governor and seven assistants "to rule and governe the said plantacons within the said
limits for one whole yeare and no more." But their authority to
govern did not include the enactment of legislation. All laws and
ordinances of the colony were to be voted on in the General
Court "by the freeman of the Corporacon and no other." [33]
Neither law altered accepted practice. Since 1621 the General
Court annually had elected a governor and assistants. And since
the institution of colony records in 1633, the Court of Assistants,
which consisted of the governor and the seven assistants, had not
enacted legislation. Nonetheless, the legislation of 1636 was an
important milestone, for no records now extant indicate that written law had earlier guaranteed a check on the magistrates' authority. Further curtailment of magisterial power followed when
in 1639 the governor and assistants lost the right to control the
granting of land. Seven years later the General Court ordered
the governor and assistants, when they sat as a court, to limit
themselves to judicial concerns.[34]

Some of the magistrates resented the lessening of their authority. When the freemen asked the governor and assistants to turn
over control of the colony lands in 1638, the magistrates
dragged their heels. Seven years later Edward Winslow bitterly
informed John Winthrop: "But . . . we are so many (since we
followed your example in one particular, which we too late repent) to consult, as tis very hard for any to say what will be
done, tho' he should know what is most wholsome for us." [35]
Bradford, too, probably felt dissatisfaction with curtailment of
his authority. Yet he and his colleagues always seemed to have
the good sense to yield when they had to. More important was
their ability to yield gracefully, and if there was bitter argument

33. *Ply. Col. Rec., I,* p. 43; *II,* pp. 7, 11.
34. Ibid., *II,* p. 54.
35. Edward Winslow to John Winthrop, Careswell (Marshfield), June 30, 1646,
Massachusetts Historical Society, *Collections,* Ser. IV, *6* (Boston, 1863), pp. 181–
83.

there were few permanent scars. When June election time came, seldom was a governor turned out of office, and once at least, when Bradford was not reelected, it was at his request. Colony law required a man elected to the governor's office to assume office or pay a fine, but between 1633 and 1639, when much of the changing of governors took place, it also allowed a man to decline election in successive years. It is probably not coincidental that after this law was repealed in 1639, only once did an incumbent fail of reelection.[36]

As the governor and assistants sitting in the Court of Assistants lost power, the General Court became the sole governing authority in the colony. Consisting of the magistrates and town deputies, and in June including all the freemen who bothered to attend, the General Court governed almost without legal restraint. Not only was it the legislative and taxing instrument of the colony, but in addition it assumed responsibility for "the management of the greatest concernes of this Common Weale." Only the General Court could make war or enter an alliance: after 1640, it controlled the distribution of land; through its required approval of men desiring to become freemen it supervised granting of the franchise. Indeed, so extensive were its powers that it had the right to change the basic form of government and did so in 1685 when it established a county system. Before 1672 the only check to its power was the requirement in the Bradford Patent that no law could be made repugnant to the law of England. But the requirement could be ignored, for, like Massachusetts, Plymouth argued that "different circumstances" in America excused the colony from a rigid adherence to English law.[37]

Even the General Court apparently recognized the dangers inherent in governing without legal restraint and in 1672 enacted legislation which, so it hoped, would limit the authority of future courts. The first chapter of the *Colony Book of General Laws* printed that year contained a bill of rights: annual free election of the governor and assistants by all the freemen, justice and right equally and impartially administered, no person damaged but by virtue or equity of some express law, the right of all men

36. Winthrop, *History of New England, I,* p. 98; *Ply. Col. Rec., I,* p. 5; *II,* p. 10. Bradford failed of reelection in 1644.
37. *Book of the General Laws* (1672), p. 15; *Ply. Col. Rec., 6,* p. 169; Gay Transcripts, *2,* p. 43.

to a jury trial, the right of the defendant to challenge the jury for cause, and in a capital crime the right to pre-emptory challenges, the prohibition of a death sentence without the testimony of at least two witnesses. Such rights, the *Book of Laws* declared, were "so Fundamentally essential to the just Rights, Liberties, Common good and special end of this Colony, as that they shall and ought to be inviolable preserved." They were apparently the rights New Plymouth's freemen in 1672 valued most. Many of these rights the Pilgrims had brought with them from the Old World.[38]

Until 1645 the General Court met in March, June, October, and December of each year; thereafter the December session was omitted. During the first twenty years of settlement the election court convened in March. But by 1640, some people were living too far from the town of Plymouth to ask the freemen to tramp through the snow and ice of a New England winter, and in 1642 colony law made June the month of election court.

The General Court was a judicial as well as legislative body and its records include judicial matters from the probating of wills to criminal trials for witchcraft and murder. The procedure followed by the Court in the disposition of judicial cases is unknown. Undoubtedly the governor and assistants sat as the bench and the deputies may sometimes have acted as jury. But more probably, juries of laymen were impaneled to hear a particular case or cases and the deputies were excused altogether from judicial deliberations.[39]

Information bearing upon voting procedure followed in enacting legislation is also fragmentary. In October 1649 the deputies proposed that a major part of the Court order adjournment and dissolution and the making and repealing of laws. Bradford, however, persuaded them to postpone the question until the election court which convened the following June. This Court appointed a committee of freemen and magistrates to consider the proposals, and "they the said Comittie declared theire minds to bee That things in respect of the aforsaid perticular doe Rest vnalltered as they are." While this would seem to indicate that

38. *Book of General Laws* (1672), preface; George L. Haskins, *Law and Authority in Early Massachusetts* (New York, 1960), pp. 163–88.

39. The evidence for this is admittedly fragmentary and consists only of the legislation guaranteeing trial under English common law procedures and a law passed in 1649 directing that at election courts, after the choice and swearing of magistrates, "the generall ocations of the Country" requiring the presence of the deputies come next. See footnote 38 supra and *Ply. Col. Rec., 11*, p. 56.

the magistrates and deputies were voting separately, the committee concluded its report: "And yet for the futuer as formerly in the making and Repealling of lawes and aiornment of Courts wherein Comitties are Requeset; the Magestraits and Comitties or Deputies bee Concidered together as one body." By 1672 law required that no act pass the General Court except by majority vote, so that by then the Court was apparently voting as a unicameral body.[40]

The most important man in the General Court was the governor, who could summon the Court into special session when he deemed it necessary. He presided once a Court convened, and he had a casting vote in case of a tie. He was also a judicial officer and could arrest and commit to prison, and was responsible for the execution of all colony laws. He had no other statutory powers.[41]

But legal power was not what mattered. The governor, through the prestige of his person and office, exercised a vigorous control over all colony policies. Whatever their voting status in the General Court, the governor and assistants commanded the attention of the deputies. As the Court sat together, the governor, with the support of the other magistrates, could present an issue about which the most articulate and prestigious element in the Court could have already reached resolution. Their views carried great weight, for the notion that every person is equally capable of declaring policy was not yet part of the popular creed. The General Court's enactment of legislation in 1655 as a sequel of Governor Bradford's ultimatum is a case in point. If Bradford could dictate such terms, he obviously could exercise a vigorous direction over colony affairs. While the moral persuasiveness of Thomas Prence was probably less, it assuredly was influential upon court proceedings. Although no court records exist showing who initiated legislation and colony policies, undoubtedly each governor was primarily responsible during his years in office.

Occasionally, however, the General Court refused to accept a governor's leadership. Early in October 1645, a Court of Assistants met at Plymouth to consider "a matter of great concernment."[42] Bradford and three assistants, William Collier, Miles

40. *Ply. Col. Rec., II*, pp. 55–57; *Book of the General Laws* (1672), p. 16.
41. *Ply. Col. Rec., II*, pp. 7, 81–82.
42. The only account of this episode is found in Edward Winslow's letter to John Winthrop, Careswell (Marshfield), November 24, 1645, *Winthrop Papers,*

Standish, and Edward Winslow, were present, and the four magistrates agreed to present the issue and their decision to the adjourned session of the June General Court meeting the third week in October. After a full day of discussion the Court voted the proposal into law. Only one deputy voted in opposition. The last week in October, the regular October General Court convened and some of the magistrates and deputies who had not attended the earlier Courts appeared. This Court began a heated discussion of the law enacted the previous week, and after what Edward Winslow termed "a tumultous order," a majority of the Court demanded repeal. Standish, who voted with Bradford earlier, reconsidered and joined the opposition. Collier was gone, but Prence had arrived and stood with Bradford and Winslow against the rest of the Court; in spite of their arguments the majority continued to press for repeal. Bradford, however, stood firm and would not allow it. If, he stated, the law was found prejudicial, a future Court could reopen the issue. The Court then listened to the petition requesting toleration in religion for all men who were not disturbers of the civil peace. Outraged, Bradford could hardly contain himself, and, supported vigorously by Prence and Winslow, spoke against allowing the petition even to come to a vote. Again, however, their arguments seemed to make little impression upon the rebellious deputies and, as a last resort, Bradford ordered the petition shelved. Winslow informed John Winthrop of these disturbing events and wrote that he was ready to move to Massachusetts.[43]

How Governor Bradford legally prevented the General Court from repealing a law enacted by a court a week earlier and forced the tabling of a petition is unknown. No grant of power under colony law gave him the authority to do either. Perhaps the deputies and opposing magistrates acquiesced because they did not choose to fight his will; perhaps unrecorded in law, he did possess a veto power. Apparently the colony freemen thought Bradford's action warranted for the next June they reelected him governor.

Thomas Prence, while governor, also experienced a stormy

5, pp. 55–56. The colony records show that the matter "of great concernment" may have been the establishment by law of a standard bushel agreed upon by the New England Confederation. This law set a fine of twelve pence for failure to use the standard bushel in commercial transactions. The law was repealed in June 1646. *Ply. Col. Rec., II* p. 46.

43. Ibid.

session at court. Prence managed to stir up the freemen by neglecting to have the colony laws read to the General Court before ordering an adjournment, and by making some comments which he later regretted. Cautioned by a friend to use more tact in the future—tact was not one of Prence's virtues—the Governor denied that he had tried to put anything over on the freemen, but accepted "lovinghly what you have observed and hinted to me." [44] The frequency with which such conflicts occurred in the General Court is a matter only of conjecture; although probably not often. If the freemen had constant and substantial grievances against the governor and assistants it seems inconceivable that they would have continued to return them to office.

Protests of actions taken by the General Court sometimes came from the towns. Denied the right to participate directly in the colony government, the men who were not freemen but could vote for deputies sometimes tried to initiate or oppose policy through their elected representatives. Marshfield in 1645 bluntly informed the Court that it would not assent to a lease of the Kennebec fur trade to noncolony residents. Marshfield did not add what action the town planned if the Court ignored the town's instructions. [45] Other towns similarly tried to influence legislation. Rehoboth in 1672 drew up a set of written instructions for its deputies, and in the following year Scituate proposed alteration or repeal of several laws. The Scituate townsmen urged amendment of the Court's authority to reject deputies at will and suggested legislating explicit reasons for not allowing elected representatives to take their seats. Establishment of a county system of government in 1685 and transfer of some taxing power to the new county courts brought vigorous protests from several towns. Duxbury declared itself "very much dissatisfied" with the new system and protested as well the severity of newly enacted laws tightening military discipline. Scituate men charged that giving rate-making power to the county courts was an infringement of their basic rights as Englishmen and looked for a threefold augmentation of the usual charges. Scituate also protested the new militia law. But the county system and the militia regulations stayed on the books. [46]

44. Winslow Papers, Massachusetts Historical Society, Boston, *61L.42*, #4, hereafter cited as *61*.

45. Marshfield Town Records, *I*, p. 53.

46. Leonard Bliss, *History of Rehoboth* p. 71; Scituate Town Records, *I*, p. 11; Duxbury Town Records, *I*, p. 3.

In spite of occasional protests from some of the towns, the same deputies seemed to return year after year to attend sessions of the General Court. Bridgewater, which (except in two years) sent only one deputy, had four representatives between 1656 and 1692; and one of the four served nineteen years. Duxbury elected the same two representatives for twelve consecutive terms.[47] The extension of such a pattern throughout the colony meant that in any given year the personnel sitting on the Court were not likely to differ greatly from the previous court. This willingness to reelect incumbents was surely one sign of the existence of a surface equilibrium in the colony for in June 1682, when no significant political stresses were apparent, twenty-four of the twenty-seven deputies were holdovers from the preceding year. In contrast, in June 1692, when the colony was in serious political turmoil, nearly forty per cent of the deputies elected to the General Court replaced incumbents.[48]

Nevertheless, the significance of reelecting the same men should not be overestimated. Only freemen could hold the office, and possibly few among them wanted it: attending three general courts a year, and in some years four, could become all too burdensome. Moreover, in a small country town and in the absence of a formal party structure, certain difficulties clearly existed for those wishing to unseat the incumbent. Nor did the reelection of incumbents, when the presence of government did not normally intrude into the everyday life of the average citizen, necessarily indicate that politically all was well in the colony.

For, despite the transfer of power and responsibility from the governor and his advisers to the General Court (a transfer largely accomplished by 1640) in the seventeenth century Plymouth had moved away from rather than toward a wider and fuller participation by its inhabitants in the political life of the colony. Some shift of this sort was of course inevitable. The expansion and proliferation of settlement, which by 1638 required the establishment of a representative form of government, meant that government necessarily became less immediate and less responsive to the needs of its people. But the tightening of the qualifications required for participation in politics also suggests a conscious effort toward exclusiveness and a determination to

47. Ebenezer Peirce, *Civil, Military and Professional Lists of Plymouth and Rhode Island Colonies* (Boston, 1881), pp. 7–60.
48. Ibid.

preserve the internal mechanism of the state from disruptive elements. Less realistic than their predecessors, the men who initiated this policy seemed less aware that, in the absence of tradition and military power, a government must command the confidence of its people. Their failure to understand would eventually plunge the colony into political crisis.

8

"The Same Spirit of Truth"

In 1667 the Plymouth Church called John Cotton to preach and eighteen months later elected and ordained him minister. His coming gave the church a stamp of respectability: no one could doubt his commitment to orthodox Puritanism. His father, the elder John Cotton, who died in 1652, had been the preeminent clergyman in the Massachusetts colony. The younger Cotton went to Harvard and graduated in 1654. Through a sister's marriage to Increase Mather, he was a close friend of both Increase and Cotton Mather, and in his letters called Increase "brother." After he was himself married, an affair with a woman caused him some personal embarrassment—he was temporarily excommunicated from the Boston Church—but his doctrinal credentials were excellent. Ruddy-faced, short, a little fat, but a commanding speaker and a scholar, John Cotton was welcome at Plymouth despite his earlier indiscretion.[1]

Cotton's presence proved beyond the shadow of a doubt what had long since become apparent: that as John Robinson predicted, the issue of separatism was dead. Speaking to the Pilgrims before they sailed from Holland in 1620, Robinson had promised, "There will be little difference between the unconformable [Robinson meant nonseparating Puritan] ministers and you when they come to the practice of the ordinances out of the

1. John L. Sibley, *Biographical Sketches of Graduates of Harvard University,* *I* (Cambridge, 1873), pp. 496-97; Josiah Cottoh, Diary, Massachusetts Historical Society, Boston.

Kingdom." And Robinson urged "by all meanes to endeavour to close with the godly part of the Kingdome of England and rather to study union than division." [2] Robinson's prophecy had been fulfilled. The split between separating and nonseparating Puritan, between the people who tried to reform within the framework of the established church and those who abandoned the establishment and its corruptions altogether—a split which had seemed so fundamental in England—did not exist in America, and the Pilgrims had followed his advice and closed with and accepted the Massachusetts churches. To the extent that they did this, they renounced their separatist heritage, for the Massachusetts churches continued to insist they were part of the English Church. The apparent reversal in their intellectual position caused the Pilgrims little concern. Even before they sailed for the New World they had begun to move, under Robinson's guidance, toward a position of fellowship with other godly men.

At one time, a few of the Pilgrims were separatists in the most rigorous sense. Separation from the Church of England preceded the flight from Scrooby to Amsterdam and was indeed the cause of exile. In 1610, a year after the Scrooby group moved to Leyden, John Robinson's *Justification of Separation from the Church of England* appeared. Robinson's treatise was a reply to an attack upon the separatists by an Anglican clergyman, Richard Bernard, and was a defense of separatist doctrine. Robinson acknowledged that the Anglican Church contained "many excellent truths of doctrine, which we also teach without commixture of error, many Christian ordinances which we also practice being purged from the pollution of antichrist." He continued that many godly persons were communicants of the church, and "could we possibly separate them from the profane, we would gladly embrace them with both arms." That was the sore spot. The profane members of the church corrupted it as "a little leaven leaveneth the whole lump." Robinson concluded:

> Lastly, The Scriptures do expressly debar men of lewd and ungodly conversation, of all fellowship, union and communion with God. "If we say, that we have fellowship with him and walk in darkness, we lie and do not truly," saith the apostle, i John i. 6, "and what fellowship," saith Paul, "hath righteousness with unrighteousness? and what com-

2. Edward Winslow, *Hypocrisie*, p. 98.

munion hath light with darkness? and what concord hath Christ with Belial? or what part hath the believer with the unbeliever or infidel?" &c., 2 Cor. vi 14–18.[3]

Because "men admitted into the church are admitted to the participation and communion of the holy things of God in the church," and because "lewd men" had no right to the holy things of God, a church that included the profane, even if it also included some of the elect, was not truly gathered and was no church at all. Since the Church of England included both saints and sinners, it was corrupt. The godly, to preserve themselves from its corruptions, had no choice but to withdraw.[4]

Within a few years, John Robinson had begun to hedge a little on the answer to his rhetorical question of what fellowship hath righteousness with unrighteousness. The year in which *A Justification of Separation* was published three prominent nonseparating Puritan clergymen, Robert Parker, William Ames, and Henry Jacob, resided in Leyden for a few months. The three argued with Robinson and tried to convince him that he was wrong to refuse communion with godly members of the Church of England. They were not immediately successful, for Robinson and Ames exchanged bitter letters on the subject in 1611.[5] Nonetheless, what the three clergymen said to Robinson apparently made some impression. In 1614 Robinson wrote that he and the people with him had separated "from the formal state of the parish assemblies" in England and continued to maintain their separation. But Robinson admitted that his position had moderated to allow private communion with some in the English Church. He explained what he meant by private communion:

> Now from these two springheads [Robinson has been discussing "faith" and "order"; see Col. ii 5], as it were, thus distinguished do issue and arise two sorts of religious actions, or exercises: which we may not unfitly, for distinction's sake, call personal and church actions. By personal actions I do understand such as arise from, and are performed immediately by the personal faith, and other graces of God, in the hearts of holy men. Of which sort are, private prayer, thanksgiving and singing of psalms, profession

3. Robinson, *Works, 2,* pp. 15, 339.
4. Ibid., p. 324.
5. Ibid., *3,* pp. 83–89.

of faith, and confession of sins, reading or opening the Scriptures, and hearing them so read, or opened, either in the family or elsewhere, without any church power, or ministry coming between. Of the second sort, are the receiving in, and casting out of members, the electing and deposing of officers, the use of a public ministry, and all communion therewith.[6]

According to Robinson "personal actions," i.e. matters of private communion, could be entered into by all godly men jointly and together, irrespective of formal church membership. Although Robinson insisted that communicants of the English Church not participate in "our church communion, service, order of government, ministry and ministrations," by agreeing to admit them to private communion he incurred the fury of the more rigid separatists of John Smyth's church in Amsterdam. Edward Winslow, writing much later, recalled that many of Smyth's church "would hardly allow" communion with the Leyden group.[7]

A decade after Robinson agreed to private communion with all godly men, he stated that for a separatist to hear an Anglican minister preach also was lawful. Two communicants of the Leyden Church attended services in England while they were away from Leyden and drew the censure of other members of the church. Robinson defended the right to hear English ministers, for, he argued, "the preaching of many ministers in the Church of England hath, and doth, ordinarily beget men to the faith of Christ."[8] Here was further compromise with separatist doctrine, although it had been anticipated in the Seven Articles of Faith assented to by Robinson and Brewster in 1617. In their attempts to secure a patent from the Virginia Company, Robinson and Brewster had stated full agreement "to the confession of fayth published in the name of the Church of England," and continued:

> As wee do acknolidg the docktryne of fayth theer taught so do wee the fruites and effeckts of the same docktryne to the begetting of saving fayth in thousands in the land (conformistes and reformistes) as they ar called with whom

6. Ibid., pp. 102, 104.
7. Ibid., p. 126; Winslow, *Hypocrisie*, p. 84.
8. Robinson, *Works, 3*, p. 349.

also as with our brethren wee do desyer to keepe spirituall communion in peace and will pracktis in our parts all lawfull thinges.[9]

Having admitted that the English Church was capable of begetting "saving fayth to thousands in the land," it was only logical for Robinson to state five years later that communicants of the Leyden Church could listen to the word of God preached by Church of England ministers.

In spite of a willingness to compromise his earlier position and to encourage fellowship with individuals who were members of the English Church, Robinson never stopped insisting that he and his people had separated from it. In 1619, the year before the Pilgrims left Leyden, Robinson's *Just and Necessary Apology of Certain Christians* was published in a Latin edition. In *The Apology* Robinson refused to accept the tangled sophistry of nonseparating Puritans who argued that a pattern of Congregational worship could exist within the framework of the Church of England. He agreed that "if by the word church be understood the catholic church dispersed upon the face of the whole earth, we do willingly acknowledge that [we are] a singular part thereof." And he noted that the Leyden Church required no one to renounce the English Church in his or her confession of faith. But he concluded:

> if by the word church be understood a spiritual and politic body, such as was in her time the Church of Israel; and in hers the Church of Rome, Corinth, the seven Churches of Asia, and others, with them, partaking of the same apostolical constitution, and as unto which do appertain the oracles of God, sacraments, censures, government and ministry ecclesiastical, with other sacred institutions of Christ; I cannot but confess and profess, though with great grief, that it is to us a matter of scruple, which we cannot overcome, to give that honour unto it which is due from the servants of Christ to the Church of Christ, rightly collected and constituted.[10]

Robinson's position until his death was one of continued separation from the Church of England; but Robinson had aban-

---

9. "Articles from the Church of Leyden, 1617," New York Historical Society, *Collections,* Ser. II, *3* (New York, 1857), p. 301.
10. Robinson, *Works, 3,* p. 64.

doned separation from all who were not also separatists. That made it possible for Robinson, according to the sworn testimony of a University of Leyden professor, to press for the merger of his church and the nonseparatist English church in Leyden; and it meant that in America there would be no fundamental split between separating and nonseparating Puritan.[11]

Proof that the Pilgrims were anxious to escape the opprobrium of separation from other godly men appears in the writings of Bradford and Winslow. Neither tried to maintain that they and their people had not separated from the Church of England; but both claimed fellowship with other "true" churches. Winslow, who lived at Leyden from 1617 to 1620, argued that Robinson always opposed separation from the churches of Christ; and Winslow added that the Leyden Church considered itself in communion with the Scotch, French, and Dutch Reformed churches, and admitted members of the three churches to its communion. Moreover, communicants of the Leyden Church who understood the language occasionally attended the Dutch Church with the approval of Robinson and the rest of the church. Winslow admitted that Robinson at first had been more rigid in his separatist beliefs than later, but insisted "that there was nothing in the world more hatefull to him" than schism and division. Dissatisfaction with the Church of England had stemmed from a hatred of the episcopacy, the liturgy, the prayers, and the communion of the unregenerate. Never had the Pilgrims approved these, nor did they in 1646. But Winslow remembered that if any joined the Leyden Church (or later the Plymouth Church) and in the course of professing their faith declared separation from the Church of England, either Robinson or Brewster had stopped them, pointing out that the Church of England was better left to the Lord "to whom wee ought to pray to reforme what was amisse amongst them." [12]

When Winslow argued that the Pilgrims were not schismatics, he was engaging in polemical argument with Samuel Gorton and was replying to Gorton's attack on the New England churches. Bradford, none of whose writings was published until more than 200 years after his death, presumably was not. Almost thirty years after the settlement of Plymouth, Bradford wrote a dialogue between "Som Younge men borne in New England and

---

11. Testimony printed in Daniel Plooij, *The Pilgrim Fathers from a Dutch Point of View* (New York, 1932), pp. 93–94.

12. Winslow, *Hypocrisie*, pp. 88–103.

sundery Ancient men that came out of holland and old England." The young men were questioning their elders on separatism and schism. Bradford, like Winslow, denied that the Leyden Church was schismatic; he denied that the Pilgrims thought all churches corrupt but their own, "for they hold all the Reformed Churches to be true churches and euen the most Ridged of them haue euer do soe." Bradford criticized the mistaken zeal of separatists who refused communion with other godly persons. He insisted that "those of the separation as they are tearmed" had not said "that wee Remember that they [the English Church] are noe Church." Bradford argued, quoting Robinson, that if the English Church be understood to mean "the Catholique, dispersed vpon the face of the whole earth," then "a singulare p^{r}te therof, and the same visible and Conspicuous, is to be found in the land." [13]

But Governor Bradford could not bring himself to accept the reasoning of the nonseparating Massachusetts Puritans. Like Robinson he insisted that as the English Church "is a Nationall Church Combined together of all in the land promisiquously vnd the hirarchicall Gournment of archbisshopps theire Courts and Canons soe farr differing from the primetiue patteren; in the Gospell," he, at least, could not count it a true church of Christ. Replying to a question put by the "young men" whether differences in doctrine or polity existed between the Leyden Church and the churches in England, Bradford could find in polity nothing of importance,

> and for matter of Judgement it is more (as we Conceiue) in words and tearmes than matter of any Great substance, for the Churches and Cheiffe of the minnisters heer hold that the Nationall Church soe Constituted and Gou^{r}ned as before is said, is not allowable according to the p^{r}mitiue order of the Gospell, but that there are some Parrish Assemblyes that are true Churches by vertue of an Implissed Couenant amongst them selues in which Regard the Church Of England may be held and Called a true Church. [14]

Bradford added that if by an implicit covenant the New England clergy meant one "which hath the substance of a Couenant in it

13. "A Dialogue or the sume of a Conference between som younge men borne in New England and sundery Ancient men that came out of holland and old England Anno dom 1648," printed in *Plymouth Church Records, I,* pp. 115–16, 140.
14. Ibid., p. 116.

some way descernable," he supposed he agreed. Then, in a statement which punctured the fabric of sophistry woven by the nonseparating Congregational clergy, he continued: "But such an
Implised as is Noe way explised is Noe better than a popish Implised faith (as some of us Conceiue) and a meer fixion or as
that which should be a Marriage Couenant; which is noe way ex-
plissed." [15]

Although Bradford would not renounce separation from the
Church of England, the English Church was too far away now to
matter. Bradford's answer to the differences existing between the
Pilgrim Church and the churches of New England was a confirmation of Robinson's promise made at Delftshaven, a promise
that in the New World division between the Pilgrims and the
godly in the Church of England would not continue. Separation
had no place in America. The Plymouth Church was not to be a
church apart; there was no need for separation because the godly
in the English Church directed and controlled the great migration to Massachusetts. Plymouth, in fact, was prepared to help
the nonseparating Puritans of the Massachusetts Colony organize and establish their churches.

Settlement at Salem by the Massachusetts Bay Company
began in 1629, and in the spring of the year some of the new arrivals, exhausted by the crossing and suffering from malnutrition,
were down with scurvy. Word of the sickness reached Plymouth,
and Bradford asked the Pilgrim physician, Deacon Samuel Fuller,
to journey to Salem and provide whatever assistance he could.
Fuller's success in checking the outbreak of scurvy and curing the
ill is not known. John Endecott, governor of the Salem settlement, acknowledged himself "much bound" to Bradford for
sending Fuller, without mentioning the efficacy of Fuller's cures.
But Fuller accomplished much in cementing a religious understanding between Plymouth and Salem. Endecott wrote to Bradford:

> Right Worthy sir,
> It is a thing not usual, that servants to one master and of
> the same household should be strangers; I assure you I de-
> sire it not, nay to speak more plainly, I cannot be so to you:
> God's people are all marked with one and the same mark,
> and sealed with one and the same seal, and have, for the

15. Ibid., pp. 116–17.

main, one and the same heart, guided by one and the same spirit of truth; and where this is there can be no discord. . . . I acknowledge . . . your kind love and care, in sending Mr. Fuller amongst us, and rejoice much that I am by him satisfied, touching your judgements, of the outward form of God's worship; it is (as far as I can yet gather) no other than is warranted by the evidence of truth, and the same which I have professed and maintained, ever since the Lord in mercy revealed himself unto me, being far differing from the common report that hath been spread of you touching that particular.[16]

What did Endecott mean that he "rejoiced much that I am by him satisfied touching your judgment of the outward form of God's worship"? Perry Miller, whose sensitivity and knowledge of Puritan thought were unequaled, argues that Endecott was telling Bradford that he was pleased to learn that Pilgrim beliefs coincided closely with his own; that he had expected the contrary but now knew that no basic split existed between Salem and Plymouth. Miller believes that the Congregational worship established by the Massachusetts Puritans was not generic to the "free aire" of the New World, nor was it established because Fuller converted the Salem settlers to Congregationalism. By 1629, Miller continues, a generation of English Puritans taught by William Ames, Robert Parker, and Henry Jacob knew non-separating Congregationalism in theory, and a few knew it in practice: since 1616 a Congregational church had existed at Southwark. Before the migration of 1629 began, men whose sympathies leaned to Congregationalism had gained control of the Massachusetts Bay Company and agreed to establish Congregational worship in America. That John Endecott, with the approval of the Massachusetts Company, had resolved to gather a Congregational church at Salem before he sailed for the New World, Miller argues, is apparent from Endecott's request for Hugh Peter to become minister of the settlement at Salem. Peter was a leading English Congregationalist. Miller concludes: "Endecott could not have spoken this way (in the letter to Bradford) had he just been converted from Presbyterian Puritanism to Congregational Separatism; his whole tone is that of a man

16. John Endecott to William Bradford, Naumkeok, May 11, 1629, *Bradford's Letter Book*, pp. 46–47. The parentheses are Endecott's.

who has received corroboration for his own belief from unexpected quarters." [17]

No one, I think, can argue persuasively that Miller's basic premise is wrong.[18] It is very unlikely that Endecott and the two ministers who sailed with him had not talked in England with the Massachusetts Company's officers on what form of church worship they should establish in the New World. Deacon Fuller could hardly have persuaded all three to become Congregationalists and to ignore the company's decision. Finally, John Cotton the elder, preaching to Winthrop and others who left in 1630, would not have urged the governor to take advice from Plymouth if earlier a decision had not been reached to establish a Congregational discipline. It seems certain that the Massachusetts Puritans had agreed upon what Miller thinks are "the two essential features of Congregational polity, restriction of church members to the proved elect and the autonomy of particular congregations," before they left England.[19]

In implementing the Congregational way the Massachusetts Puritan unquestionably learned from the Pilgrim, perhaps more than Perry Miller admits. I do not think that Endecott, as Miller suggests, referred to general church polity when he informed Bradford he was satisfied "touching your judgments of the outward form of God's worship." For Endecott added that such was contrary "to the common report that hath been spread of you touching that particular." What was the common report? Almost certainly that the Pilgrims were separatists and denied communion with all other churches. Fuller's assurances that the report was false probably prompted Endecott's statement to Bradford. And Fuller's assurances to Endecott probably meant that church practice at Plymouth, as Fuller explained it, was influential upon the gathering of a church at Salem.

Most Massachusetts Puritans had no prior practical experience with Congregationalism; even communicants of Henry Jacob's church in Southwark discovered that Congregational worship was different in America. James Cudworth, who had be-

---

17. Miller, *Orthodoxy*, pp. 127–29.

18. Larzer Ziff tries to in "The Salem Puritans in the 'Free Aire of a New World'," Huntington Library *Quarterly, 20* (1957), pp. 373–84. In his recent book, *The Career of John Cotton* (Princeton, 1962), Ziff is closer to Perry Miller's position.

19. Miller, *Orthodoxy*, 77; *Bradford's Letter Book*, pp. 56–57.

longed to the Southwark Church, wrote in 1634 that since arriving in the New World the Lord had acquainted him "how and in what manar hee will be worshiped in." [20] Moreover, no *Cambridge Platform of Church Discipline* existed in 1629 to help resolve problems. But advice from men who had practiced Congregationalism for two decades could be had for the asking. The common sense of the matter indicates that Endecott and his ministers asked.

Apparently they not only asked but followed Fuller's advice to an extent that prompted quick reprimands from the members of the Massachusetts Company who were still in England. The latter were anxious to prevent reports of religious radicalism in Salem from jeopardizing their own plans for relocating to America. John Cotton Sr. wrote from England to Samuel Skelton, minister at Salem, cautioning: "Your change hath sprung from New-Plymouth men, whom though I much esteem as godly living Christians; yet their grounds which for this Tenant they received from Master Robinson, do not satisfy me, though the man I reverence as godly and learned." [21]

While the question of whether to admit godly men to church communion if they were not in covenant was not basic to an acceptance of Congregational worship (and does not therefore make Miller's argument untenable), it was a question that had to be resolved. Robinson and William Ames, both Congregationalists, argued the point earlier and Ames insisted that a visible communion could exist even outside of a visible church.[22] Robinson and the Pilgrim Church, however, continued to refuse public communion to members of the English Church. And in America the Salem Church apparently concurred in Pilgrim practice, much to John Cotton's annoyance. Cotton's letter, then, is not proof that the Salem colonists learned Congregationalism from

---

20. James Cudworth to John Stoughton, Scituate, December, 1634, printed in *New England Historical and Genealogical Register, 14* (Boston, 1860), p. 102.

21. John Cotton to Samuel Skelton, Oct. 2, 1630. The text of this letter is printed in Thaddeus M. Harris, *Memorials of the First Church in Dorchester* (Boston, 1830), pp. 53–57. Reference to and excerpts from this letter also appear in Robert Baillie, *A Dissuassive from the Errours of the Time* (London, 1645), p. 65. For John Cotton's conclusions about the influence of the Plymouth Church on Massachusetts Congregationalism, see John Cotton, *The Way of the Congregational Churches* (London, 1642), pp. 13–17.

22. Robinson, *Works, 3*, pp. 85–86.

Plymouth in the "free aire" of the New World. But it does indicate that in implementing Congregationalism, the Massachusetts Puritans learned much from Fuller and the Pilgrims.

Further proof exists that Cotton objected to the separatist rather than Congregational ways Salem had learned from the Pilgrims. Cotton's letter written to the Salem church warned: "Your other Errour that our Congregations in England are none of them particular Reformed Churches requireth a Book then a Letter to answer it." [23] Cotton sternly admonished the Salem minister for adopting Robinson's form of separatism since it undercut the professed nonseparating position of the Massachusetts Bay Company and gave ammunition to the company's enemies, and since many of the nonseparating Congregationalists sincerely believed withdrawal from the English Church was wrong.

The civil leaders of the Bay Company were still in England planning their great exodus for the following year. They were equally upset by hints of separatism from Salem. In the autumn of 1629 the governor and deputies of the company wrote from London cautioning the two Salem ministers to be more circumspect for "we are tender of the least Aspersion which either directly or obliquely may be cast upon the State heere." A letter also went to Endecott warning: "you are in a Government newly founded, and want that Assistance which the waight of such a Business doth require, wee may have Leaue to thinke that it is possible some Vndigested Councells haue too Sodainely bin put in Execucon which may haue ill Construccon with the State heere and make vs obnoxious to any Adversary." [24]

Salem continued, however, to seek advice from Plymouth. Fuller, Isaac Allerton, and Edward Winslow were at Salem in July 1630, when news arrived there of sickness at Charlestown. Governor Winthrop, who had arrived in America a few weeks earlier, had written telling of disease and death, and requested prayers by the people at Salem. Fuller and Winslow wrote to Bradford: "It was therefore . . . taken into the godly consideration of the best here what was to be done to pacify the Lord's

23. Harris, *Memorials,* p. 55. That Salem later settled Roger Williams suggests that Cotton's fears about separatism at Salem were well-founded.

24. These letters are printed in Ebenezer Hazard, *Historical Collections Consisting of State Papers* (2 vols. Philadelphia, 1792), *I,* pp. 287–89.

wrath; and they would do nothing without our advice, I mean those members of our church, there known unto them, viz. Mr. Fuller, Mr. Allerton and myself." [25]

Fuller did not confine his proselyting to Salem. Earlier in the year he was at Dorchester letting blood and arguing church polity. He talked with Mr. Warham, "till I was weary," about whether a visible church could consist of the godly and openly ungodly. Fuller hoped the "Lord would give a blessing" to their conversation. He met Winthrop and liked the Massachusetts leader. Fuller found some "opposers" in the Bay Colony but more friends; he sounded optimistic.[26]

Both Bradford and Winslow later insisted that the Massachusetts Puritans learned much from the Pilgrim Church. In *Hypocrisie Unmasked* (London, 1646), Winslow stated:

> And for the many plantations that came over to us upon notice of Gods blessing upon us, whereas 'tis falsely said they tooke Plimouth for their precedent as fast as they came. 'Tis true I confesse that some of the chiefe of them advised with us (comming over to be freed from the burthensome ceremonies then imposed in England) how they should doe to fall upon a right platforme of worship, and desired to that end since God had honoured us to lay the foundation of a Commonweale, and to settle a Church in it, to shew them whereupon our practice was grounded.[27]

Winslow continued that Plymouth had shown the Massachusetts settlers Pilgrim Church practice and its biblical warrant; the new arrivals had agreed that it was right and adopted it for themselves. He concluded: "So that there also thou mayest see they set not the Church at Plimouth before them for example, but the Primitive Churches were and are their and our mutuall patternes and examples." [28]

Bradford was more restrained in giving Plymouth credit for the establishment of true churches of Christ in Massachusetts. He concurred with John Cotton, who argued that no formal agreement or consultation had taken place between the Massachusetts churches and Plymouth. But Bradford admitted "It is

25. *Bradford's Letter Book,* p. 57.
26. Ibid., pp. 56–57.
27. Winslow, *Hypocrisie,* p. 92.
28. Ibid.

true they did, as if they had agreed by the same spiritt of truth and vnity sett vp by the healp of Christ; The same modle of Churches one like another." Bradford suggested that if Plymouth had influenced the establishment of the first churches in the Bay Colony, then, as in the parable of the woman who had leavened the bags of meal, the Scriptures were fulfilled.[29]

Bradford and Winslow were not alone in believing that the first Massachusetts settlers benefited greatly from Plymouth's example. William Hubbard, a seventeenth-century Massachusetts clergyman, argued that the Bay Colony was settled by men who did not arrive with a definite commitment to a particular form of church government. Hubbard insisted they had come knowing only what they disliked in the government and ceremonies of the Church of England, and at Salem "a virtual tabula rasa" existed when Deacon Fuller arrived. Hubbard concluded that later the Massachusetts clergy were not willing to admit "that they had received their platform of church order from those of Plymouth; although there is no small appearance that in whole or in part they did (further than some wise men wish they had done)."[30]

Possibly Winslow's statement, certainly Hubbard's, give excessive credit to Plymouth for the development of a Congregational order at Salem. Neither Winslow nor Hubbard was at Salem in 1629 when Endecott and the first settlers of the Massachusetts Company arrived. Winslow was there the next year and could remember the advice given by himself, Fuller, and Allerton to the Salem Church in keeping a day of humiliation. Perhaps Winslow meant such advice rather than teaching the basic doctrine of Congregationalism when he asserted that Plymouth had counseled the Salem Church, "how they do fall upon a right platform of church discipline." Hubbard came to New England in 1635 at the age of fourteen and did not write his manuscript history until forty years later. By then the distinction between what Miller calls the essential features of Congregationalism (which the Massachusetts Puritans brought with them) and the implementing of Congregational polity (which they learned from Plymouth) had apparently become blurred.

The Pilgrims share some of the responsibility for the practical working out of New England church polity. For the Plymouth

29. *Plymouth Church Records, I*, p. 123.
30. Hubbard, *History*, p. 117.

Church had the largest experience in practicing Congregationalism. John Cotton admitted as much when he urged Winthrop and others to take advice from them at Plymouth (before Cotton knew the extent to which the Salem people would follow his suggestion). Had Massachusetts not drawn upon Plymouth's experience, it is very unlikely that the New England way of church worship would have developed as it did; but it is also very unlikely that the organization of religion would have been along Presbyterian rather than Congregational lines. The intellectual roots of Congregational worship ultimately did go back to the Leyden Church and the other separatist congregations in Holland; but the transplanting was accomplished in the Old World.[31]

31. The most recent book to examine in detail the impact of Plymouth upon the Massachusetts churches is Edmund S. Morgan, *Visible Saints: The History of a Puritan Idea* (New York, 1963).

9

"A Pious Orthadox Minnestry"

THE younger Cotton's settlement at Plymouth in 1667 was important in another respect. Although the Massachusetts clergy had acted as John Robinson said they would and accepted fellowship with the Plymouth Church, they had been continually irritated by what they considered the absence of official zeal in Plymouth Colony. In particular, they disapproved of the manifest delinquency of some New Plymouth churches in providing their ministers adequate support. In September 1656, Massachusetts appealed to the commissioners of the New England Confederation. Plymouth Colony, Massachusetts had complained, seemed "to bee wanting to themselues in a due acknowlidgement of and Incurragement to the Minnesters of the Gosspell soe as many pious Minnesters of the Gosspell have (how Justly wee know not) deserted theire stations callings and Relations." The Bay Colony hoped that something might be done "that a pious Orthadox Minnestry may bee Restated amongst them." [1] This blast of public criticism was in particular intended to remind the General Court of its responsibilities, but it must also have caused embarrassment in the Plymouth Church which was again without a minister and had been so for more than a year. Its problems in finding and keeping a clergyman were all too familiar.

In spite of the paramount importance of religion in their lives, the Pilgrims had come to America in 1620 without a minister.

1. *Ply. Col. Rec., 10*, pp. 155–56.

John Robinson, who probably wanted to come, had earlier agreed not to separate himself from the majority of the church and the majority had voted not to go. The Pilgrims hoped that Robinson would join them later but they attempted to engage another clergyman in England. Their efforts, however, failed, and in the months of first settlement at Plymouth, the Pilgrims confronted the problem of establishing a permanent form of worship without a settled minister.

Certain things were clear. The Sabbath meeting did not require an ordained minister. A layman could lead the singing and read from the Bible—a deacon might well do both even if a minister was conducting the service—and, if necessary, a layman could read the prayers. Preaching the sermon, the very heart of the service for the Puritan, presented more difficulty. A layman could preach; the practice of "prophecying," i.e. lay preaching, was a long-established separatist practice and continued at Plymouth even after the settlement of a minister. But expounding, interpreting, and explaining the word of God could not be permanently entrusted to laymen. Like other Puritans, the Pilgrims believed that a clergyman must have a university education; and Robinson wrote in 1623 from Leyden and cautioned against settling anyone who was not a learned man.[2] Yet someone had to preach for the sermon could not be omitted. The Plymouth Church had no choice but to turn to educated laymen.

Unfortunately, there were few educated laymen. Not one of the early settlers was a university graduate. Elder Brewster had spent some time in residence at Peterhouse College, Cambridge, but he was apparently the only Pilgrim even to matriculate at a university. Brewster did his best. As Elder of the church and the only university-trained person, Brewster gave the plantation spiritual guidance in the early years. He conducted the services and Governor Bradford recalled that "he taught twise every Saboth, and that both powerfully and profitably to the great contentment of the hearers and their comfortable edification." Brewster also conducted the prayers and, Bradford noted with satisfaction, thought that it was better "for ministers to pray oftener, and devide their preyars than be longe and tedious in the same." The governor was positive that Brewster did more to bring people to God in a year "than many that have their hundreds a year doe in

2. Bradford, *History, I,* p. 371.

all their lives." [3] Bradford never said why Brewster did not become Plymouth's minister, but the failure to hold a university degree probably was responsible.

While Brewster could conduct worship on the Sabbath, he could not administer the sacraments. After three years at Plymouth, he wrote Robinson asking if as ruling elder he could baptize and give communion. Robinson answered no: only the clergy, "the elders that teache and exhort and labore in the word and doctrine to which the sacraments are annexed," could administer them.[4] Lyford may have baptized in 1625, but since the Plymouth Church had not ordained him minister, he did so illegally. Under Congregational doctrine, only the ordained minister of a particular church could use the sacraments in that church, and the settlers at Plymouth continued to do without them until the arrival and ordination of the Reverend Ralph Smith in 1629.

Ralph Smith, Plymouth's first settled minister, came to the plantation from Salem. William Hubbard wrote that Smith left Salem because he was a separatist and therefore unacceptable to the nonseparating Puritans of the Massachusetts Bay Colony. Bradford does not mention ecclesiastical differences but says only that Smith and his wife stayed a short time at Nantasket "with some stragling people," and that growing "wearie of being in that uncoth place and in a poore house that would neither keep him nor his goods drie," they had sought passage to Plymouth.[5] If Smith's separatism, in fact, forced him out of Salem in 1629, during his residence at Plymouth he evidently decided that there was not much point in worrying further about whether the Church of England was a true church. In 1638 Smith wrote his friend Hugh Goodyear in Holland that he had given up the ministry at Plymouth about two years before and was spending much of his time in Boston, "where, besides Our Synod . . . much of my business had bene." [6] It is very unlikely that Smith would have agreed or been permitted to attend synods of the Massachusetts clergy if he had persisted in maintaining such a rigid separatist position. Ralph Smith's stay at Plymouth was not al-

3. *Ibid.*, *2*, pp. 348, 350.
4. *Ibid.*, *1*, p. 371.
5. Hubbard, *History*, p. 97; Bradford, *History*, *2*, p. 88.
6. Ralph Smith to Hugh Goodyear, Boston, 1638, printed in Plooij, *Pilgrim Fathers*, p. 114.

together happy nor was the church happy with him. His departure in 1636 was mutually satisfactory.

Still, Plymouth could hardly have helped wondering if God was displeased with them: their experience in trying to establish a permanent minister had been so disappointing. Neither of the two clergymen who had been at Plymouth as so-called "teachers" during Smith's pastorate remained. John Norton, whom Winslow had persuaded to come to Plymouth from England and whose transportation the Pilgrims financed, stayed one winter and left for Ipswich. Roger Williams, who departed Massachusetts in hopes of finding more purity at Plymouth, found Pilgrim practices less to his liking than what he knew at Salem and returned to the Bay Colony.

After Smith left, the Plymouth Church turned to John Reyner, a graduate of Magdalene College, Cambridge. Reyner, whom Bradford thought "of a meeke and humble spirite," preached at Plymouth until 1654 when the church asked for his resignation.[7] Why Plymouth forced Reyner out is unknown; Nathaniel Morton, Bradford's nephew and Secretary of the colony, later wrote that both the people and Reyner were to blame, but Morton did not elaborate.[8] Reyner left reluctantly and, hoping that the church would take him back, returned to Plymouth in the spring of 1655. The church declined and he again departed to settle eventually at Dover, Massachusetts. It was shortly after his departure that Massachusetts appealed to the New England Confederation to remind the Plymouth government of its responsibilities.

The Plymouth Church failed to settle another minister for a decade. While several clergymen helped out on an interim basis, the burden of carrying the church fell upon Elder Thomas Cushman (Brewster died in 1644) and several of the magistrates. Not a Sunday passed, Morton proudly wrote, without two public meetings in which a neighboring minister, or Cushman, or one of the magistrates preached. Nonetheless, the Plymouth Church, in attempting to confound sectarianism and the influence of the Quakers, missed a clergyman. One of its deacons began to have doubts about Congregational orthodoxy and became an Anabaptist; he was excommunicated. Shortly thereafter, a member questioned some of the ordinances of Christ, and although lacking a

7. Bradford, *History, 2*, p. 237.
8. *Plymouth Church Records, I*, p. 107.

minister, the church tried to answer him. The attempt was not a notable success and Morton sadly noted, that "as in the prouerbe it is ezier for a Child yea a foole to Cast Stones into a well then for a wise man to Gett them out; In which Respect it had ben better to haue qvelled and stiffled such qvestions Rather; then to haue disputed them." [9]

By 1665 the failure of the Plymouth Church to secure a clergyman was a matter of grave concern. The vacancy, of course, was not unique: other New England towns had, and continued to have, similar troubles. But it was humiliating for the capital of a Puritan colony, consecrated to the end of building a godly society, to be destitute of an ordained minister.

The church extended an invitation to at least one of the several men who preached temporarily at Plymouth after Reyner left. The offer was turned down, and in September 1666, John Cotton received an invitation to come to Plymouth. Cotton was working among the Indians on Martha's Vineyard and could not accept; but in July of the next year the church again extended an offer, and the following November, Cotton and his family moved to Plymouth. Cotton remained at Plymouth for three decades.

The difficulties encountered by the Plymouth Church in settling a minister also developed in some other colony towns, while in still others, vacancies were of only short duration. Sandwich had no minister from 1653, when Leverich left for Long Island, until 1675. Taunton, on the other hand, ordained Samuel Danforth in 1687 within six months of the decease of his predecessor. Marshfield filled a vacancy in 1658 within a year; but Barnstable spent five years finding a replacement for Thomas Walley, who died in 1678.[10] Because Puritan theology required a learned ministry and because after 1640 the arrival of Puritan ministers from England had dropped off sharply, trouble and delay in finding a minister sometimes occurred in the other New England colonies. Harvard was the only local source of trained men, and there were not enough graduates to fill all positions. Still, the reports of Quaker difficulties and doubt about the willingness of a particular town to support a minister seem to have

9. Ibid., p. 92.

10. For evidence that Leverich's successor, John Smith, did not settle at Sandwich until 1675, see F. Freeman, *History of Cape Cod, 2,* footnote 2, p. 69 and footnote 1, p. 70.

accentuated the problem for some Plymouth Colony churches. The point is not that a significant number of churches were permanently without settled ministers, for they were not; rather it is that in some instances the difficulties always present in persuading a man to accept a call to a rural church may have been increased.

Some towns, trying to escape the burden of support, in fact waited for years after settlement had begun even to gather a church. Settlement began in Little Compton before 1680, but a church was not formed there until after 1700. Dartmouth, where settlers were in residence by 1660, did not organize a Congregational church until 1694.[11] Little Compton and Dartmouth were new towns, and making the prospects of settlement attractive to young clergymen was not easy. Moreover, as Puritan ardor cooled—to the General Court it apparently seemed of a negligible quantity in Dartmouth from the date of first settlement— even the devout probably sometimes wondered about the additional tax burden placed upon a town by the settlement of a minister. For, once the minister was settled, the church, and eventually the whole town, confronted the responsibility of paying for his support.

The legislation enacted in 1657 and amended in 1670 was intended to guarantee collection of clergymen's salaries, but this intent was not always realized. Even among the church members (who benefited directly when all the taxpayers were forced to support the minister) there existed strong opposition to compulsory maintenance. The question of whether to support their churches by forced contributions was not one which Congregationalists confronted in Europe. As dissenters they could place no reliance upon the state to force contributions. Therefore they had become accustomed to voluntary support for their churches. Nor was their position one of mere expediency: John Robinson had insisted that the clergy must content themselves "with the peoples' voluntary contribution whether it be less or more." [12] As heirs to such thought some New Plymouth churchmen, even when the churches were clearly in a declining condition, did not want compulsory support.

11. However, a Quaker meeting and possibly a Baptist church were organized in Dartmouth before 1700. See *History of Bristol County, Massachusetts,* D. H. Hurd, compiler (Philadelphia, 1883), p. 195.

12. Robinson, *Works, 2,* p. 467.

When a petition came from Rehoboth in 1655 asking the General Court to force men to contribute, James Brown, a magistrate from the town, offered to engage himself for those who had not paid, thus temporarily solving the problem there. In 1657, shortly after the Court passed legislation ordering compulsory maintenance, James Cudworth, a member of the Scituate Church, wrote bitterly to England: "But now we must have a State-Religion . . . a State-Minister and a stateway of Maintenance; And we must worship and serve the Lord Jesus as the World shall appoint." [13] Opposition to the new law also appeared in the town of Plymouth. Lieutenant Fuller, son of Deacon Fuller and a colony assistant, denounced it as wicked and thought "the diuell satt att the sterne when it was enacted." Fuller paid a fine of fifty shillings to the colony for his thoughts, but his point was understood; and in 1663 when the town of Plymouth levied a tax to enlarge and furnish the minister's house, the town provided "that in case som few that may scruple the way of gathering or levying the said sum by rate," they could pay voluntarily according to their just proportion.[14]

Although passage of legislation ordering compulsory support gave the towns a more regular means for raising the minister's salary, some towns, influenced by the kind of thinking articulated by the outspoken Fuller, continued voluntary contributions for a few years. Scituate did not begin to support its two ministers by taxation until 1665. Four years later Rehoboth was still trying to raise the money freely and in 1677 the town voted to send the church deacons around from house to house to see if they could persuade men to contribute £50. In 1679 Middleboro was paying Samuel Fuller, a candidate for the ministry, by contribution, although threatening legal action against anyone who would not make good on his promise.[15]

The problem in many towns seems not to have been one of requiring unwilling and sullen inhabitants who were not church members to pay; rather it was one of compelling men who had promised voluntary support to meet their commitments. Most people were of good intent; many of the towns voted adequate support, and did so without notable opposition. Bridgewater

13. This letter is printed in Bishop, *New England Judged*, pp. 131–32.
14. *Ply. Col. Rec.*, *3*, p. 150; *Plymouth Town Records, I*, p. 58.
15. Scituate Town Records, *I*, pp. 1–2; Bliss, *Rehoboth*, pp. 68–69; Middleboro Town Records, Middleboro, Massachusetts, *I*, p. 11.

voted to pay its first minister, James Keith, £40 and to give him his wood, a house, and a purchase right in the town. When the town later proposed raising his salary to £50, only "four or five" opposed. The younger Cotton's salary at Plymouth was £50 in 1667, the first year of his settlement, but soon rose to £80. The town unanimously agreed in 1668 to provide for Cotton's wife and children in case of his decease. Rehoboth paid a salary of £60; Eastham paid £60. Duxbury gave Mr. Wiswall £50, and in 1687, when Sir Edmund Andros governed all New England and the forcible collection of a clergyman's rate was illegal, only seven persons refused to pay for Wiswall's support.[16] Salaries of between £50 and £80 were not high, but they were not far below Massachusetts levels. Charlestown paid £100 and Salem £125, but Braintree and Dedham gave their ministers salaries about equal to those paid in New Plymouth.[17] A minister who received a salary of £70 in the Plymouth Colony received—if he collected—£20 more than the salary paid to the governor of the colony.

Collection was indeed the problem, and in many of the towns, ministers' salaries were continually in arrears. Plymouth in 1679 was trying to collect £6-3-0 due John Cotton in 1677. To solve its problem of getting the money in on time, Rehoboth tried collecting every Sabbath. Yarmouth in 1679 agreed that failure to meet its minister's salary was "a blemish" on the town, and voted "to do something about it." Bridgewater seemed always to be behind in its payments to James Keith. In 1670 the town met and "did once more promise to get in his pay." Eight years later the town voted "to take account that it may be known what is due from the time of his beginning." [18]

When delinquencies occurred some of the towns seemed reluctant to initiate judicial proceedings. Eastham voted in 1691 to make up what the Quakers owed and refused to pay. With the

16. Bridgewater Town Records, *I*, pp. 34, 51, 79, 91; *Plymouth Town Records, I*, pp. 87, 111–12, 164; Bliss, *Rehoboth*, p. 120; Eastham Town Records, Eastham, Massachusetts, *I*, p. 40; Duxbury Town Records, p. 182.

17. Richard Frothingham Jr., *The History of Charlestown* (Boston, 1845), p. 185; *Records of the Town of Braintree, I* (Randolph, 1886), p. 12; *The Early Records of the Town of Dedham, Massachusetts, 1672–1706, 5* (Dedham, 1899), p. 9.

18. *Plymouth Town Records, I*, p. 160; Bliss, *Rehoboth*, p. 71; Yarmouth Town Records, Yarmouth, Massachusetts, *2*, n.p.; Bridgewater Town Records, *I*, pp. 70, 74.

agreement of the town selectmen, Bristol instructed its assessors to tax, more heavily in apportioning other charges, those persons who refused to pay. Marshfield, at least once, sought redress through the courts, for in 1669 four Marshfield men were found guilty of not paying their church taxes; three were sentenced to pay double their assessed rates; one was let off because of old age.[19] Relatively few instances appear in the colony's court records of men hailed to court for refusal to support the church.

The ministers usually accepted the towns' unfulfilled promises with long-suffering patience, and no evidence that I have come across even hints that a minister sued his town to collect back pay. On the contrary, they sometimes offered to write off part of their promised salaries. Mr. Treat of Eastham voluntarily forgave £10 because of bad crops in 1683. The next year Bristol's Benjamin Woodbridge offered to accept a reduced salary when payment of the full amount excited controversy in the town.[20] The clergy were accommodating, provided they received sufficient funds to live on; they were, after all, students of human nature. In spite of the discouragements which existed in particular towns, most Plymouth Colony churches were able to attract Harvard graduates.

John Cotton was the first Harvard graduate to settle in Plymouth Colony and others followed: Samuel Treat went to Eastham in 1672; Jonathan Russell to Barnstable in 1683; Thomas Mighill to Scituate the following year; Samuel Danforth to Taunton in 1687. In 1691 John Cotton Jr. settled at Yarmouth, and the following year his brother Rowland went to Sandwich.

One consequence of this arrival of Harvard-educated men to fill Plymouth Colony pulpits was the strengthening of the ties of personal friendship between the clergy in the two colonies. Since the settlement at Salem in 1629, ministers from the two colonies had corresponded and consulted. John Reyner and Elder Brewster had written to the "Reverend Brethren of the Church of Christ in Boston" asking for advice on the problem of maintaining church worship as the population scattered. When Charles Chauncy argued for baptism by immersion, Reyner and the

---

19. Eastham Town Records, *I*, p. 59; Wilfred H. Munro, *The History of Bristol, Rhode Island* (Providence, 1880), pp. 126-27; *Ply. Col. Rec.*, *5*, p. 28.
20. Eastham Town Records, *I*, p. 10; Munroe, *Bristol*, pp. 126-27.

Plymouth Church wrote to the clergy and churches in Connecticut, Massachusetts, and New Haven.[21] But such correspondence and consultation were probably more official than personal. Although some of the first ministers in both colonies had been good friends in England they had not shared a common training in the New England way. Their successors, on the other hand, learned their orthodoxy at Harvard, and as the young graduate went out to preach the word of God, he carried with him not only a shared academic training, but the bonds of fellowship forged in four years at college. The New England ministers who had gone to Harvard constituted a fraternity that made colony bounds inconsequential.

John Cotton, for example, exchanged pulpits with both Mathers, and Cotton Mather boarded one of Cotton's sons when the boy was at grammar school in Cambridge. While Cotton's strong family tie to the Mathers gave him a unique connection with the Boston clergy, other New Plymouth ministers also maintained close contact with the Massachusetts world. Jonathan Russell of Barnstable and Samuel Danforth of Taunton were the sons of prominent Massachusetts ministers. Ichabod Wiswall, Duxbury's minister, accepted an invitation to preach in the Boston First Church and in 1687 was sent to England on Massachusetts' business. The following year the Harvard Corporation asked Samuel Lee of Bristol to conduct the college commencement.[22]

When viewed in retrospect Cotton's settlement at Plymouth in 1667 symbolized the arrival of respectability. Although separatism at Plymouth was long since dead, the call to Cotton gave the final assurance; doubts about orthodoxy in the Plymouth Church could now cease. His presence in the citadel of government could help stiffen the civil authority to meet its responsibilities in the future. Cotton's acceptance of the call to Plymouth was also an indication that other Harvard graduates would follow and settle in the colony; and the arrival of men who shared the experience of a common education and who would continue

21. John Cotton Papers, Boston Public Library, Boston, *2*, #116–17; Winthrop, *History of New England, I*, p. 398.

22. "Diary of Increase Mather," Massachusetts Historical Society, *Proceedings,* Ser. II, *13* (Boston, 1900), pp. 345, 363, 371; Mather Papers, MSS, Boston Public Library, *4*, #9; Cotton Papers, *8*, #18; Massachusetts Historical Society, *Collections*, Ser. IV, 8, *The Mather Papers* (Boston, 1868), p. 502.

to maintain their fraternal ties after graduation, in turn, seemed to promise that church practices in New Plymouth would become institutionalized. Thus more pressures toward uniformity existed after 1670 than were evident earlier; but the effectiveness of those pressures in imposing a single pattern of church worship should not be exaggerated.

I O

"The Right Worship of God"

For the Puritan, church polity was always of cardinal importance. His quarrel with the Anglican, at least until the tide of
Arminianism swept through the English Church, was not over
doctrinal fundamentals. Before the Pilgrims sailed for America,
they insisted they were quite willing to acknowledge their acceptance of Anglican doctrine: "to the confession of fayth published
in the name of the Church of England and to every artikell
thereof wee do with the reformed churches weer we live and also
els wheer assent wholly." [1] But church polity was something else.
The very essence of Puritan protest projected cleansing the Anglican Church of the government and ceremonies left over from
Catholicism, of returning to the pristine simplicity of the early
days of Christianity and, by using and interpreting the Bible, establishing "a discipline out of the word." The issues of the
church's organization and government precipitated the Pilgrim
flight to Holland.

The Pilgrims and other Congregationalists argued that organization of a church could be accomplished in one way only. A
number of persons covenanted and formed a church to which
others seeking membership and able to meet the necessary requirements were afterwards admitted. Although Congregational
theory directed that a sifting take place to determine, through
discussion, who were among the godly and therefore capable of

1. "Articles from the Church of Leyden, 1617," New York Historical Society,
Collections, Ser. II, *3*, p. 301.

gathering a church, in practice earlier membership in another church eliminated the need for testing. John Lothrop, Scituate's first minister, noted in his diary: "Uppon January 8th [1635] wee had a day of humiliation and then at night joined in Covenant together so many of us as had beene in Covenant before." [2] The criterion used at Scituate to determine the qualifications of first members was not unique. For more than half the churches formed in Plymouth Colony before 1692, at least a hint exists to suggest that they were formed with an initial membership of people who had been in covenant in another church. Before leaving Holland the Plymouth Church organized as a separate body with many, if not most, of its members drawn from the Leyden Church. Plymouth's church in turn claimed four direct offshoots in the Old Colony: the Duxbury, Marshfield, Eastham, and Middleboro Churches all formed from a nucleus of Plymouth saints.

One of the basic doctrines of Congregational worship was selectivity in church worship. Puritans—Presbyterians and Congregationalists alike—believed only certain men to be regenerate and capable of salvation. But the Presbyterians never attempted to distinguish between the elect and the damned; that was, they argued, better left to God. The Congregationalists disagreed; while at first they did not require evidence of election for membership, by 1640 they were insisting that since the unregenerate were forever barred from entering a covenant with God, a true church could include only proven saints:

> The doors of the churches of Christ upon earth do not by God's appointment stand so wide open, that all sorts of people, good and bad, may freely enter therein at their pleasure, (2 Chr XXIX. 19; Mat XIII. 25, and XXII. 12,) but such as are admitted thereto, as members, ought to be examin'd and tryed first, whether they be fit and meet to be received into church-society or not.[3]

At one time New England Puritans hoped that most settlers would be "fit and meet." James Cudworth wrote from Scituate in

---

2. Diary of John Lothrop, copied by Ezra Stiles from a manuscript Stiles found in the possession of Elijah Lothrop of Gilead, Connecticut, and since lost. Stiles' copy is in Stiles Papers (bound with a copy of Winthrop's History of New England), pp. 323–63, Yale University, New Haven, Connecticut.

3. Cotton Mather, *Magnalia, 2,* p. 225.

1634 urging a friend in London to promote the sending of men fit to be received into church fellowship.[4] And limitation of the franchise in Massachusetts to church members was probably done in the belief, certainly the hope, that many of the males coming to settle the colony would join the church and be entitled to a vote. The hope had not materialized: along with the godly had come more who were not. They attended Sabbath worship; they helped support the minister; they probably formed a majority of the congregation in many towns, but they were not church members.

By 1645 the distinction between saint and sinner, so far as evidence is available, was maintained in every New Plymouth town except those in which Quaker meetings were organized. Edward Winslow acknowledged in 1646 that Plymouth churches desired "to see the grace of God shining forth (at least seemingly, leaving secret things to God) in all we admit into church fellowship with us, and to keep off such as openly wallow in the mire of their sins, that neither the holy things of God, nor the communion of the Saints may be leavened or polluted thereby." [5] But how much a church demanded of the candidate for church membership and whether many, if any, were rejected, varied from one church to another. In Holland and during the early years at Plymouth, all that was required of the candidate was agreement to the confession of faith and acceptance of the covenant.[6] In time, some kind of a testimonial of God's grace, at first given publicly, later, in some churches at least, privately, was asked; some assurance that the supplicant in fact was truly one of God's elect. Samuel Newman, Rehoboth's minister, suggested "NOTES, OR THE MARKS OF GRACE, I FIND IN MYSELF." He included: a love of God and a desire to love God for Himself, a desire to requite evil with good, a looking up to God, and a greater fear of displeasing God than of displeasing the world.[7]

If we can believe Charles Chauncy, the standards which Newman set for himself were not followed in the Second Scituate Church. Chauncy who moved from Plymouth to Scituate in 1641, and whose policies split the Scituate Church, wrote to the Church

4. James Cudworth to John Stoughton, Scituate, December, 1634, *New England Historical and Genealogical Register, 14,* p. 103.
5. Edward Winslow, *Hypocrisie,* p. 98.
6. E. S. Morgan, *Visible Saints,* pp. 43–44.
7. Cotton Mather, *Magnalia, I,* p. 432.

of Roxbury that the dissident church "have since great multitudes
added to them, (as we hear) nine or ten in a day concerning di-
verse of whom we have just cause to doubt, that they are not
lively stones for such a spiritual house." [8] William Vassall,
lay leader of the Second Church and subsequent critic of the exclusiveness of religion in New England, admitted "we shall not
refuse into our society such of God's people whose hearts God
shall incline to joyne themselves with us for the furtherance of the
worship of God amongst us and the good of their souls." [9] Use
of the sacraments was one of the privileges of church membership usually denied to men not in church covenant. The Scituate
Second Church, Vassall affirmed, ignored this policy and admitted men and women who were not in particular fellowship to the
sacraments. But even the Second Church observed the form of asking for evidence of regeneracy before allowing a person to share
in the Lord's Supper.

A liberal policy of admission to church membership also existed in more respectable churches. Plymouth's church, for one,
was not rigorous in asking proof of election. In Bradford's
"Dialogue" between the Young Men of New England and the
Ancient Men who came from Holland and Old England, the
Young Men asked: "Wherein doe they (the separatist churches)
differ then from the Judgement or practice of our churches hear
in New England?" To this the Ancient Men replied: "Truly for
matter of practice Nothing att all that is in any thinge materiall
these being Rather more strict and Ridged in some proceedings
about admission of Members and things of such Nature than the
other." [10] John Robinson had written in *A Justification of Separation from the Church of England* that concerning salvation "a
man can say this onely of himself certaynly because he onely
knows his own heart but of others morally and in the judgment
of charity which is according to outward appearance and which
may deceive." These words are underlined in Bradford's copy of
Robinson's book.[11]

Following Cotton's settlement in 1667, when Bradford and the
others who had belonged to Robinson's church were dead, some
tightening seems to have taken place in the procedural require-

8. Printed in Deane, *Scituate,* p. 64.
9. Norwell First Church Records.
10. *Plymouth Church Records, I,* p. 116.
11. Bradford's copy of Robinson, *Justification,* p. 433.

ments for admission to the Plymouth Church. Individuals desiring church membership were asked to make a public statement to the church recounting the experience of the awakening of God's grace within them, an experience called by the Puritans "conversion." Presumably those whose experiences were shams would be exposed in the process of disclosure and in the questioning of the church which sometimes followed. If this requirement in fact made actual admission more difficult, it was not because candidates failed to satisfy the church, but because they failed to satisfy themselves. John Cotton later insisted that while he was Plymouth's minister, no one seeking church membership was ever refused.[12] Cotton's statement, if it is true—and I see no reason to doubt him—is important for it sheds new light on the division in seventeenth-century New England between saints and sinners, a division which unsympathetic historians have exploited with such enthusiasm. Cotton, of course, spoke only for Plymouth, but his statement could have a wider significance.

While the church records for many towns no longer exist, those which have survived the ravages of three centuries suggest that in some towns a substantial proportion of the adult citizens were church members. In 1667, the year of Cotton's settlement, the Plymouth Church, after more than a decade without a resident minister, numbered only forty-seven communicants. But in the thirty years which followed, 178 more people joined. Although exact population figures for the town are lacking, in 1688 the town's militia company, which included most of the males between sixteen and sixty, counted 155 men. This suggests that the total adult population of the town was probably less than 350.[13] At Barnstable, when Jonathan Russell settled as minister in 1683, seventy men and women were communicants of the Church, twelve of them being members "in remote places." Between 1683 and 1692, the Barnstable Church admitted fifty-nine new members. Barnstable was the county seat and the largest town on the Cape, but Barnstable's militia company in 1688 numbered only 134 men. Sandwich had a considerably smaller number of church members. In 1694, Rowland Cotton, Sandwich's newly settled minister, recorded the names of twenty-one members, and in the next six years, only six more joined the

12. *Plymouth Church Records, I*, pp. 181–82.
13. Ibid., *I*, pp. 143, 180; Greene and Harrington, *Population*, p. 21.

church.[14] But existence of a Quaker church in Sandwich and the religious contention which had existed in the town for a quarter century help to account for the small number of members there.

Membership in the church was important to an individual not only for the promise of his own salvation, but because it entitled his or her children to baptism. Before 1662 Congregational theory directed that baptism could be given only to the children of church members in full communion. While baptism would not ensure that the baptized child was one of the elect the sacrament provided for temporary acceptance of the child into the covenant of grace. This could be of some comfort to a father and mother whose child died, and if the child lived to maturity, although baptism in theory had no influence on conversion, in practice it probably made it more likely.

The problem of excluding children from baptism because their parents were not in full communion had not existed for Congregationalists in the Old World. There Congregational churches were dissenting and the members were presumably in full communion. But in America the situation was different. Congregationalism in New England was the state religion, and, until the middle of the seventeenth century, the only religion. And even after 1670, although Baptist and Quaker churches existed in Plymouth Colony, Congregationalism was the only choice for most people. Since the Congregational churches were supposed to admit only the children of proven saints to baptism, most other children were in theory excluded.

By 1660 the number of church members in Massachusetts was declining and the future was looking bleak for some of the churches. The children of the first generation had found it increasingly difficult to recapture the intensity of their parents, and by 1660 the presumption of the covenant continuing through the children of saints to the grandchildren was proving unwarranted. If the number of saints continued to decline, God would surely forsake New England as He had forsaken other people, and the great experiment would crash in ruins. Of more immediate and practical concern, the authority of the church as a moral force in the disciplining of youth would disintegrate if there were no children in covenant to look after.

14. Records of the West Parish of Barnstable, Massachusetts. Photostatic copy in the Massachusetts Historical Society; Sandwich Church Records, pp. 1–15.

In 1662 the Massachusetts clergy found a solution for their perplexing problem. At the request of the colony's General Court, the clergy met in a synod and altered requirements for baptism. Through a new "Half-Way Covenant" the grandchildren of members in full communion could be accepted into the church covenant and baptized even if their parents were not in full communion. The parents must only profess their assent to the covenant and renew their allegiance to the church. The Half-Way Covenant made no compromise, however, and denied baptism to children whose parents had not "owned" the covenant. Such was Congregational doctrine: the actual practice was sometimes different.

John Lothrop, minister of Scituate and later of Barnstable, went so far as to ignore doctrine completely and occasionally baptized the children of men and women who had no connection with the church whatsoever.[15] But Lothrop's liberalism was unusual. Some of the churches in New Plymouth not only refused baptism to the children of the unregenerate but rejected use of the Half-Way Covenant.

In Holland, John Robinson had administered baptism to children one of whose parents was a member in full communion of a reformed church, and in America the Plymouth Church continued to insist upon this requirement. The Plymouth saints did not accept the Half-Way Covenant until 1731; even then, Nathaniel Leonard, who had succeeded to the ministry in 1723, needed seven years of argument to convince the church. According to his grandson, John Cotton accepted the Half-Way Covenant but never managed to persuade his church.[16]

Other New Plymouth churches also rejected the Half-Way Covenant. The Barnstable Church under Jonathan Russell baptized only the children of members in full communion, and efforts by Thomas Thornton to introduce the Covenant at Yarmouth encountered stiff opposition. John Cotton wrote to Increase Mather in 1678 and asked for twenty copies of the book Mather had written in support of the Half-Way Covenant; Cotton thought they might be of great use in quieting the contention at Yarmouth, although Mather ironically was himself a late convert to the doctrine. In the Bristol Church from 1688 until 1691

15. Lothrop's Diary, pp. 322–36. Stiles noted this, see Stiles Papers, pp. 365–66.
16. Bradford, *History, I*, p. 82; John Cotton, *The General Practice of the Churches of New-England Relating to Baptism Vindicated* (Boston, 1772), p. 10; *Plymouth Church Records, I*, pp. 230–43.

the children of saints alone received baptism. Until 1704 the names of all baptized children at Sandwich have the same surname as that of a church member. Middleboro's Church Covenant of 1694 pledged that baptism be administered to visible church members and their children, and the Kingston Church, Yale President Ezra Stiles later noted, refused to accept the Half-Way Covenant until the middle of the eighteenth century.[17]

As in Massachusetts, opposition to the Half-Way Covenant in New Plymouth apparently came from lay membership rather than from the clergy. Cotton and Thornton favored it, and it seems very likely that their Harvard-trained colleagues, who by 1690 were occupying a number of Plymouth Colony pulpits, also approved. Failure of the Covenant to win acceptance in New Plymouth may indicate that the clergy were less powerful than in Massachusetts where, in the Boston churches at least, after initial rejection, the ministers persuaded their congregations to accept it. John Cotton's grandson, who wrote an essay in the eighteenth century favoring adoption of the Covenant, suggested that perhaps the reason why it had not become polity earlier at Plymouth was because none of "this sort" applied to have their children baptized.[18] Perhaps there is another reason. The Half-Way Covenant had not developed in a vacuum: declining church membership in Massachusetts had forced the clergy to come up with an expedient, a compromise. If in fact the admission requirements were less rigorous in some New Plymouth churches than in the Bay Colony, the Half-Way Covenant may have been unnecessary to assure a continuing membership.

In their efforts to show that the Puritan religion in New England followed a pattern from which deviation was not allowed, sympathetic and unsympathetic historians alike have emphasized the informal control exercised over supposedly Congregational churches by a consensus of ministers agreeing in a synod. While decisions agreed upon in such synods were not binding upon the individual churches no one can deny their importance in formu-

17. Barnstable Church Records; *Mather Papers,* p. 247. Stiles copied the names of the early communicants of the Bristol Church, see Stiles, Itineraries, Yale University Library, *3,* p. 8. Early baptisms at Bristol in *New England Historical and Genealogical Register, 34* (1880), pp. 132–33; *Book of the First Church of Christ in Middleborough* (Boston, 1859), p. 19; Stiles, Itin., *2,* p. 388.
18. John Cotton, *General Practice,* p. 21.

lating and stabilizing a New England way; but the emphasis, I think, has gone too far.

Some New Plymouth churches distrusted the idea of ministers even meeting in synods. Massachusetts called the first formally-convened synod of clergy in 1646 to write a platform of Congregational worship and invited clergy from the four Puritan colonies. Ralph Partrich, Duxbury's minister, was apparently the only Plymouth Colony clergyman to attend.[19] Partrich played a prominent part and, along with the elder John Cotton and Richard Mather, wrote the Cambridge Platform. But elsewhere in New Plymouth John Lothrop, the old Congregationalist from Southwark, and his Barnstable Church, held a day of humiliation "partly for Old England, partly for the State of this Country to preventing evill that might come by their Synod or discontented persons and partly for ourselves." [20]

Governor Bradford also had doubts about the calling of synods. In the back of his copy of Robinson's *Separation Justified* he wrote that councils of ministers were permissible so long as they did not infringe upon the orders of Christ or the liberties of the brethren. When and if they decreed against the testimony of the Scriptures they should be ignored: "It seems unto men not the part of Christian man to appeal from the Scriptures of God to man's judgement." Bradford may have been responsible for legislation protecting the colony churches from outside interference. In 1646, when he was governor, the General Court agreed to act "to mayntaine the libertys of the churches without intermedleing or wronging eich other, according to the statutes of England, that they may liue in peace." [21]

Plymouth Colony's suspicion of synods seems to have continued and there is no evidence that any colony ministers attended the Massachusetts synod called in 1657 to discuss baptism. Cotton Mather later wrote that the Plymouth clergy "regularly" met to resolve questions of doctrine, and while Mather may be correct, he may also have overstated the case. Only once is there record of an attempt to convene the colony clergy. In 1676 John

19. *Records of Massachusetts Bay, 2*, p. 156; *A Sermon Preached at the Ordination of the Reverend Mr. Chandler Robbins by his Father Philemon Robbins with an Appendix Containing an Account of the Church of Christ in Plymouth by a member of the said Church* (Boston, 1760), Appendix, p. 28.

20. Lothrop's Diary, p. 347.

21. Bradford's copy of Robinson, *Justification*, back flyleaf; *Ply. Col. Rec., 2*, p. 106.

Cotton suggested a meeting of all the colony ministers and the next year Governor Winslow asked the churches for an opinion on the extent of tolerance permissible to dissenters. Some of the ministers and ruling elders assembled and tried to come to a resolution of the question, but many were absent; moreover, the problem under consideration was not one that had any bearing on church practices.[22]

The individual church then was not subject to external ecclesiastical control. If internal dissension existed and attempts to heal it failed, a church could ask for the convention of a council of ministers and lay brethren from other churches to advise a solution. When a new minister was ordained, usually the clergy from neighboring churches were present and one extended "the right hand of fellowship" showing approval of the new man. If a church deviated too far from accepted doctrine, other churches could refuse to have communion with it; but that was the extent of control available to the clergy and churches over practices and policy in a particular church.

Ultimately each church could ordain or depose its minister without recourse to higher authority. Churches usually ordained only men of academic training, but they occasionally settled non-university men. In 1660 Vassall's old church called Nicholas Baker who was not a university graduate. Customarily the clergy from other churches "laid on hands" at an ordination to indicate approval, and, at least by implication, the affirmation of apostolic succession; but Baker, according to tradition—there is no other evidence—was ordained by the laying on of lay hands. If the story is true, perhaps Baker's lack of proper academic training may have prompted the clergy to refuse to participate. Yet the Scituate Second Church went ahead and ordained Baker by itself. Middleboro also settled a man without university training; Plymouth's church approved and sent Cotton and four members to attend.[23]

In Massachusetts the clergy did not approve of preaching by the lay brethren. Although the ministers acknowledged that in the years of first settlement the practice might have been justified they later insisted that it no longer was acceptable. But several

22. John G. Palfrey, *History of New England* (Boston, 1860), *2*, p. 488. Palfrey states that no Plymouth ministers attended and I have found nothing to indicate they did; Mather, *Magnalia, 1*, p. 62; Cotton Papers, *7*, #13, 30.

23. Stiles, Itin., *2*, pp. 389–92; *Plymouth Church Records, 1*, p. 176.

Plymouth Colony churches allowed laymen to preach. When John Winthrop worshipped with the Pilgrim Church in October 1632, he heard Bradford and "some two or three more" speak and then was invited to do so himself. After John Reyner left in 1654, laymen preached regularly to the Plymouth Church. Bridgewater's lay elder also preached to his church when its minister was ill for several months in the winter of 1668.[24]

A church could also decide upon the conduct of its service. While Charles Chauncy was minister, the Scituate Church held communion in the evening and, given Chauncy's reason for leaving Plymouth, probably practiced baptism by immersion.[25] Marshfield's church also celebrated communion in the evening. The Plymouth Church in 1680 discussed whether to read a psalm before singing it, and when the argument became heated, asked John Cotton to preach on the subject. Cotton favored a prior reading, but it was the church members who had to decide. In this instance, Cotton's preaching persuaded them, and they voted to change earlier practice and have Cotton read the psalm before the congregation sang it. Until the end of the century, however, the Plymouth Church continued to use the *Ainsworth Psalm Book,* which the Pilgrims brought with them from Holland, instead of the newer *Bay Psalm Book* used by the Massachusetts churches.[26]

To conduct its administrative business the Plymouth Church met monthly, and probably other churches similarly convened at regular intervals. Such meetings at Plymouth began and ended with a prayer but they were not services of worship. Policies were discussed and voted, the church sometimes voting by hand, sometimes agreeing by not voicing disapproval as in the admission of "old Goodman Briant" to church membership; sometimes every man spoke in turn, as in the election of a deacon. Topics for discussion covered a wide variety of matters: whether the blessing should precede or follow the sacrament, whether to allow reticent men to make their confession in private, whether to renew the covenant, whether to deal with the offending chil-

24. Hubbard, *History,* pp. 65–66; Winthrop, *History of New England, I,* p. 109; *Plymouth Church Records, I,* p. 109; Nahum Mitchell, *History of the Town of Bridgewater* (Boston, 1849), p. 64.

25. See Chapter 5, p. 62.

26. *Plymouth Church Records, I,* pp. 156–57, 171; "Marshfield Church Records," *Mayflower Descendant, II,* p. 38.

dren of members in private only, what to do with church contributions; the church even argued about whether the first Christians were in covenant.[27]

When troubles came and it appeared that God was angry, the church discussed the probable cause of His wrath, and when conditions seemed to warrant it ordered a day of humiliation. Twice during King Philip's War and again in 1692 when civil order was disintegrating, the church found the state of the colony so distressing that it tried renewing the covenant as a means of assuaging God's anger.[28] Nor were God's blessings forgotten. During good times or when a general sickness or threat of trouble had passed, the church held a day of thanksgiving. John Lothrop recorded a day of thanksgiving observed at Scituate in December 1636, "the day being very cold." After Lothrop said a short prayer there came the singing of a psalm, followed by more lengthy prayers and another psalm. Lothrop preached and the service concluded with a prayer and final psalm. The purpose of a thanksgiving day for the early Puritan was, of course, to give thanks to Almighty God, but the turkey dinner was not forgotten. At Scituate, after the service all made merry feasting, the rich hosting "the poorer sort." [29]

Churches not only acted upon administrative matters: they also discussed and sat in judgment on the conduct of their members, a practice which has given the New England Puritans an unenviable reputation in the history books of their descendants. The sour, prying Puritan in his black stovepipe hat, peering around corners, is all too familiar. The Puritan did pry— although he did not wear the black stove-pipe except to church —but he pried for a reason. As a member of his church, he and the others in the church were knit together in covenant with God. Should one of them sin and the church fail to act then all bore the taint of the sin. New Englanders established their churches on the principle that only the elect could form a true church of Christ. They would not admit people who did not show proof of regeneracy; and even those who were the elect and supposedly predestined to salvation had to maintain a high standard of conduct, for the chance always existed that a pretender had joined the church.

27. *Plymouth Church Records, I*, pp. 143–89, 249–82.
28. Ibid., pp. 148, 169.
29. Lothrop's Diary, p. 351.

The Puritan freely admitted that churches were not infallible in distinguishing the elect from the hypocrite. But when a pretender did slip in and his hypocrisy became apparent the church had to eject him; and what would be better evidence of a false saint than one who sinned and refused to profess contriteness? The Puritans were not so hardheaded that they ignored human frailty; on the contrary, they taught the inherent depravity and corruption of all men. But though a man might sin, a true saint would repent and then, if the sin was not too grievous, be permitted to continue within the covenant. The Roman Catholic confessional had contributed to Protestant revolt, but by 1650 the Puritan in New England, although from a different point of view, also was giving emphasis to the public confession of a sinner.

John Cotton recorded for posterity the excommunication of a Plymouth saint in 1681.

> A brother formerly failing by intemperance was againe overtaken in the same kinde, he not attending the chh that Sabbath the Elders ordered him, he was appointed to come to a private chh-meeting, his expressions and behaviours were offensive to the chh then, soe they were the Sabbath after; He was then bidden to come the next Sabbath but he absented; The chh met in private and he not humbling himselfe, yet exercised patience towards him for 2 Sabbaths more, at the Sabbath when he was expected He came not to meeting and though sent for came not, for all which He was by the Elder in the name of the chh excommunicated, and within 2 years after upon his manifestation of repentance was reconciled to the chh.[30]

Cotton's patience was apparently stretched in this particular case for he wrote Governor Hinckley in 1681 that God had finally given the church strength to excommunicate "the old drunkard," Samuel Dunham.[31] The Scituate Church acted with similar restraint against Christopher Winter. Winter finally suffered excommunication for marrying Mrs. Cooper, a woman "of scandalous carriage being light vain proud, much given to scoffing." The church took the decision only after hours spent arguing with Winter trying to convince him to give up the idea of marrying

30. *Plymouth Church Records, I*, p. 157.
31. Cotton Papers, *6*, #6.

this frivolous lady. But when the church excommunicated him, several of the members registered their dissent by stalking out of the meeting.[32]

Of course, for some offenses excommunication was quick and almost automatic. Scituate hastily excommunicated a man for homosexuality; Barnstable purged Roger Goodspeed for bearing false witness and John Smith Jr. for refusing to join with the church in communion. But John Lothrop's Scituate and Barnstable churches may have been unusually quick to excommunicate. Between 1634 and 1652, Lothrop's churches expelled seven saints. Plymouth's church, while Cotton was its minister, excommunicated only six members in a quarter century; and three of the six were persons who had left town and subsequently refused to acknowledge any continuing tie to the church.[33]

Even for the man whose conscience was clear, excommunication was not something casually shrugged off. Arthur Howland, who was purged from the Marshfield Church, insisted that Marshfield's minister had instructed all the church members not to eat or drink with him and had directed "the neighbours of the town that they should not carry femillery to him." [34] As in Massachusetts, no civil penalties followed excommunication unless a civil or criminal law had been broken; but even if the state did not act, and even if such extreme proscription as occurred in Marshfield was not usually the fate of a fallen sinner, some social alienation must have followed.

Free to order their polity as they saw fit, the Congregational churches in New Plymouth Colony were in practice, as well as theory, "congregational." Of course, limits existed beyond which a church could not go without incurring the disapproval of the other churches in the colony, and especially after 1650 the government kept a watchful eye open for the bloom of heterodoxy. But provided that a church stayed within the basic structure of Congregationalism it could exercise certain freedoms. Each church could set its own standards for the admission of members and decide who and for what it would excommunicate; it could accept or reject the Half-Way Covenant as it saw fit; it could choose and dismiss its minister; it could establish when it would

32. Lothrop's Diary, pp. 354–55, 359.
33. Ibid., pp. 354–58; *Plymouth Church Records, I*, pp. 143–69.
34. This letter is printed in Joseph Hager, *Marshfield: The Autobiography of a Plymouth Town* (Marshfield, 1940), pp. 39–41.

celebrate the Lord's Supper, when it would say the blessing, whether it would sing the psalms.

In the context of our own time these freedoms do not seem very impressive, particularly when we remember that churches which challenged the basic premises of Congregational worship were for some time the targets of state persecution. In the context of the seventeenth century, however, they were perhaps more substantial. They were certainly greater than those which existed within the Anglican and Roman Catholic churches, the two major religious institutions whose practices were familiar to the settlers of Puritan New England. Moreover, the Puritan, by stripping away the hierarchy which stood between man and his maker, demanded that the individual take a more positive and active role in his relationship with God. In the late sixteenth century and the early decades of the seventeenth century this was a role which some men accepted with enthusiasm.

For the people who left England to settle Plymouth, the working out of this relationship with God in a new world offered the excitement and the challenge of great adventure. By 1650 the adventure was over, the spontaneity which had fired the hearts of the early settlers gone. To protect their churches, men therefore found it necessary to compromise some of their beliefs and to force what once was voluntary. Sometimes compromise and regularization met opposition and sometimes they were checked for a period; but the trend was certain in a society for which the prospects of building a prosperous and comfortable life became increasingly important.

I I

"Much Imployment About the Things of This Life"

THE challenge which worldly success presented to the intensity of religious commitment soon became apparent. Richard Mather, progenitor of the breed of Mathers who alternately comforted and threatened three generations of New Englanders, warned his Dorchester congregation in 1657 that "experience shews that it is an easy thing in the middest of worldly business to lose the life and power of Religion, that nothing thereof should be left but only the external form." [1] Mather and his fellow clergy, of course, did not counsel poverty. Prosperity, they assured their congregations, was a sign collectively and individually of God's favor; and poverty, while not a sin in itself, was acceptable only when it occurred because of circumstances beyond an individual's control. But they hoped that wealth and piety could live comfortably together. Richard Mather died in 1669; by then, whatever his doubts that this hope would be realized, he knew Massachusetts was an economic success.

Had Mather lived in Plymouth Colony he would have seen fewer signs of material prosperity; for Plymouth was poor by comparison with Massachusetts and never developed the substantial wealth which accumulated in the great trading port of Boston. Sir Robert Carr, one of four commissioners sent from

1. Richard Mather, *A Farewel-Exhortation to the Church and People of Dorchester in New England* (Cambridge, 1657). The quotation appears in Perry Miller's *The New England Mind, 2, From Colony to Province* (Cambridge, 1953), p. 4.

England to New England in 1665, wrote to the Earl of Arlington after a visit to Plymouth that the colony had "neither good river, nor good harbor," and that some towns were so poor that they used lay preachers because not enough money was available to support a trained ministry. Plymouth, the commissioners concluded, was "certainly by much the poorest [New England] colony." Plymouth concurred in this judgment: in 1644/45, in a negotiation with Massachusetts, Connecticut, and New Haven, the colony insisted upon a recognition of its comparative poverty.[2]

Plymouth's failure to develop an expanding economy was due in part to geography. Unlike the other New England colonies, Plymouth lacked good port facilities for ships engaged in overseas commerce. Shipping could enter the harbor at Provincetown (where the *Mayflower* had lain at anchor in November and December 1620), but Provincetown was not well-located to become a commercial center. South of the Cape, Buzzards Bay provided a safe anchorage for large ships. The Pilgrims had built a trading station at Manomet at the head of the Bay in 1627, and for a number of years carried on an extensive trade with the Indian tribes of Connecticut and Long Island. But to reach Buzzards Bay, a ship bound from Europe had to undertake the long voyage around the Cape and skirt the shoals which guarded the approaches to the Bay. Ships trading to Europe and the West Indies could enter the harbor at Plymouth—one Plymouth Governor called it "tollerably good for such as are well acquainted with it." [3] Nevertheless, even for those familiar with the harbor, the spits of land which projected out from the entrance made access difficult in certain kinds of weather, and the shallowness in the Bay forced shipping to anchor at some distance from the shore. In the western reaches of the colony a good harbor existed at Mount Hope on Narragansett Bay, but Mount Hope was the tribal seat of the Wampanoag Indians, and settlement did not begin there until after King Philip's War.

Development of overseas commerce in Plymouth Colony also suffered from a scarcity of men with capital and, perhaps even more important, of contacts in English commercial circles. English associations were critical to the establishment of mercantile

2. *Cal. of State Papers, Col. Ser., 1661–1668,* #10000, #1103.

3. Manuscripts in the Public Record Office, London, England, Colonial Office 5, vol. 904, pp. 56–67, hereafter cited as C.O.

operations in North America since American merchants depended upon English credit; and Americans who were without family connections or friends in the great English trading houses found it almost impossible to establish the credit necessary to trade overseas.[4] Few, if any, men with commercial contact in England seem to have settled in Plymouth Colony until after the opening of the Mount Hope lands in the 1680's.

Although the absence of mercantile contacts in England and the limits imposed by geography prevented the establishment of a trans-atlantic commerce, a small number of Plymouth merchants traded to the Caribbean islands. In 1681 the bark *Adventure,* including among her owners five Plymouth Colony men, sailed for the West Indies. Scattered traces in colony deeds and wills indicate that a few other men shared in trading enterprises there, and after the settlement of the Mount Hope lands in the 1680's, this number increased; by 1690, the number of ships owned by Bristol (Mount Hope) merchants trading to the Caribbean had reached fifteen.[5] But for the most part Plymouth remained dependent upon Boston for goods brought from beyond the sea.[6]

In many towns, settlement at the entrances to small rivers or inlets favored the development of coastal shipping. Sloops and ketches of twenty or thirty tons, suitable for working in and out of small harbors along the New England coast, sailed from these towns to fish the waters of Cape Cod Bay or carry produce and fish, chiefly to Boston, bringing in return goods imported into Massachusetts from overseas. Coastal vessels carried pork, beef, mutton, hides, and tallow, a small amount of grain in good years, hemp, flax, tar, and timber from Plymouth; by 1680 the colony had also begun to ship horses to Boston where they were reexported to the West Indies. Fish exports included cod, striped bass, mackerel, sturgeon, oysters, and oil extracted from small whales washed ashore or killed in Cape Cod Bay.[7] Occasionally this export of whale oil reached sizable proportions. In January

4. Bernard Bailyn, *The New England Merchants in the Seventeenth Century* (Cambridge, 1955), pp. 34–35.

5. *Ply. Col. Rec., 6,* p. 68; Plymouth Colony Deeds, vol. 2, pt. I; *Mayflower Descendant, 14* (1912), p. 68; Wilfred H. Munro, *Tales of an Old Sea Port* (Princeton, 1917), p. 31.

6. C.O. 5, vol. 904, pp. 56–57.

7. Ibid.

1687, Edward Randolph estimated that since the middle of December, Plymouth fishermen had taken nearly 200 tons of oil for shipment to England.[8]

Shipbuilding furnished a livelihood to a small number of persons. Materials needed for ship construction, timber, hemp, flax, and iron, could be obtained locally, and men who listed their occupation as "shipwright" lived in a number of colony towns. Scituate, in part because of its proximity to the Boston market, quickly became the major center for the industry, and Scituate yards seem to have operated on a continuous basis in the last quarter of the seventeenth century and perhaps earlier. Vessels built here sailed chiefly in the coastal trade and seldom exceeded fifty tons; in most cases they were apparently sold to Boston owners.[9]

Taunton provided the site of the only major ironworks in the colony although several other towns tried to promote the industry. Shortly after the settlement of Taunton the inhabitants became aware of local deposits of bog iron. Undeterred by the difficulties experienced in the Massachusetts iron enterprise at Saugus, twenty-two settlers formed a company to establish an ironworks on the Two Mile River. A full share cost £20, and the first stock offering brought in almost £300 subscribed in amounts from £5 to £20. The partners hired James and Henry Leonard of Braintree as bloomers (Henry soon left to begin the manufacture of iron in New Jersey), and by 1656 production at the ironworks had begun.[10]

In the first quarter-century of its operation the ironworks paid only irregular dividends and the price of shares fluctuated between £20 and £30. The partners rented the works in 1660 to a small group from among their own number for a rental of four tons of iron per year. No dividends were paid between 1668 and 1671, and again between 1675 and 1677. In spite of the difficulties which marked its early years of operation the furnace, over the fifty-seven year period from 1656 to 1713, returned dividends averaging approximately twelve per cent per annum; and

8. Edward Randolph to Mr. Povey, Boston, January 24, 1687, *Collection of Original Papers Relative to the History of the Colony of Massachusetts Bay,* Thomas Hutchinson, ed. (Boston, 1769), pp. 558, 559.

9. Vernon L. Briggs, *History of Shipbuilding on North River, Plymouth County, Massachusetts, 1640–1872* (Boston, 1882), p. 284. The records which Briggs used for the seventeenth century were fragmentary.

10. Scrapbook #2, Old Colony Historical Society, p. 108.

from 1683 to 1713, payments averaged fifteen per cent.[11] The Leonard family was one which prospered, and when Thomas Leonard, who succeeded his father as manager of the furnace, died in 1717, he left an estate of more than £2500, chiefly tied up in the ironworks.[12] The colony as a whole also benefited from the manufacture of iron at Taunton. In addition to its use in the making of agricultural tools and in shipbuilding, iron circulated as a medium of exchange in a society which was chronically currency-poor.

A few men in Plymouth Colony made their living through the operation of local industries or services considered important to the welfare of the towns in which they lived. Probably most important was the flour or grist mill; to give men incentive to set up such a mill, many towns offered some form of encouragement. Duxbury, for example, promised persons who built a mill at their own expense that no other mill would be allowed to begin operation until the first mill could no longer supply the need of the town. Duxbury also voted £6 for the purchase of lands adjacent to the mill site and agreed to make a further grant of additional lands. Marshfield and Scituate both voted land to men who would establish grist mills; Sandwich agreed to contribute £20 toward building a mill, and the inhabitants promised to take their grain there or pay a penalty for taking it elsewhere.[13]

A few men in the colony operated saw mills and fulling mills; others worked as tanners, coopers, weavers, handicraftsmen, or blacksmiths. The blacksmith played a particularly important role in the economic life of a seventeenth-century town, and in at least two towns—Plymouth and Taunton—the settlement of a smith became a matter of town concern. Plymouth voted £10 spent on a bellows and tools for a smith, and Taunton agreed to pay £5 toward bringing a blacksmith from Boston.[14] One enterprise which presented special and, for seventeenth-century America, unusual difficulties, involved the extraction of spermaceti from dead whales. Governor Prence, one of the promoters of this project, received a letter in June 1659 from a Boston partner stating that instructions had arrived from England "how to

11. Ibid., p. 113.
12. Ibid., p. 89.
13. *Ply. Col. Rec., 12*, pp. 72, 73; Scituate Town Records, *2*, p. 17; Marshfield Town Records, *1*, p. 47; Sandwich Town Records, MSS, Sandwich, Mass., *1*, p. 9.
14. *Plymouth Town Records, 1*, p. 45; Taunton Town Records, Old Colony Historical Society, MSS T193 1649.

make and order the business and in what part of the fish to find it." But the letter warned Prence that "our care must be that the people employed may not understand what they do so far as to be able to communicate to others." [15]

But for most men, including many whose primary occupations were in the skilled trades, agriculture was the base for economic existence. The pattern of farming which developed in Plymouth Colony proceeded from the assumption that family units would group together in compact settlements. This assumption followed in part from the need for protection in case of Indian attack; in part it rested upon the conviction that community living placed a necessary restraint upon human behavior. Thus when the settlement of a new town began, each man received a house lot, varying in size from one acre to twenty or more, depending upon the town and the estate of the individual.

On this house lot the settler built his home, usually a simple frame structure covered with boards or shingles, with a central chimney rising in its center. Downstairs, two or three rooms, more in a few cases, provided living and cooking quarters for the family, and often sleeping facilities for senior members of the household; upstairs, in most homes, was either a sleeping loft or bedrooms for other members of the family. The house lot also contained several outlying buildings which provided space for the storage of tools and shelter for animals. Behind the buildings frequently lay a vegetable garden and perhaps a small orchard of fruit trees.[16] In addition to his house lot each settler received title to lands lying beyond the limits of the town. Here the farmer grew the staple crops, wheat, corn, hay, barley, and rye, which were suited to the sandy soil of southeastern New England.

The pattern of agriculture that developed in Plymouth Colony usually included the raising of livestock. Taunton, for example, toward the close of the century, with about 150 taxpayers in the town, counted a population of 414 cows two years old and less. 561 full-grown cows, 254 horses including thirty-two yearlings, 800 sheep, and 338 pigs.[17] A study of eighty-eight inventories

15. Winslow Papers, *61*, #8.

16. See the *Mayflower Descendant,* passim, for inventories taken by room.

17. Old Colony Historical Society, MSS T1931. The list is not broken down by individual owner and is undated. From a comparison of the handwriting with other manuscripts and from the information given, I have concluded that the list was compiled late in the seventeenth century, probably between 1685 and 1692.

filed in the probating of Plymouth Colony wills between 1620 and 1658 showed that sixty-five listed cattle, including oxen, and forty-eight listed swine. The numbers of persons owning other kinds of animals were much smaller. Before 1641 not one of the inventories studied showed possession of a horse, and of sixty-six inventories filed between 1641 and 1659, only thirteen included horses. Six of the eighty-eight inventories listed poultry, eleven listed goats, twelve listed sheep. Both sheep and goats were more commonly owned in the early years of settlement than later in the century; eight of the eleven inventories listing the ownership of goats and five of the twelve which included sheep were filed before 1641.[18]

Settlement in villages required different procedures in the raising of livestock than those which would be followed by subsequent generations of farmers. Frequently the grazing of cattle and horses followed a communal pattern, with daily care of the livestock left to a single herdsman who grazed the animals on town commons. In the winter months some towns sent their cattle under the care of the herdsman to pasturage on town-owned lands in another part of the colony.

Because of its communal character and the assumptions which governed the role of the state, the agricultural pattern that developed in Plymouth Colony, and in other Puritan colonies as well, differed from the independent yeomen society which eighteenth-century America, and Thomas Jefferson in particular, later admired. The concept of the priority of the public good and the readiness to assign to government certain regulatory functions brought a structure to economic life which the Jeffersonian thought unnecessary. Jefferson and his followers believed that concentration of power in government caused oppression and that men freed from all but the minimum number of restraints

18. The statistical analysis of eighty-eight inventories is on file at Pilgrim Memorial Hall in Plymouth. The inventories studied do not necessarily represent a cross-section of Plymouth society, and I am fully aware of the perils of generalizing from a statistical sample apparently compiled on the basis of inventories previously printed in the *Plymouth Scrapbook* and the *Mayflower Descendant*. The inventories studied, however, include those of a number of people whose estates were small; the fact that even so nearly seventy-five per cent of the inventories included cattle is, I think, meaningful. One cannot, of course, then go on to conclude that for the population as a whole, the percentage of adult males owning cattle (only a few women are included in the eighty-eight) was necessarily this high.

would develop a productive society in which they lived together with a due concern for the rights of others. The Puritan, on the other hand, assuming that man could not be trusted and that harm to the public welfare would follow without active intervention by the government, insisted that the state play a positive role in the regulation of economic life.

During the early years of settlement at Plymouth, the government attempted to set the general price and wage levels for the colony and to regulate the margin of profit on business transactions. In 1635 the General Court authorized the governor and assistants "to sett shuch rates on goods to be sould, and labourers for their hire, as should be meete and juste." [19] Four years later Thomas Clark of Plymouth paid a thirty shilling fine because he had purchased a pair of boots and spurs for ten shillings and sold them for fifteen.[20] But this close supervision over the price and wage structure did not continue. The mechanics of setting prices on goods sold in the colony and of enforcing those prices went beyond the capability of a government lacking bureaucratic structure. Moreover, economic prosperity and the growth of business opportunity, especially in the Massachusetts Colony, placed a considerable strain upon the concept of the just price. In the second half of the seventeenth century, Plymouth, therefore, like Massachusetts, gave practical acceptance to a free market and abandoned further efforts at general price-wage regulation.

The regulation of economic life extended to the establishment of conditions under which various enterprises might operate; and because the public good was more important than the individual's profit, the state maintained firm control over certain industries. As early as 1626, in one of the first recorded laws passed at Plymouth, the government prohibited the export of handicrafts from the colony.[21] No explanation accompanied passage of this law, but presumably the colony wanted to assure that products needed at home were not sold abroad. The government also insisted that certain goods manufactured within the colony meet established specifications. Coopers were required to make their casks tight and to London gauge, and the colony ordered sealers of leather to distinguish clearly between good and bad leather.[22] In 1665 the government heard a complaint that

19. *Ply. Col. Rec., I*, p. 36.
20. Ibid., p. 137.
21. Ibid., *II*, p. 4.
22. Ibid., p. 60; *3*, p. 38; *Book of General Laws* (1685), pp. 276, 277.

the Taunton ironworks had turned out a poor grade of iron and promptly ordered the owners to take necessary corrective action.[23]

Because her capital resources were limited, Plymouth Colony could not afford the luxury of competition in industries which were considered vital to the well-being of society. Thus, when circumstances indicated that the grant of a monopoly served the public welfare, government, either at the colony or town level, encouraged its existence. The first monopoly established in the colony dated from 1627 when the Undertakers agreed to pay off the plantation debt in return for an exclusive grant of the fur trade. After that debt was finally paid, the colony continued the practice of granting the right to the trade to a few individuals who paid a fixed rent. The government followed a similar procedure in selling the privilege of seining fish at Cape Cod for a set term of years, and used the money paid in rent toward the maintenance of grammar schools in the colony.[24]

The towns also established local monopolies, and in return insisted that the grantees meet certain conditions. Towns which encouraged and subsidized the building of grist mills often set the price which could be charged by the owner and required that construction of the mill not interfere with other activities dependent upon the water supply of the river or stream.[25] The towns in particular wanted assurance that there be no interference with the passage of the herring, or alewives, which swam into the rivers of southeastern New England by the tens of thousands in the spring of the year. Because herring were the primary source of fertilizer and vital to the prosperity of the community, several towns organized the construction of herring weirs, designated a few individuals to undertake the project, set the price per thousand, and barred all others from obstructing the passage of the fish.[26]

Other town monopolies existed. Plymouth agreed in 1641 to give John Jenny the sole right to cut wood on Clark's Island in support of efforts to produce salt from sea water. Jenny in return promised to sell salt for two shillings a bushel to inhabitants of the town. Sandwich granted an exclusive right for the cutting up

23. *Ply. Col. Rec., 4,* p. 98.
24. Ibid., *3,* pp. 13, 14; *5,* pp. 244, 245.
25. Ibid., *12,* pp. 72, 73; *6,* pp. 111, 112.
26. *Plymouth Town Records, 1,* p. 172; Bridgewater Town Records, *1,* p. 42; Sandwich Town Records, MSS, *1,* p. 13.

of drift whales. Middleboro even established a monopoly to supply the bait for the town's fishermen.[27] The town of Taunton gave Henry Andrews permission to build a saw mill only if he agreed not to take any partners from outside the town. Although in this case the right to build the saw mill did not include the grant of a monopoly, Taunton still wanted the ownership of an enterprise of such importance to the town in the hands of persons presumably responsive to local pressures.[28] An agricultural people with little capital available, working for their survival in a soil inferior even by comparison with other lands in southern New England, the farmers of Plymouth expected public intervention in the economy to protect the public interest.

Lacking the combination of investment capital and either good harbors on the Atlantic or rich lands, few Plymouth Colony residents became even moderately wealthy during the seventeenth century. Governor Josias Winslow wrote to England in 1680 that while some estates amounted to £1000, "if any are worth two thousand, such are very rarely found." [29] With the exception of a few years when drought, crop disease, or war occurred, the standard of living at Plymouth represented an improvement for many of the settlers over what they had known in the Old World. Governor Bradford, who on occasion tried his hand at verse, wrote of Plymouth:

> All sorts of grain which our own land doth yield,
> Was hither brought and sown in many a field:
> As wheat and rye, barley, oats, beans and pease
> Here all thrive, and they profit from them raise.
> All sorts of roots and herbs in gardens grow,
> Parsnips, carrots, turnips, or what you'll sow,
> Onions, melons, cucumbers, radishes,
> Skirets, beets, coleworts and fair cabbages.[30]

Bradford was no fool; he knew full well that Plymouth was not an agricultural paradise. But his verses are not the work of a man living in the midst of economic privation. More than twenty years after Bradford's death, Governor Winslow reported that

27. *Plymouth Town Records, I*, p. 7; Sandwich Town Records, MSS, *I*, p. 5a; Middleboro Town Records, *I*, 252.
28. Old Colony Historical Society, MSS AN26H, 1690.
29. C.O. 5, vol. 904, pp. 56–57.
30. *Mayflower Descendant*, 7 (1905), pp. 152, 153.

there was little poverty, that "we are fed and Cloathed and our people are Generally Growing in their estates." Winslow continued that few men were tenants and most were freeholders whose goods lay principally in livestock and lands.[31]

Although by Richard Mather's standards they did not live in the midst of worldly riches, Plymouth saints, like their friends in the Massachusetts Colony, found it increasingly difficult to live with their eyes riveted upon heaven. In the daily tasks of coaxing a living from their environment and seeking to improve their economic standing, some men inevitably came to think more of earthly rewards and less of the life to come. Long before Mather admonished his Dorchester congregation, Governor Bradford saw that the greed of men for more and better lands might in time "be the ruine of New England, at least of the churches of God ther." [32] Thus, when Indian war burst upon all New England in 1675, the Puritan understood: God in His infinite wisdom had chosen this means to chastise an erring people.

31. C.O. 5, vol. 904, pp. 56–57.
32. Bradford, *History, 2,* p. 153.

I 2

"Mischiefe from the Indians"

A FORTY-YEAR peace had continued between the Wampanoag Indians and the colony ever since the dreary spring of 1621 when Massassoit and his warriors first appeared at Plymouth Plantation. Welcomed with all the fanfare the little settlement could muster, Massassoit had exchanged presents with his English hosts and signed a treaty promising peace; the English, in turn, promised support in the event that the Wampanoags were unjustly attacked by another tribe.[1]

John Carver had negotiated this agreement for the Pilgrims and after Carver's death Governor Bradford continued to follow a policy of firmness and friendship. In 1640 the Governor and the other "Old Comers" insisted that General Court grant them jurisdiction over the Wampanoag lands at Mount Hope, the tribal seat, and they had then reserved Mount Hope to Massassoit and his people forever.[2] But promises made "forever" are sometimes difficult for subsequent generations to keep, and by 1660 the old friendship which had been so important to the first settlers was failing. It depended upon the personal friendship and respect of men of good will, and by 1660 the two leaders who knew and trusted each other were dead. Bradford died

1. Bradford, *History, I*, pp. 201–02; *Mount's Relation*, p. 193. Alden T. Vaughan's book, *New England Frontier: Puritans and Indians 1620–1675* (Boston, 1965) appeared after completion of this book.
2. See Chapter 4, pp. 41–44.

in 1657; Massassoit three years later. Their successors never became friends.

The first indication of trouble came in 1662. Wamsutta had succeeded his father Massassoit as chief, and in March 1662 the Plymouth General Court took notice that Wamsutta was alienating land and not selling it to the colony. Concerned by this seeming reversal of Wampanoag policy, the government asked Wamsutta to come to Plymouth, and when he did not, sent a force of armed troopers commanded by Major Josias Winslow to bring him in. Whether Wamsutta came willingly was later a source of dispute. William Hubbard, writing in 1676, accused Winslow of ambushing Wamsutta and a number of his men, disarming them, and taking the Wampanoag chief from the place of ambush as a prisoner. John Cotton promptly insisted that this account was inaccurate; that in fact no ambush had taken place, that Wamsutta assured Winslow he had always intended to go to Plymouth, and returned willingly.[3]

Much to the colony's embarrassment, Wamsutta died shortly thereafter. Hubbard stated that a fever caused by cholera and anger was the cause of death. Cotton countered that Plymouth's treatment of Wamsutta was fair and friendly, that the Indian had left in good health for home, but before he traveled far had changed his mind and decided to go to Boston. On the way there he was stricken with a fever and taken to Winslow's house in Marshfield, where arrangements were made to take him to Sowams as he wished. This was accomplished, and Wamsutta was returned to Sowams and there died.[4]

Within a few days rumors began to circulate at Plymouth that Wamsutta's brother Philip, who succeeded him as Chief, was angry, and the Wampanoags were plotting trouble. Fearing there might be some substance to these reports, Governor Prence summoned Philip to appear at Plymouth in August. The Indian came and insisted he was not plotting trouble; he professed his love for the colony, and even offered one brother as a hostage. Reassured, the government declined the offer and, after Philip pledged himself to continue the covenant made by his father, allowed him to return to Sowams.[5]

3. *Ply. Col. Rec., 4,* p. 8; William Hubbard, *A Narrative of the Indian Wars in New England* (Danbury, 1803), pp. 59, 60; *The Mather Papers,* pp. 232, 233.
4. Ibid.
5. *Ply. Col. Rec., 4,* pp. 25–26.

In spite of the trouble in 1662, it seemed for a time that friendly relations between the Wampanoags and Plymouth Colony would resume. When two of Philip's wives caused him concern by entertaining several Narragansett Indians while he was away from home, Philip asked for colony help, and three magistrates recommended a settlement which supported his authority. Several years later the General Court gave Philip a horse, which under colony law could not be given or sold to an Indian.[6] Yet it now seems clear that after the death of Massassoit, the foundation for a firm and sincere peace between Plymouth Colony and the Wampanoags no longer existed. Philip was determined not to submit to the encroachments of the white man and was not so ready as his father to search for the ways of peace. Governor Prence was rigorous and lacked the tact and patience of Bradford. Both Prence and Philip knew a tradition of amity and concord to look to for precedent, but to solve the problems ahead, tradition would not be enough.

Prence and Philip admittedly faced more critical problems than had their predecessors. Gradually most of the lands once belonging to the Wampanoags were being settled by white men. Although such lands were almost always purchased, and although there is little reason to suppose that the Indians were unaware of the full implications of land sale, the amount of land in their possession was steadily shrinking.

The colony attempted to follow a policy which would protect the rights of the Indians. The Pilgrims had naturally assumed that a chief could dispose of tribal lands, since Massassoit himself had given them their lands at Plymouth.[7] Thereafter, because they thought it was right and because they did not want to antagonize the Indians, the Pilgrims insisted upon payment to the Indian owner before settlement could begin. In 1643, to give further protection to the Indian owner, the General Court directed that no one could buy land from an Indian without prior court approval:

> Whereas it is holden very vnlawfull and of dangerous consequence and it hath beene the constant custome from our first begining That no person or persons haue or euer did

6. Ibid., pp. 24–25, 93.
7. So Nathaniel Morton claimed. See Morton, *New Englands Memoriall*, p. 24.

purchase Rent or hire any lands herbage wood or tymber of the Natiues but by the Majestrates consent. It is therefore enacted by the Court that if any person or persons do here-after purchase rent or hyre . . . without the consent and assent of the Court Euery such person or persons shall for-fait fiue pounds for euery acree.[8]

It was a heavy penalty; £5 probably was, at minimum, five times the worth of any acre of virgin land in the colony. In 1660 the General Court further interpreted the law to include receiv-ing gifts of land; and the colony enforced compliance. The Court fined one man £200 in 1664 for buying without court approval, although it allowed him to keep part of the land. But ten years later a Massachusetts man, who "hath caused great disturbance amongst vs by produceing a deed of gift of lands to him from an Indian sachem," went to prison. The Court of Assistants subse-quently ordered him released when he surrendered the deed and disclaimed any right to the gift.[9]

To prevent fraud and safeguard the Indians' interests the government usually appointed two or three trustworthy men to negotiate a sale. Often these men were colony assistants; some-times they were among the grantees, but frequently they were not. Barnstable signed an agreement in 1658 with Paupumun-nuck transferring land "in the presence and with the help of" two assistants, neither of whom apparently had any personal interest in the purchase. Several years later, Josias Winslow, a colony as-sistant, bought a piece of land from the Massachusetts Indians and deeded the land to the proprietors of Marshfield. Winslow was one of the proprietors, but as a magistrate he could be pre-sumed to deal fairly and honestly with the Indian owners.[10]

While colony policy required full recognition of the Indian's title, the price paid to him seldom, of course, represented the land's value to the white man. Massassoit in 1649 sold 150 square miles for seven coats, nine hatchets, eight hoes, twenty knives, four moose skins, and ten and one-half yards of cotton. Twenty-three years later his son, Philip, sold twelve square miles to Taunton for £143, considerably less than a shilling an acre.[11]

8. *Ply. Col. Rec., II*, p. 41.
9. Ibid., *4*, pp. 59, 64; *5*, p. 151.
10. *Barnstable Town Records*, 5; Marshfield Town Records, *1*, p. 100.
11. Mitchell, *Bridgewater*, pp. 11–12; *Ply. Col. Rec., 5*, pp. 100, 106. The pay-ment also included "a yard a half in a coat." Emery, *Taunton*, pp. 114, 115.

Payment to an Indian in manufactured goods was usual, although a small sum of money was often included. What many Indians wanted most, munitions and liquor, were not offered—except in far-away Maine, where at least once, two colony magistrates included a couple of bottles of wine and a bottle of liquor in payment for land along the Kennebec River.[12]

In the seventeenth century, as later, men differed about whether the white man cheated the Indian. In 1659 the Plymouth General Court heard that some men in the colony had given several Indians additional sums above the price paid by court-appointed intermediaries. The Court ordered disciplinary action taken against anyone who "in an vnderhand way" had given the Indians money or goods for "their lands formerly Purchased according to order of Court by the majistrates therby Insinuating as if they had dealt vnjustly with them." [13]

Whether the price paid to the Indian, in fact, meant that he was cheated is a subjective question. Perhaps, considering the value of land to the Indian and the value to him of the goods given for land, the purchase price often was fair. Douglas Leach, who confronts the problem of Indian land sales in his history of King Philip's War, suggests that Indian landowners were sometimes the victims of fraud, for he argues that the Indians' concept of land ownership was entirely different from that of the white man. No Indian really owned land as an individual, but the tribe held jurisdiction over an area, and Indians of the tribe used the land as was convenient for them. By deeding land to the white man, the Indian gave the buyer the right to use but not a preemptive right.[14] Leach's assumption may be valid for the earliest years of white settlement. Perhaps the Indian at first did experience difficulty understanding the meaning of a land deed; but by mid-century Indian sachems (chiefs) who usually negotiated the sale of tribal lands must have realized that conveyance of land title meant eventual loss of the land to the Indian forever. Some Indian deeds contain stipulations that the Indians reserved rights to hunt, fish, and cut firewood, and some set apart acreage for agricultural use. One deed even included right of access to the Taunton River at the turn of the herring run. By 1664

12. Plymouth Colony Deeds, vol. *2*, pt. I, p. 102.
13. *Ply. Col. Rec., II,* p. 124.
14. Douglas Leach, *Flintlock and Tomahawk* (New York, 1958), pp. 16, 18.

the Indians themselves were recording in a colony record book deeds of land given and sold to each other.[15]

The policy of close supervision of Indian land sales, established by Bradford and continued by his successors, was an attempt to protect the Indian from fraud and exploitation. According to modern standards that attempt sometimes failed. But Plymouth's government, according to the standards which it believed were just, thought this policy had been faithfully carried out; and when Governor Winslow wrote shortly after the outbreak of King Philip's War that Plymouth had dealt fairly with the Wampanoags, there was no reason to question his sincerity.[16] What Winslow never understood was that protection of the Indian in a particular land sale was not the crucial issue; rather it was the proximity of settlement.

By the middle 1660's the amount of public land still available in Plymouth Colony was almost exhausted; the demand for it, however, continued. The General Court, therefore, while trying to protect the Indians, at the same time gave its approval to settlement near the entrance to the Mount Hope Peninsula where Philip's village of Sowams was located. To prevent unscrupulous persons from taking advantage of their nearness to Philip, the Court thought it necessary to remind people that "noe person neither Inhabitant of this Jurisdiction nor any other shall att any time either by vertue of libertie from the Court to purchase lands of the Indians or vpon any pretense whatsoeuer shalbe suffered to buy or receiue (in any way of the Indians) any of those lands . . . as there is a body of Indians vpon; and the Court shall judge they can not liue without." Yet the General Court consented that "for the accomodateing of more inhabitants in the said township, that all such lands as the Indians can well spare shalbe purchased," provided Governor Prence first approved.[17]

Other issues embittered the relationship between Indian and white. As white settlement crept closer to Indian homes and fields, friction between the two races inevitably increased. The settlers' cattle and pigs seemed to have an appetite for Wam-

15. *Mayflower Descendant, 18* (Boston, 1915), p. 244; Plymouth Colony Deeds, vol. *3*, pt. I, p. 94; *Ply. Col. Rec., 12*, p. 239.
16. Davis Papers, #83.
17. *Ply. Col. Rec., 11*, p. 221; *5*, p. 24.

panoag crops, and efforts to keep the livestock away from the Indian fields were not always successful. In 1662 the General Court ordered townships where the problem existed to help the Indians fence their fields or take other steps to secure the safety of Indian crops. Cases of trespass, however, were tried in select or local town courts where the plaintiff may have experienced difficulty in collecting damages.[18]

John Cotton's persistent efforts to convert the western Indians in the colony to Christianity may also have contributed to Philip's growing bellicosity. Cotton arrived at Plymouth in 1667, fresh from a year of proselyting among Indians on the Vineyard, and promptly began to spread the gospel in Philip's back yard. Before his settlement no evidence exists to show that white missionaries had made sustained efforts to convert Plymouth Colony's western Indians. But between 1668 and 1675, John Cotton preached an average of more than twenty-five sermons a year to the Indians of the colony. Sometimes he preached to them at his home in Plymouth; at other times he traveled to the Indian villages. Although his Journal does not show that he ever visited Philip's village of Sowams, he spoke in Indian towns nearby. Once, at least, when Cotton preached at Plymouth, Philip and some of his people were present.[19] Proof that Philip himself was hostile to Cotton's efforts is not certain, but when the Puritan missionary John Eliot talked of Christianity to Philip, the Indian reportedly took hold of a button on Eliot's coat and gravely informed the clergyman that he cared for Christianity no more than for that button. One thing is certain: Eliot later expressed full support for Plymouth's tough policy toward Philip.[20] Another Indian sachem, Josiah of Matakesset, was hostile to Cotton's preaching. Cotton recorded in his Journal: "I went to Josiah . . . to preach to the Indians but because many of his Indians would forsake him and he should lose much tribute he would not hearken." [21]

Philip responded with increasing belligerence to the increasing manifestations of the white man's presence. The colony was aware of this development, and when in June 1667 a rumor reached Plymouth that Philip had agreed to help the French at-

18. Ibid., *3*, p. 21; *11*, pp. 208–09, 227–28.
19. John Cotton's Journal, Massachusetts Historical Society.
20. Cotton Mather, *Magnalia, 1*, p. 566; Davis Papers, #60.
21. John Cotton, Journal.

tack New England, the government decided that it could take no chances and sent a troop of horse to escort Philip to Plymouth. The Indian came willingly. He denied the rumor, and insisted that to make trouble between himself and the English, the Narragansett Indians had hired one of his men to feign hostility. He agreed that the colony was justified in showing concern but he again professed his love and friendship. Deciding that although "there was great probabillitie that his tongue had bine runing out," the General Court accepted his professions of friendship, but ordered him to assume part of the expense of the expedition sent to bring him to Plymouth. The colony further warned him not to make trouble in the future.[22]

Four years later, alarming news reached Plymouth. In March, one of the colony rangers patrolling near Sowams reported to the General Court that Philip had marched up Mount Hope neck toward Swansea with a band of armed warriors. Although the Indians had turned back, the colony called Philip to an accounting and ordered him to come to Taunton. He came and, so the General Court later insisted, acknowledged that he was guilty of preparing to make war "and that not grounded vpon any injury sustained from vs, nor prouocation giuen by vs, but from theire own naughty harts." The colony promptly ordered the Wampanoags to turn in all their guns and began efforts to secure promises of peace from other Indians living in New Plymouth.[23]

Suspicion of Philip's intentions continued, however, and in June 1671 the General Court accused him of breaking the promises he had made at Taunton: he kept weapons which he had agreed to surrender; he refused to come and negotiate, "notwithstanding his late engagement, as well as former, to submitt to the kings authoritie, and the authoritie of this collonie;" he had complained to Massachusetts and rendered "vs odiouse to our naighbour collonie." For such offenses, the Court declared the arms which had been turned in forfeit. The Court also ordered an expedition to march against his allies, the Sakonnet Indians, and to bring in their arms by force if necessary.[24]

July and August were anxious months. The expedition against the Sakonnets never left, for Awashuncks, their squaw sachem,

22. *Ply. Col. Rec., 4*, pp. 165–66.
23. Ibid., *5*, p. 63; Massachusetts Historical Society, *Collections*, Ser. I, *6* (Boston, 1846), p. 211.
24. *Ply. Col. Rec., 5*, pp. 63–64.

promised peace; but doubt as to Philip's next move continued to keep the colony in a state of tension. John Tomson, a Middleboro selectman, sent word to Plymouth that Indians had been seen lurking about that town, and hopefully suggested that Middleboro would be a very convenient place to keep a colony garrison. On the 23rd of August the government decided to make a new effort to persuade Philip to come and talk: two men, Harvey Walker and James Brown, left for Mount Hope with letters for Philip; a letter also was sent to Roger Williams asking him to join Walker and Brown. All the towns were now warned to expect trouble.[25]

The mission to Philip was unsuccessful. Walker and Brown, without waiting for Roger Williams to join them, traveled to Sowams and found Philip and many of his men sitting around drinking. In spite of such unpropitious circumstances, and although they probably hazarded their lives, Walker and Brown carried out their instructions and ordered Philip to come to Plymouth on September 13th. Philip replied insolently, angry words passed, and in a rage the Indian rose and struck Brown's hat from his head. The insult ended further conversation and the white men withdrew. The following day, accompanied by Roger Williams, they returned and found that Philip was leaving for Boston.[26]

After Walker and Brown communicated their report of the meeting at Mount Hope to Governor Prence, probably no one expected Philip to appear on September 13th. But neither did anyone expect the letters which came from the Massachusetts Colony's Secretary, Jonathan Rawson, advising moderation in dealing with Philip and stating that Massachusetts doubted whether the Wampanoags were subject to New Plymouth's authority as the colony claimed. Rawson added that his letter was not from any disposition to fail Plymouth in a time of stress, "we not knowing how soon we may have need of yours," but that "considering the juncture of affairs in this day we do not think it is for the common interest to put ourselves or be put into blood." [27]

This letter was read with dismay at Plymouth. Repudiated by the Massachusetts General Court and anxious to vindicate its

25. Davis Papers, #84.
26. Massachusetts Historical Society, *Collections,* Ser. I, *6,* pp. 197–98.
27. *Ply. Col. Rec., 5,* p. 77; Winslow Papers, *61,* #69.

treatment of Philip, the government decided that something should be done to convince the other Puritan colonies that Plymouth had the right to exercise control over Philip's people. Plymouth therefore requested that Massachusetts and Connecticut send men to Plymouth to hear the controversy which existed between the colony and Philip. The plan was a complete success. On September 24th these people arrived and began a hearing: their judgment was that Plymouth's treatment of Philip was just. They concluded that "such had bine the wronge and damage that hee [Philip] had done and procured vnto the collonie as ought not to be bourne without competent repairation and satisfaction; yea that hee by his insolencyes had in probabillitie occationed more mischeife from the Indians amongst them than had fallen out in many yeares before." They ordered Philip to humble himself to the colony magistrates and to mend his ways.[28]

Subsequently Plymouth offered Philip a new treaty which he signed. He acknowledged himself subject to the King of England and to the government of New Plymouth and its laws. Furthermore, he promised to pay £100 to the colony treasury within three years and to send in five wolf heads annually. He agreed that in case of trouble between his people and the English settlers he would submit the matter to the colony governor. He promised not to make war without the governor's approval and not to sell any of the lands at his disposal without permission from the General Court. He thus placed himself and his tribe in a position of total subjection to Governor Prence and the Plymouth General Court. This treaty he was supposed to have been "left to accept of or reject, as hee should see cause"; that a free choice in fact was his hardly seems possible. The treaty dictated harsh terms, unacceptably harsh for Philip to have signed freely. Such coercion as may have been used to secure his consent, the Secretary of the General Court, Nathaniel Morton, did not choose to record.

During the four years following the signing of the treaty, Philip gave no further trouble. He paid the fine due the colony by first mortgaging and then selling the mortgage to a tract of land near Taunton. In 1672 he complained to Governor Prence about the continuing sale of Indian lands to white men and asked that if any Indians or white settlers spoke about land he prayed

28. *Ply. Col. Rec.,* 5, pp. 78–79.

Prence "would give them no answer." Concerned by the purchase and settlement of lands belonging to his ally, Awashuncks, Philip reminded the governor of his promise (probably given in 1671) that Plymouth would make no further grants for a period of seven years.[29] Philip, in spite of this complaint, seems to have kept the promises he made in the treaty, and for a time, although lacking their earlier warmth, relations between the Wampanoag Tribe and the colony were stable.

In part, this stability was probably the result of a change in Plymouth's governor. Stern and tough-minded to the end, Thomas Prence died in 1672 and was succeeded as governor by Josias Winslow. Winslow, a kinder and more moderate man, was the son of Edward Winslow, himself a former governor of the colony and Bradford's chief lieutenant in dealing with the Indians. Edward Winslow and Massassoit had been friends and Philip may have hoped that under the younger Winslow, Plymouth's policy towards the Wampanoags would soften. This, in fact, did not occur. No overtures were made to Philip in the hope of improving the relationship between the Indians and the colony, and no changes were made in the treaty negotiated in 1671.

The events which led directly to King Philip's War began in January 1674/5 with the murder of an Indian called John Sassamon. Sassamon had become a convert to Christianity, what men then termed "a praying Indian." Although he was himself not a Wampanoag, Sassamon had lived for a number of years at Sowams, and since he could read and write, acted as an adviser and interpreter for Philip. Sassamon eventually left Sowams and became the teacher of an Indian church at Nemsaket (Middleboro). In January 1674/5 he journeyed from Nemsaket to see Governor Winslow and inform him that Philip was preparing to make war upon the colony. On his way home from Marshfield, Sassamon was murdered and his body stuffed under the ice of Assowamsett Pond. Unknown to the three braves who committed the murder, another Indian witnessed the crime and reported the identity of Sassamon's murderers to the authorities at Plymouth. In June 1675 the three Indians, two of whom were Philip's men, went on trial and were found guilty. Two were hanged on June 8th—John Cotton preached this day to the Indians who had

29. Philip to Prence, written by John Sassamon, Mt. Hope, n.d., Massachusetts Historical Society, *Collections*, Ser. I, 2 (Boston, 1810), p. 48. The original is at Pilgrim Memorial Hall in Plymouth.

gathered at Plymouth for the hanging—and the third Indian, whose rope broke, was shot a month later. Three days after the hangings at Plymouth, James Brown, a magistrate living at Rehoboth, wrote to Winslow that the Wampanoags had sent their wives to the Narragansetts and were preparing for war.[30]

30. William Hubbard, *Narrative of the Indian Wars*, pp. 68–70; *A Report of the Record Commissioners Containing the Roxbury Land and Church Records* (Boston, 1881), pp. 192–93; *Ply. Col. Rec., 10*, p. 362; *5*, pp. 167–68.

13

"The Greate Indian Warre"

THE sentencing and execution of Sassamon's murderers were not followed by an immediate tightening of security measures in the colony. Governor Winslow seems to have assumed that Philip would not choose to make this a cause for war. Still, the news which reached Plymouth of the Wampanoags' reaction to the hangings was unquestionably disturbing. On June 11, James Brown informed the Governor that warriors from other tribes were joining Philip. The warnings, however, were not considered sufficiently alarming to prompt the taking of precautionary measures. Winslow wrote to Weetamoo and Ben, sachems of the Pocasset Indians who lived across the Sakonnet River from Philip's village on Mount Hope Peninsula, and asked for intelligence; and he wrote a conciliatory letter to Philip promising that Plymouth had no hostile intentions against him. But no warnings were sent to outlying towns and the militia was not alerted.[1]

In Rhode Island, the government was more concerned about the possibilities of war. In an attempt to head off trouble a number of Rhode Islanders, including Deputy Governor Easton, visited the Wampanoag Chief and urged him to submit his disputes with Plymouth Colony to two neutral persons, one to be an Indian picked by him. Philip rejected their proposal.[2]

On June 16th, Governor Winslow received further informa-

1. Winslow Papers, *61*, #89.
2. John Easton, "A Relacion of the Indyan Warre," *Narratives of the Indian Wars 1675–99*, Charles Lincoln, ed. (New York, 1913), pp. 8–9.

tion that Philip was plotting war. About a year earlier Benjamin Church had settled on lands recently acquired from the Sakonnet Indians. Church soon became friendly with Awashuncks, squaw sachem of the Sakonnets, and gained her confidence. When in June 1675 six of Philip's warriors, wearing their war paint, arrived to persuade her to join Philip in war, Queen Awashuncks held a dance and invited Church. Church arrived to find a heavily-perspiring Awashuncks, who promptly used the opportunity of his presence to call off the dancing and chanting to the great spirit in favor of more earthly consultations. She asked Church whether Plymouth Colony was gathering an army to attack the Indians as Philip's warriors claimed. Church replied no; he pointed out that he had just returned from Plymouth where he had attended the meeting of the General Court, and that there had been no talk of an attack; and he in turn asked Awashuncks if she thought he would have brought all his goods and settled if he knew the colony was preparing for war with a close neighbor. Church's reply reassured Awashuncks and she promised to remain neutral. He now left for Pocasset where he learned that Philip also had recently held a dance, another indication of approaching trouble. Church promptly hurried on to Marshfield where on June 16th he communicated all his information to Governor Winslow. Winslow still took no action.[3]

Four days later Philip's warriors attacked the outlying houses scattered south of Swansea, a village sprawled across the entrance to Mount Hope Peninsula and closest to the Indians. Some persons had already left their homes in this section of Swansea, and when Philip's men appeared, the rest of the settlers retreated north. The Indians looted and burned the abandoned houses and then marched toward the main settlement. Swansea sent word to Winslow at Marshfield and grimly settled into the several garrison houses built for such an emergency.

The messenger sent to bring Winslow the news of the attack rode into Marshfield late the same day. The Governor at once ordered seventy-five men from Taunton and Bridgewater to leave for Swansea, and he called for an additional 150 men from other towns in the colony to march June 22nd. He also sent a letter to Massachusetts asking that colony to use its influence to re-

3. Benjamin Church, *The History of Philip's War* (2d ed. Boston, 1829), pp. 19–29.

strain the Narragansett and Nipmuck Indians. He was certain that if Plymouth faced only Wampanoag braves, the colony would give a good account of itself.[4]

Winslow's statement reflected a confidence in the militia system which Plymouth Colony had developed for the situation. For seventy-five years the Pilgrims and their descendants had known that they could not discount the possibility of attack by the Indians, and in preparation for an emergency, the colony had required enrollment of the great majority of able-bodied adult males into militia companies organized in each town. Few were excused from this requirement until after King Philip's War and removal of the threat of attack from Indians located within the borders of the colony. Even servants were included in the companies, and so difficult was it to escape this military obligation that Ezekiel Mayne of Scituate needed the approval of the General Court before he could be excused from militia duty. Mayne had only one eye and reported that the Scituate company supported his request since "It is difficult and in som respects dangerouse for him to be in armes, and to traine as others." [5]

Impressive as this organization of potential manpower may have been, the military system of the colony was hardly one which would have inspired confidence in a seasoned commander. The officers of the militia, nominated by the towns and appointed by the General Court, were almost without exception lacking in military experience. While many of them no doubt conducted the training of their men as best they could, that training was probably not of great value in accustoming the men to combat conditions in the forest.

The truth of the matter was that as yet no one in Plymouth Colony, nor for that matter in any of the New England colonies, really knew what kind of training or tactics were required for the conduct of warfare in the forest. Although their settlement went back more than fifty years, the Puritan colonies had thus far escaped a major Indian war. Massachusetts and Connecticut fought the Pequot Tribe in 1637, but the major battle of the Pequot War took place when the English forces attacked the Indian fort at Mystic, Connecticut; in the course of that attack the

---

4. Massachusetts Archives, *67, #202*. Douglas Leach states that the messenger bringing the news arrived early on the morning of June 21; Leach, *Flintlock,* p. 37. Church says the messenger arrived June 20; Church, *History,* p. 30.
5. *Ply. Col. Rec., 5,* p. 8.

fort caught fire and 500 Pequots perished in the flames. Thus, less than a year after it had begun, the war ended in complete success for the English. The experience gained in attacking a fortified position, however, was not very useful in teaching men how to fight in the forest; these lessons were not yet learned when war broke out in June 1675.[6]

Equally important in limiting the effectiveness of the colony militia were the difficulties in maintaining a force in the field. Since there was no permanent quartermaster, supply of the army had to be improvised. Worse still, in a subsistence economy where almost the whole population was engaged in producing its own food, to call up all able-bodied males in a town and keep them from their fields for more than a few days at a time could have disastrous consequences. Furthermore, if all the men in a town were called out on service in another part of the colony, the town itself became vulnerable to attack. The government of Plymouth recognized the problem, and when there was a need for troops to fight in offensive operations, each town was required to send only a few men to serve in a composite force. But while this offered an alternative to stripping a single town of its adult males, it had the distinct disadvantage of requiring men and officers to function as a unit in combat without previous opportunity to train and work together.

In spite of these inadequacies—which were perhaps more apparent in retrospect—Governor Winslow remained confident that Plymouth's militia would give a good account of itself. He had been an officer in the Marshfield company and in 1658, a few years after the death of Miles Standish, was appointed to the command of all the militia in the colony. Since his appointment to this command, Winslow had sat as a member of the Supreme War Council, a body of eleven men authorized by the General Court to act, in the event of war, in the impressment of manpower and supplies and to plan and direct military campaigns. Governor Winslow, from his personal knowledge of the system and knowing that it had been designed for just such an eventuality as faced him in late June 1675, thus confronted the prospect of war against the Wampanoags with some measure of optimism.

6. For the history of the Pequot War see Lion Gardiner, *A History of the Pequot War* (Cincinnati, 1860); for a modern analysis of the causes of the war see Alden T. Vaughan, "Pequots and Puritans: the Causes of the War of 1637," *William and Mary Quarterly, 21* (April 1964), pp. 256–69.

On June 21st, the troops ordered by Winslow to Swansea from Taunton and Bridgewater filed out of the forest. Morale in the beleaguered town immediately improved. Furthermore, the Wampanoag braves had not followed up their attack of the previous day and there were still no casualties, either white or Indian. Emboldened by continued Indian inactivity, the settlers began sorties from the garrison houses to fetch food and other belongings from their abandoned homes. On June 24th the Indians ambushed one of these foraging parties and killed six. Two other Englishmen were killed in another part of town. Swansea buried its dead and sent two men to Rehoboth for a doctor to care for the wounded. It was now perfectly clear Plymouth faced a major Indian War.[7]

Meanwhile, Massachusetts came to the aid of her sister colony. On June 21st, Governor Leverett received Winslow's letter requesting help in keeping the Narragansetts and Nipmucks out of the war and called an immediate meeting of the Massachusetts Council. The Council agreed to send missions to the Narragansetts and Nipmucks, and further decided to attempt mediation of the trouble between Philip and Plymouth. On June 22nd, the three missions left for their separate destinations. Leverett and the Council also called up two companies of Massachusetts troops and ordered them to prepare to leave for Swansea. On June 24th, Leverett informed Winslow that guns and ammunition were being sent to Plymouth, and four days later the sloops *Swansey* and *Joseph* began to load provisions.[8]

The missions sent by Massachusetts to the Nipmucks and Narragansetts were, according to the assurances given by the Indians, a success. Of course no one could be certain, but the Narragansett and Nipmuck promises to remain neutral were a cause for cautious optimism. The mission sent to conciliate Philip, however, probably knew before it reached Mount Hope that its journey was futile. On June 25th, a few miles north of Swansea, the Massachusetts emissaries came upon the horribly mutilated corpses of the two men sent from Swansea the day before to obtain a doctor. Shocked by this grisly sight, the Massachusetts men continued on to Swansea, but they knew it was too

7. Massachusetts Archives, Capitol Building, Boston, *67, #203*, hereafter cited as Mass. Archives. Some confusion exists on just how many Englishmen died June 24. Nine persons were buried in Swansea on that day, *Ply. Col. Rec., 8*, p. 6.
8. Mass. Archives, *47, #205*, 211, 211a; Davis Papers, #81.

late for conciliation. June 26th they started home to Boston. That evening Governor Leverett called for 100 volunteers to follow the two companies already on their way to Plymouth.[9]

Since the Indian ambushes of the 24th, the situation had improved at Swansea. Captain James Cudworth marched in with an additional eighty men on the 24th and distributed them among the garrison houses. There they stayed. He was now in overall command of the forces at Swansea, and although Winslow offered the command to any Massachusetts officer whom Governor Leverett and the Council should select, Leverett insisted Cudworth continue in command of all troops.[10]

While there were probably no men then in Plymouth who were experienced in leading troops in the field, the appointment of Cudworth was unfortunate. Cudworth had settled in Scituate before 1634, and was now well past sixty. Unaccustomed to life in the field, he was too old to direct sustained campaigning. Moreover, Cudworth had no apparent military ability or training. In 1673 he had declined command of the Plymouth forces being mustered to move against the Dutch, claiming that he was ill and knew nothing whatever about military tactics. He continued: "Learned, judicious, and worthy Mr. Ward, in his animadversions to war, says, that the inexperience of a captain hath been the ruin of armies and the destruction of commonwealths."[11] This self-effacing man commanded all the forces on the scene in what was unquestionably to be the most critical phase of King Philip's War.

Between June 24th and June 28th, when the first Massachusetts troopers arrived, Cudworth held his Plymouth militia in garrison. That was perhaps prudent, for he probably had few more than 100 men to oppose a force of well-armed Indians whose strength he—and later historians—could only guess. On June 28th, however, the coming of the Massachusetts soldiers built up the army to more than 300 men, and Cudworth prepared to move his army down Mount Hope Peninsula toward the Indians' camp. For some reason—probably to rest the Massachusetts companies which had marched hard to reach Swansea— Cudworth did not attack on the 29th but waited until the following day. Shortly before noon on June 30th, with horsemen

9. Leach, *Flintlock,* pp. 40–42.
10. Mass. Archives, *67, #203;* Winslow Papers, *61, #90.*
11. Massachusetts Historical Society, *Collections,* Ser. I, *6,* pp. 80–83.

patrolling the flanks to prevent an ambush, the army swept south past the blackened ruins of the houses burned on June 24th, past eight English heads impaled on poles. The angry troopers, determined on vengeance, plunged through the undergrowth searching for their foes. They found only the emptiness of the forest and the sandy beaches of Narragansett Bay. The Indians had abandoned their village at Mount Hope and escaped east across the Sakonnet River to the mainland.[12]

Knowledge that Philip and his warriors had made good their escape to the mainland, and were now loose to ravage at will, sent chills up the spines of the Plymouth militia. What would be the fate of the people living in the small and isolated western towns? Would other Indians who had as yet not taken up the tomahawk now join the Wampanoags? Such apprehensions had already occurred to some men. June 25th, the day after the first killing at Swansea, an officer in garrison there wrote Governor Winslow and urged that he not send more soldiers to Swansea but use them to guard other towns. At that time Philip was confined to Mount Hope Peninsula; now he and his warriors could attack the white settlements, and the carnage soon began. On July 3rd, John Freeman, commanding a garrison of soldiers at Taunton, wrote Winslow that Indians had attacked the town, killed several persons, and burned some buildings. On July 9th a band of warriors sacked and burned in Dartmouth. Two days later the inhabitants of Middleboro, who had already withstood one Indian raid, evacuated their town; Middleboro was only fourteen miles from Plymouth itself. In the coastal town of Marshfield, Governor Winslow, fearing an Indian threat to himself and his family, sent his wife and children to Salem; he also fortified his house and detailed twenty men to guard it.[13]

While Plymouth Colony families huddled in their town garrison houses, the Plymouth and Massachusetts troops at Mount Hope hurriedly constructed a fort. Then on July 5th, the Massachusetts troops, acting under instructions from home, headed west for Narragansett country—Philip had escaped to the east—to give the Narragansetts a show of force. Cudworth, with only Plymouth soldiers available to follow Philip, decided against a vigorous pursuit and returned with some of the army to Plymouth. But under the pressure of repeated urgings from

12. Church, *History,* pp. 34–35.
13. Massachusetts Historical Society, *Collections,* Ser. I, *6,* pp. 86–87, 91.

some of his officers, he agreed that the troops left behind at
Mount Hope could throw a probing expedition across the Sakonnet River to look for Philip.[14] July 7th or 8th an expedition,
commanded by Captain Fuller of Plymouth with Benjamin
Church second in command, crossed from Mount Hope. The
expedition was nearly a catastrophe. Fuller, brave but inept, divided his force of less than forty men into two patrols. Both
were soon under attack from Indian war parties and were forced
to retreat to the water's edge where they waited for rescue.
Church's patrol—if that energetic Indian fighter's account is
accurate—had an especially close call. Firing from behind piles
of rocks, he and his men were evacuated one at a time by a
Rhode Island sloop which lay offshore beyond the range of Indian musketry.[15]

Meanwhile, Captain Cudworth's decision to ignore orders to
"range after the enemy" and his return to Plymouth with some
of the army angered Governor Winslow. Winslow allowed Cudworth and his troops one night at Plymouth, then sent them back
into the field.[16] On July 16th, the pursuit of Philip by Plymouth
forces began, and on July 19th, Plymouth and Massachusetts
soldiers, who had by now returned from the Narragansett expedition, tried to follow Philip's trail into a swamp. The attempt
was a failure, and while his soldiers blundered about in the bog,
Cudworth wrote to Winslow and requested permission to bring
his forces home. Cudworth reported that his men were tired and
worn out from travel, labor, and want of provisions. He suggested that instead of the seemingly fruitless pursuit of Philip in
the forest, the colony maintain small forces in forts at Mount
Hope and in the Pocasset country across the Sakonnet River, and
that a flying army be created to gather the crops in towns subject
to Indian raids.[17] Cudworth had no way of knowing that the
continuing harassment of Philip which had begun July 16th had
cut the number of warriors in the Wampanoags' band to a mere
handful, and that on several occasions Philip had nearly been
captured.

Winslow now believed, as did Cudworth, that vigorous pursuit of Philip should be abandoned. The Governor had already

14. Winslow Papers, *61*, #94.
15. Ibid.; Church, *History*, pp. 37–47.
16. Winslow Papers, *61*, #96.
17. Massachusetts Historical Society, *Collections*, Ser. I, *6*, pp. 84–85.

ordered Cudworth to send most of the Massachusetts troops home and to cut Plymouth forces to 100 men.[18] He knew that if the colony were to survive the following winter the crops must be harvested; he also knew that the colony did not have sufficient manpower to gather the harvest and send a large force after Philip. Acting on Winslow's orders, all the Massachusetts troops except for Captain Henchman's company, which went into garrison at the Pocasset fort, departed for home.

Although the number of soldiers harrying Philip was now substantially diminished, Cudworth retained more than 100 men under his command as Winslow had insisted that some troops be kept in the field. On July 29th, following Winslow's orders that a column of soldiers visit Dartmouth to boost morale in the devastated town, Cudworth led his men from the fort on Mount Hope.[19] Philip watched the soldiers march southeast for Dartmouth and started northwest with his own people toward the Nipmuck country of central Massachusetts and safety.

On July 30th, Philip and a small band were seen hurrying north across the broad plain lying west of Rehoboth. A company of Rehoboth militia, including the town's minister, Noah Newman, gave chase. Hard-riding posts were sent to Mount Hope where Lieutenant Thomas and twenty men had been left by Cudworth, and to Pocasset, where Captain Henchman and 100 Massachusetts troopers were defending Fort Leverett. Thomas and his men left immediately to join the Rehoboth troops. On the 31st, they joined up, and early the following morning, supported by a number of friendly Mohegan Indians, the combined force attacked Philip's band. By nine o'clock, Philip and his warriors were routed but managed to escape to the temporary safety of a swamp. At this point Captain Henchman and his soldiers arrived, and Henchman assumed command. Philip was cornered and there seemed every likelihood that he would be dead or captured by evening. Henchman's troops, however, were tired from a forced march, and the Massachusetts Captain decided to delay attack until the next day. During the night the Wampanoags slipped past the white sentinels and made their escape; for the third time in five weeks Philip eluded the grasp of the men who were trying so hard to catch him.[20]

18. Winslow Papers, *61*, #96.
19. William Bradford to John Cotton, Mount Hope, July 21, 1675, John Carter Brown Library, Brown University; Church, *History*, pp. 50–51.
20. Mass. Archives, *67*, #130a–131; Davis Papers, #86–88.

An assessment of the decisions taken by Plymouth and Massachusetts Colonies and by their field commanders, during the six weeks from mid-June until Philip's escape August 1st, reveals serious blundering. Winslow was negligent in failing to mobilize at least one or two companies of militia when clear evidence was presented to him that the Wampanoags were preparing for war. Cudworth's tactical handling of his troops during the first ten days of the war was inept; his failure to organize a prompt and vigorous pursuit once he knew Philip had escaped to the mainland is difficult to understand. The diversion of all the Massachusetts troops to the expedition into the Narragansett country between July 5th and July 16th was a mistake. So were the failures to follow up pursuit of Philip, which began on July 16th, and reduction of the army after July 20th. Finally, Cudworth's march to Dartmouth July 29th and Captain Henchman's delay in attacking on August 1st allowed Philip to make good his escape and to carry the message of war to the Indians of central and western Massachusetts.

But some of the information now known was not available to the confused and perplexed men making policy in the hectic weeks of June and July 1675. Governor Winslow, for example, did not know that war would come until a rider carrying news of the attack upon Swansea arrived at his home in Marshfield on June 20th. Until he knew, Winslow, fearing that mobilization of the militia would make war a certainty, hoping still that it could be avoided, may have deliberately avoided calling up colony troops. Cudworth's decision to use his army between July 1st and July 5th to construct a fort near Philip's old village at Mount Hope could have seemed proper, since it seemed advisable that measures be taken to deny the Indians access to corn presumed hidden near the village; and in fact, when Captain Church and his patrol finally caught up with Philip more than a year later, it was at Mount Hope where the Wampanoag and a band of his men were foraging for food. Dispatch of the Massachusetts troops to the Narragansett country may well have seemed necessary in July 1675. The Narragansetts were the most powerful tribe in southern New England and potentially far more dangerous than Philip and his Wampanoags; nor did they enter the war until Winslow's troops stormed their fort the following December.

While the Massachusetts companies were engaged in the expedition against the Narragansetts, Cudworth pulled some of his remaining troops back to the town of Plymouth. This action, which now seems so extraordinary, may have been necessitated by a shortage of provisions, for sustained supply of an army in the field was something about which men knew very little. To feed and resupply his men, Cudworth may have had no choice but to return briefly to one of the coastal towns. After a month of war, Winslow's decision to reduce the size of the army pursuing Philip was a choice of policy for which there was no acceptable alternative. The men were desperately needed at home to harvest crops which otherwise would have rotted in the fields. Cudworth's march to Dartmouth and Henchman's failure to renew the attack upon Philip on August 1st were mistakes. But when Cudworth left for Dartmouth, no one knew that Philip would try to flee to the Nipmuck country; and when Henchman arrived an hour after Philip had fled into a swamp, the soldiers there were tired after a sharp early-morning firefight, and his own troops exhausted after a twenty-four hour march. The conduct of the first six weeks of war reflects little credit upon the tactical skill of the commanders in the field; but the decisions, made on the basis of available information, were not as incredibly poor as they now appear.[21]

After Philip's escape, the war which hitherto had been localized in Plymouth Colony began to spread through New England. Early in August the Nipmuck Indians, inhabitants of central Massachusetts, went on the warpath, and by October 1st the Connecticut River Valley north of Springfield had become a battleground. On October 5th, Springfield itself, the largest settlement in the valley north of Hartford, was attacked and burned by Indians who had been thought friendly. The people of western and central Massachusetts grimly hung on and awaited the onset of winter's cold and snow to bring temporary relief from Indian raiding parties.

After August 1st, Plymouth Colony settled into a period of watchful waiting. Philip's flight north seemed to have brought an end to active skirmishing but no one knew whether or when the enemy would strike again; and if men were not to starve the crops must be harvested. While some men tensely gripped their weapons and peered toward the forest, others gathered the har-

21. See Leach, *Flintlock,* chapter 4, for a more severe assessment.

vest which lay ripe in the fields. The towns continued to maintain watches at night, and some families who lived outside town moved into the settlements.

In November the commissioners from Massachusetts, Connecticut, and Plymouth met in Boston and agreed to attack the Narragansett Indians before that tribe could enter the war. The problem of what to do about the Narragansetts had puzzled the English since June. They were the most powerful Indians west of the Hudson River and their actions since the beginning of the war had been unfriendly. They had provided shelter to the Wampanoag women and children and to fugitive and wounded warriors. Moreover, evidence had begun to accumulate that they were planning to take an active part in the fighting. On the basis of such evidence, and the apparent willingness of the Narragansetts to give aid and comfort to the enemy, the commissioners agreed to strike first. They appointed Governor Winslow of Plymouth commander-in-chief, and ordered him to take an army into the Narragansett country and destroy the military effectiveness of the tribe.[22]

Early in December, Winslow's army, which was supposed to number 1000 men, began to collect. Plymouth Colony contributed 150 infantrymen divided into two companies, one commanded by Captain John Gorum of Yarmouth and the other by Major William Bradford of Plymouth. On December 6, the Colony Council of War issued a declaration to the colony. The Council requested the people to express "theire woonted chearfulnes and currage," and added that men who volunteered for service against the Narragansetts or were pressed for that service "shalbe looked vpon with singular respect." The Council assured the men that land and other profits of the war would be kept as security for their pay.[23]

On December 10, the Plymouth companies joined up with troops from Massachusetts at Rehoboth, and by the middle of December, Winslow established his main base at Wickford, Rhode Island, about a day's march from the heart of Narragansett country. After a few days of skirmishing, Winslow moved his soldiers into a swamp where the Indians were building a palisade around a large village. There, on December 19, in a

22. Meeting of the Commissioners of the New England Confederation, Boston, November 2, 1675. Minutes are at the John Carter Brown Library.
23. *Ply. Col. Rec.,* 5, pp. 182–83.

fresh fall of deep snow, the English and Narragansetts clashed in what men later would call the Great Swamp Fight.

Pouring through a hole in the still uncompleted palisade, 1000 English troops, supported by some friendly Indians, burst upon the Narragansetts. After several hours of bitter fighting, the military power of the Narragansetts was broken. Hundreds of Narragansett warriors died and the rest scattered, their shelter and food supplies gone, to endure the cruel months of a New England winter. More than seventy English died, including half of the company commanders, and many were wounded. In vain, Captain Church of Plymouth tried to persuade Winslow to occupy the Narragansett camp and give the army a chance to lick its wounds, but Winslow, fearful of an Indian counterattack, ordered the army back to Wickford. Exhausted after an eighteen mile march that morning and a hard fight, the troops carrying the wounded stumbled through the snow back to their base.[24]

A crucial battle had been fought and won, but to the tired and hungry men of Winslow's army, there seemed little cause for rejoicing. Even before all of them had returned to their homes, the New England Confederation sent out a call for another 1000 men to carry the war against the Indians in central and western Massachusetts. Plymouth was asked to send 122 soldiers. The colony pressed the men and sent them off, and early in February the Massachusetts General Court forwarded warrants to the constables of Sudbury, Marlboro, and other towns, ordering them to take care of the billeting of Plymouth forces passing through their towns.[25]

During the winter of 1675/6, Plymouth continued on its guard. Bridgewater fortified its meeting house and also the minister's home. Like their fathers before them, the inhabitants of the town of Plymouth constructed a palisade upon Fort Hill. The structure was 100 feet square, with ten-foot stakes sunk two and a half feet in the ground. Inside this stockade, the town built a new watch-house and mounted cannon to sweep the surrounding terrain.[26]

24. Mass. Archives, *48*, #101–04; a letter from Capt. Bradford describing the fight is in Thomas Hutchinson, *The History of The Colony and Province of Massachusetts Bay* (3 vols. Cambridge, 1936), *I*, footnote, p. 254.
25. Mass. Archives, *48*, #105, 131.
26. Bridgewater Town Records, *I*, p. 71; *Plymouth Town Records, I*, pp. 146–47.

As the cold and snow of winter gave way to early signs of spring, Indian raiding parties reappeared in the colony. Although people were prepared for trouble, casualties and property damage began to mount. On March 12th, William Clark's isolated garrison house at Eel River, three miles south of the town of Plymouth, was attacked and destroyed: eleven died. Less than two weeks later, a company of militia, commanded by Captain Michael Pierce, pursuing what it believed to be a small band of Indians, was cornered on the Pawtucket River by an estimated 1000 warriors, and before help could arrive—the story later was told that a messenger sent to Providence for help waited until after the service was over to deliver his information—the company was wiped out. Between forty and fifty militiamen died in this disaster. Pierce's men died fighting bravely but this was little consolation to the towns which had lost the flower of their manhood. Scituate alone lost eighteen men in the fight on the Pawtucket.[27]

As a consequence of these disasters, Governor Winslow's confidence of the preceding June had given way to deep pessimism. On March 27th, he wrote to Massachusetts that he expected hourly to hear of Indian assaults upon Plymouth's western towns or perhaps even those nearer to the sea. He continued: "We are very weak and unable to defend ourselves." Should God not intercede, Winslow feared that the people of his colony would be cut to pieces in their towns. The Governor pleaded for help but Massachusetts had enough trouble of its own and could send no troops to Plymouth. Plymouth Colony was now so short of manpower that the Council of War ordered all youths under sixteen who were capable of performing guard duty be required to do so. And the council advised all persons to gather in fewer garrisons so that ten or twelve men would be available at each for defense.[28]

Two days after the annihilation of Pierce's company, the Indians hit Rehoboth and burned the town; the next morning they moved on toward Providence. Plymouth, to counter the new aggressiveness of the Indian raiders "whoe haue fiered the greatest p̃te of one of our fronteer townes, and . . . wee haue reason to expect that they may persist," ordered 300 men into

27. Noah Newman to John Cotton, Rehoboth, March 27, 1676, printed in Bowen, *Rehoboth,* vol. *3,* pp. 14–15.
28. Mass. Archives, *68,* #177; *Ply. Col. Rec.,* *5,* p. 193.

the field. This was the greatest military effort by the colony yet: thirty soldiers to come from Plymouth, fifty from Scituate, thirty from Rehoboth; the balance to come from the remaining towns.[29]

But the point had been reached beyond which some men would not go. The effort to send an army into the field and into combat against the Indians who were then operating in the western regions of the colony failed. Scituate, which suffered most heavily of all the towns in Pierce's defeat, and Sandwich, the Quaker center on the Cape, held their men at home.[30] There was some excuse for this. Dark days had descended upon the colony; men who went out on the country's service would of course worry about what would happen at home in their absence, and people left behind would know that their own security against Indian attack was less sure. The Council of War noted in April that "in this time of our callamitie, wee can not but be in dayly expectation of the Indians theire invadeing and assaulting our townes." [31]

There were a few souls who proved more staunch. John Cotton was outraged by the pessimism of the government, and on April 17th he wrote to Thomas Walley at Barnstable that he was "exceedingly afflicted to think that we should reel and stagger in our councils as drunken men that so precious a people as Rehoboth should be so forsaken for our own selfish interests." He continued "If I were in your study alone I would tell you how much blemish some have gotten for being so backward to maintain a garrison at Rehoboth. This morning the governor (being much encouraged by Captain Bradford and the treasurer) hath sent two men to Rehoboth to signify an escort or a garrison." [32]

The offer of escort which Cotton mentioned in his letter referred to a decision made by the Council of War suggesting that the inhabitants of Taunton, Rehoboth, and Bridgewater remove to the coastal towns and abandon the frontier to the Indians. Had this offer been accepted, all of the colony except the immediate seacoast would have been given over to the enemy, for Dartmouth, Swansea, and Middleboro were long deserted. The inhabitants of Taunton, Rehoboth, and Bridgewater were of sterner stuff than the men who refused to come to their relief. Thomas Cooper, one of Rehoboth's selectmen, wrote on April 14th to express thanks for the offer, but signified the quiet deter-

29. *Ply. Col. Rec., 5*, p. 192.
30. Ibid., p. 193; Mass. Archives, *68*, #234.
31. *Ply. Col. Rec., 5*, p. 194.
32. Cotton Papers, *7*, #6.

mination of Rehoboth people to stick it out. Richard Wiliams, a Taunton selectman, and the minister of Bridgewater, James Keith, sent similar messages, although Keith added that if Taunton and Rehoboth were abandoned, Bridgewater would have to be evacuated.[33] Noah Newman, minister of Rehoboth, informed his friend and colleague John Cotton that, "If I should not take heart and be incouraged at such a time as this is who should for I perceive my wealth increaseth and I find more falling into my lap than I can possibly improve." Newman reported to Cotton that he was being given so many houses that he hardly knew what to do with them.[34]

After the burning of Rehoboth on March 28th, Indian raiding parties continued to range through the colony, and in late April the Council of War ordered one-fifth of all armed men in each town to be on alert for immediate duty. May 1st the remaining houses in Middleboro, long since evacuated, were burned by a band of warriors. On May 23rd four men were killed at Taunton, leaving thirty-two fatherless children, and late in May part of the town of Scituate was burned. In Boston news circulated that Plymouth, Duxbury, and Bridgewater were all destroyed. All communications between Plymouth and Boston had ceased and the writer of a letter home to England could only hope that the news was not as bad as reported; he added that hitherto it usually had proved worse.[35] Writing from Rehoboth early in June, John Kingsley informed an old friend in Hartford that times were desperate in Plymouth Colony. He stated that he was not "able to beare the sad stories of ovr woeful days, when the lord made ovr wolfish heathen to be our Lordes, to fier our towne, shout and holow to cal us to com out of our garisones." He continued that "Som of our suoldiers are removed, nobodey comes to say, how doe ye," and he asked that Connecticut send meal to Plymouth, for Rhode Island refused to help without being paid, "which won of 40 hath not it to pay tho thay starve."[36]

Although Indian war parties still ranged through the colony in the early summer of 1676, the worst was now over. Time was working inexorably in favor of the white man. Pitted against an

33. Massachusetts Historical Society, *Collections,* Ser. IV, *5, The Hinckley Papers* (Boston, 1861), pp. 2–8.

34. Noah Newman to John Cotton, Rehoboth, April 19, 1676, printed in Bowen, *Rehoboth, 3,* pp. 15–16.

35. Davis Papers, p. 101; *Cal. of State Papers, Col. Ser., 1675–1676,* #928.

36. John Kingsley to the Preacher of the Gospell at Hartford, Connecticut, Rehoboth, May 4 or 5, 1676, printed in Bowen, *Rehoboth, 3,* pp. 20–23.

organized society, with greater economic resources and greater manpower, the Indian ultimately had no chance. Moreover, some white men had by now learned from the Indians something about fighting in the forest. In late May, Governor Winslow, sensing that the extreme pessimism and fear of a few weeks earlier was gone, informed two colony assistants living on the Cape that the people of all towns with the exception of Scituate "are very desirous to be ranging after the enemy." [37]

In June the General Court called up 150 militiamen and fifty friendly Indians to scour the colony for Indian war parties.[38] Friendly Indians had accompanied Plymouth troops before but this was the first time that an official draft included them. The white man had learned a lot about fighting in the forest during the year that had passed since Philip's warriors struck at Swansea. To move through wooded terrain and avoid ambush called for skilled scouts flung out to the front and flanks of the main body of troops, and no one was better qualified for such duty than an Indian. When King Philip's War began, even friendly Indians in Plymouth Colony were immediately suspected of plotting against the white settlers and Plymouth's treatment of them reflected that suspicion. Now, in the closing months of the war, Indians, and in particular those living on the Cape, were being asked to serve in the colony forces; and it was probably not mere coincidence that both the greater use of friendly warriors and Plymouth's military successes began in the early summer of 1676.

The early summer of 1676 brought a cessation of deaths by Indian raids. Troops called up in June were in the field during most of July in continuous pursuit of enemy Indians, now desperately short of food. One of the soldiers, Anthony Collymore of Scituate, wrote to his wife on July 16th from the army's base camp at Taunton: " . . . [we] have killed and taken upward of one hundred Indians but never an English slain nor wounded only one or two bewildered in the woods and captured. We intend to be in pursuit of Philip again tomorrow; we have pursued him from swamp to swamp so that he is enforced to fly with a very small quantity of men." [39] While the main army operated

37. *Hinckley Papers,* pp. 8–9.
38. *Ply. Col. Rec.,* 5, p. 197.
39. Anthony Collymore to his wife, Taunton, July 16, 1676, copy at the Old Colony Historical Society. The original apparently has been lost.

in the western part of the colony, Captain Benjamin Church, commanding a detachment of tough English soldiers and friendly Indian warriors, ranged through the woods of southern and eastern Plymouth. Church's men traveled light and struck from ambush, thus in effect beating the enemy at his own game.

Early in August, Church learned that Philip and a band of warriors had returned to Mount Hope. Church, after recall of the main army and demobilization late in July, was patrolling in the western sections of the colony and moved his men across the Sakonnet River to set an ambush for Philip. Although one of the enemy discovered the ambush and gave enough warning for most of the war party to escape, Philip himself was shot down by one of Church's Indians. Church ordered Philip's corpse quartered and left to rot on the ground. Two weeks later Church's men caught up with the last of Philip's captains. Mopping up operations continued for a few months, but the war in Plymouth Colony was over.[40]

Although the war ended in Plymouth and in central New England, fighting continued in Maine (then a part of the Massachusetts Colony and known as the eastern plantations). Plymouth, in spite of requests for help from Massachusetts, refused to participate in the war in this region. Nathaniel Morton, Secretary of Plymouth Colony, wrote to Governor Leverett of Massachusetts that while Plymouth thought the defense of the English settlements in Maine to be a worthwhile project, there were "insuperable obstructions" to Plymouth soldiers fighting there. This letter drew a biting reply from Massachusetts which had risked her men and resources to support Plymouth in June 1675.[41]

King Philip's War caused heavy physical devastation, suffering, and loss of life in New Plymouth. No reliable statistics are available to indicate precisely how many persons were killed by the Indians but the total number was probably not less than 100; it may well have been more. In 1680 Governor Winslow estimated that the total number of men in the colony between sixteen and sixty years of age was about 1200.[42] If Winslow's estimate is correct, and if, as seems likely, most of the people killed during

40. Church, *History*, pp. 121–26.
41. Mass. Archives, *69*, #164; Winslow Papers, *61*, #107; Davis Papers, #103.
42. *Cal. of State Papers, Col. Ser., 1677–1680*, #1349. Each town in the colony was required to keep a list of the men capable of bearing arms. As Governor, Winslow had access to these lists, his estimate was probably accurate.

King Philip's War in Plymouth Colony were males—a massacre a few miles south of the town of Plymouth is the only recorded instance when women and children were slain—the colony lost roughly between five and eight per cent of its adult men. In comparison, United States losses in World War II were less than one per cent of the total number of males twenty years of age and older.

Property losses, especially in the western frontier towns, were also severe. Three towns, Swansea, Middleboro, and Dartmouth, were abandoned and subsequently burned by Indian raiding parties. Rehoboth, Taunton, and Scituate also suffered extensive damage. Thirty houses were burned in Rehoboth, twelve homes and their barns in Scituate. Indian bands attacked Bridgewater and some of the outlying farms near the town of Plymouth, but apparently neither town suffered heavy damage to its main settlement. Marshfield, Duxbury, and the four towns on Cape Cod were never attacked. Thus in a colony of fourteen towns, three were abandoned, three more suffered considerable damage, two others were raided, and six escaped damage altogether.[43] Confronted by the problem of financing an expensive war, the colony had a diminished tax base from which to raise the money.

Just what this war cost Plymouth in pounds and shillings is impossible to determine. In 1678, two years after the fighting had ended in southern New England, the colony presented an account of the charges of the war to the commissioners of the New England Confederation in Boston. The total figure presented was £11,743, including money spent by individual towns and colony disbursements of £3000. This total does not, I think, include the physical property damage suffered in those towns attacked by the Indians, nor is it probably wholly accurate. For the account of money paid out by some of the towns was in round figures, £200, £500, £1000, which casts some doubt on whether the town official making the report himself knew how much had been spent. In some towns, however, accurate figures apparently were kept. Plymouth reported expenditures of £601, Yarmouth a figure of £498, Bridgewater £245. These totals did not include the amount raised in each of the towns towards the £3000 spent by the colony government.[44]

43. Davis Papers, #101.
44. *Ply. Col. Rec., 10,* p. 392.

While it is impossible to assess the total financial strain placed upon the colony by King Philip's War, or even to estimate the actual cost of the physical destruction caused by the Indians, it is possible to compare the tax burden placed upon several of the individual towns with taxes paid before the war. In 1667, Marshfield taxed its inhabitants a total of £87, including a £23 assessment to be used in clapboarding the minister's house. In contrast, during the twelve months beginning August 1, 1675 and ending July 31, 1676, the people of Marshfield paid £386 in taxes. A year before the war began, Scituate collected a rate of £133; between September 1, 1675 and August 31, 1676, the tax burden in the town jumped to £883.[45]

Taxpayers in Plymouth Colony received some help in underwriting the war. Lands opened up by the defeat of the Indians were sold, and in the case of Philip's Mount Hope lands, the proceeds were distributed to the various towns. A subscription was taken in Ireland and sent to be divided among the people in the colony. But the majority of the cost was borne by the inhabitants. What this meant to the individual taxpayer can be seen from a copy of the so-called "Great Rate" taken in Yarmouth in the autumn of 1676. The total paid by Yarmouth was £297; the tax was levied on ninety-eight people. Five persons paid more than £5, and the wealthiest person in the town paid £13; seven more paid between £4 and £5; only fourteen paid less than £1. For people who were subsistence farmers, a tax of £3 was heavy. Moreover, no inflation had occurred to ease the difficulty of paying. An "indifferent" cow was appraised in March 1675/6 at forty-five shillings, just about what an "indifferent" cow had been worth for thirty years. At the going rate of two shillings six pence for a bushel of corn, a tax of £3 meant twenty-six bushels, or the yield of nearly two acres. The "Great Rate" of November was not the only tax paid in Yarmouth in 1676, although it was the heaviest.[46]

Nonetheless, Plymouth managed to pay for the war without destroying the economic life of the Colony. Rebuilding began at once and there is no evidence that any town defaulted on pay-

45. Marshfield Town Records, *1*, pp. 112, 141–44; Scituate Book of Accounts, *1*, pp. 133–45.

46. *Ply. Col. Rec.*, *5*, pp. 191, 222–23; *6*, p. 50. Yarmouth Town Records, *2*. The list is printed in Freeman, *Cape Cod*, *2*, pp. 194–95. Taunton Proprietor Records, *2*, chapter 4. Marshfield Town Records, *1*, p. 51.

ment. People went back to their fields and planted for the next year. By 1680 ministers' salaries were being raised and new meetinghouses built, and the economic life of the colony seemed to have returned to normal.

Even more awful than the physical desolation was the thought that something had gone wrong, that God had visited his wrath upon New England as punishment for its wickedness. For more than twenty years the clergy had warned New Englanders that they were showing a declension from the piety and godliness of their ancestors, and had warned that this deterioration was displeasing to God. In 1630, John Winthrop had preached to some of the people on their way to settle the Massachusetts Colony:

> Thus stands the cause betweene God and vs, wee are entered into Covenant with him for this worke. . . . Now if the Lord shall please to heare vs, and bring vs in peace to the place wee desire, then hath hee ratified this Covenant and sealed our Commission, [and] will expect a strickt performance of the Articles contained in it, but if wee shall neglect the observacion of these Articles which are the ends wee haue propounded, and dissembling with our God, shall fall to embrace this present world and prosecute our carnall intencions seekeing greate things for our selues and our posterity, the Lord will surely breake out in wrathe against vs be revenged of such a periured people and make vs knowe the price of the breache of such a Covenant.[47]

Speaking to the New Plymouth General Court in 1669, Thomas Walley of Barnstable warned that men had not lived up to the promise of their covenant. Walley entitled his sermon, *Balm in Giliad to Heal Sions Wounds or A Treatise wherein there is a clear Discovery of the most prevailing Sickness of New England both in the Civill and Ecclesiastical State*. Walley examined the state of sin which he saw existing all around him and concluded that the country was full of healthy bodies and sick souls: "Faith is dead and Love is cold. The power of godliness decays, the trumpet sounds, the alarm is given yet the most sleep on."[48]

47. John Winthrop, "A Modell of Christian Charity," in *The Puritans,* Miller and Johnson, eds., revised edition (New York, 1963), *1,* p. 198.
48. Thomas Walley, *Balm in Giliad to Heal Sions Wounds* (Cambridge, 1669), p. 8.

After King Philip's War began, few could doubt that the prophecies of the clergy were fulfilled. Governor Wislow wrote to John Winthrop, Jr. shortly after the outbreak of the war: "We doubt not but that you haue heard how it hath pleased God to exercise us under very aflictiue dispensations improveing our neighbour Indians to scourge and chasten us . . . [;] our punishment is less, far less, then our iniquiteys haue deserved." [49] In Plymouth churches men prayed to God for forgiveness and promised to walk more lovingly toward him in the future. John Cotton wrote in the *Plymouth Church Records*: "Whereas the Holy and Righteous God hath many wayes in yeares lately past changed the course of his favourable dispensations towards us and manifested sad signes of his displeasure against us, wee desire to be deeply humbled in his sight under his mighty hand." Cotton went on and listed what he believed were the sins which had provoked·God to bring this war upon the people in New England: "Wee have greatly lost our first love to and pretious esteem of the Gospel and ordinances of the Lord Jesus," and "wee have also polluted the Holy Sabbaths"; the "loosneesse of our conversations soe unbecoming the Gospel of Christ," and "unbrotherly chidings and contendings one with another," were transgressions certain to have angered the Lord. For these and other sins the Plymouth Church solemnly pledged to "lye in the dust before God," and to renew the covenant of the Church. Upon the recommendation of the General Court, other colony churches also renewed their early covenants. Cotton believed that renewal of the Plymouth Covenant was very effective, for "God turned his hand against our Heathen-enemies and subdued them wonderfully." [50] Even so, the belief that God had especially favored the people of New England received a shock in 1675 from which it never fully recovered.

Of at least one thing the Plymouth government was confident: it had not been mistreatment of the Indians that had caused this war. Winslow wrote to Governor Leverett of Massachusetts: "I do solomenly [sic] profess we know not any thing from us that might put Philip upon these notions nor have we heard that he pretends to have suffered any wrong from us only that we had killed some Indians and intended to seek for himself

49. Josias Winslow to John Winthrop, Junior, Massachusetts Historical Society, *Collections*, Ser. V, *I* (Boston, 1871), p. 428.
50. *Plymouth Church Records, I*, pp. 149–52.

the murder[er] of John Sassamon." [51] The governor was wrong: Plymouth had given the Wampanoags provocation for war and the colony must undeniably bear a share of the guilt. The establishment of a settlement near the Wampanoag village at Mount Hope and the humiliation of Philip in 1671 were actions which had surely stirred Indian resentment and anger. Yet the view of contemporaries like Deputy Governor Easton of Rhode Island that Plymouth alone was responsible for the war was equally wrong. Philip and his chiefs had been bellicose and provocative in their dealings with the white man, and they had shown little desire to search for the ways of peace. King Philip's War occurred because men of good will were succeeded by men who had neither the desire nor the tact to continue a tradition of friendship and peace.

Once the tomahawk was raised, the defeat of the Indians who fought in King Philip's War seems in retrospect to have been inevitable. Courageous as they may have been, the Indian warriors were too few and poorly organized to stand against the strength of the New England colonies. Their unhappy experience in battle anticipated a recurring pattern of conflict in which the final results were always the same.

The treatment given the Indians captured in King Philip's War would also become familiar. Convinced that the Wampanoag attack was perfidious and without provocation, the colony treated those Indians whom it captured without mercy. In August 1675 the Council of War ordered 112 Indians—men, women and children—sold into slavery, because "seuerall of them haue bine actors in the late rising and warr of the Indians against vs, and the rest complyers with them therin which they haue done contrary to engagement . . . alsoe in that they did not discouer that pernisious plott which Philip, with others, completed against vs." [52] Even in the summer of 1676, when the tide of war had turned and many Indians were captured, the colony continued to ship all male captives over fourteen years of age to the West Indies. When Philip's young son, age nine, was captured in the summer of 1676, the colony debated whether to kill him or sell him, and asked several ministers for advice. The child apparently was sold. Another practice at Plymouth was that of

51. Davis Papers, #83.
52. *Ply. Col. Rec., 5,* p. 173.

executing Indians who were known to have commanded raiding parties.[53]

There was probably some justification for selling prisoners of war into slavery. Plymouth had no place to keep a large number of captives nor the men to guard them. Nevertheless, such treatment, given to Indians who voluntarily surrendered, and whose only crime was that they were red-skinned, seemed unjust to some people even then. Thomas Walley wrote bitterly to John Cotton about the actions taken against Indian captives, and Benjamin Church argued for more conciliatory policies, but apparently with little success.[54]

Long after the fighting ended, people remembered King Philip's War. And as the years passed the horrors were forgotten, and the stories of painted warriors burning and killing, of Pierce's gallant last stand, of the march through the deep snow to the Great Swamp Fight and the return, of the skill and cunning of Captain Church, of the killing of Philip, and countless others were told and retold in Plymouth Colony homes. But on bitter winter nights while the fire crackled in the hearth, some men and women looked into the leaping flames and remembered the terror of those days when God had loosed his awful wrath upon New England.

53. Ibid., pp. 209–10; *II*, pp. 242–43; Massachusetts Historical Society, *Collections*, Ser. IV, *8* (Boston, 1868), pp. 689–90.
54. Davis Papers, #92, 94; Church, *History*, pp. 140, 146.

14

"Our Old and Indeed Imperfect Grant"

Even as the postwar rebuilding and resettlement proceeded, Governor Winslow and the General Court turned to meet the accusation reported in England that Plymouth's unwarranted provocation of King Philip had caused the war. Plymouth had an immediate interest at stake which made it vital that the accusation be countered. The colony sought a grant of the Mount Hope lands, formerly occupied by Philip and his Wampanoags. Since the decision rested with the crown, the common sense of the matter dictated that criticism of Plymouth be met and a favorable climate of opinion established. Moreover, Winslow and the Court may have suspected that other claimants to the Mount Hope lands would materialize—as in fact they did. Winslow also recognized that Plymouth's own position as a claimant was considerably weakened by the absence of a royal charter giving the colony clear and certain title to its lands.

The absence of a charter was something which the colony had been sensitive about for a number of years and which it had tried on a number of occasions to correct. Under instructions from Governor Bradford, Isaac Allerton had petitioned Charles I in 1629 to approve the new patent Allerton had just obtained from the New England Council. Bradford knew that the council, under the terms of its crown grant had authority to give land patents; this was certain. But Bradford, or some of the people advising him, knew enough law to question whether the council, a private corporation, could legally create another corporation and confer upon it the power of self-government. Moreover, the possibilities of royal approval looked auspicious, for the Massachusetts Bay Company had recently been successful in securing the crown's approval of their grant.

Allerton's endeavors were not so successful. While the king received Plymouth's application "graciously" and may well have intended to grant its request, the business bogged down in the delays of government bureaucracy. Lacking the financial resources to plant the necessary bribes and apparently without friends highly placed in court circles, Allerton could not persuade the royal treasurer to approve the customary seven years' freedom from custom duties. The treasurer referred approval on this question to the Privy Council, and although Allerton attended session after session of the council, he was unable to obtain a hearing. Eventually he sailed for home leaving the matter in a solicitor's hands. The solicitor proved no more adept than Allerton in guiding the application through the various levels of bureaucracy, and Plymouth Colony had no choice but to rest its legal existence on the Bradford Patent.[1]

Plymouth almost saw its worst fears confirmed a few years later. The Council of New England offered to resign its patent to the king if the king in turn would give the members of the council land grants extending fifty miles into the hinterland. The council wanted to substitute proprietary government for the civil governments of Plymouth and Massachusetts and convert them into feudal domains. Although the king accepted the offer to dissolve the New England Council, he at first refused to consider a reorganization of government. But by 1635, under the urging of Archbishop Laud, who wanted to check the rise of Puritanism in America, the king reversed his position. He initiated proceedings to revoke the Massachusetts Charter as the first step toward the appointment of a royal governor to rule New England. This plan was not realized, for the coming of civil war in Britain in 1638 ended all efforts towards change for a generation.

As long as Parliament and (later) Cromwell ruled England, the Puritan colonies knew they were safe from home interference. The restoration of Charles II in 1660, however, threw into

1. *Bradford's Letterbook,* pp. 51, 52. Charles M. Andrews suggests that the Pilgrims' efforts to obtain a charter may have been lost because of an internal struggle for power in the Council for New England; Andrews, *The Colonial Period of American History* (New Haven, 1934), *I,* p. 403.

doubt the legal status of the three New England colonies without royal charters—Plymouth, Connecticut, and Rhode Island. Connecticut and Rhode Island promptly sent their governors, John Winthrop, Jr. and Roger Williams, to persuade Charles II to grant them charters. Both were successful, and in light of their success it seems quite probable that similar energetic action by Plymouth at this time would have produced a similar result. But Plymouth sent only a petition asking for the king's favor.[2]

In vain Plymouth waited three years for an answer to this letter. Charles II was busy restoring and consolidating royal power after two decades of civil war and rule by Cromwell; moreover, the wheels of colonial administration turned slowly in response to communications from across the Atlantic. The absence of a reply probably bothered Governor Prence and the General Court little, if indeed they thought about it at all: no news from England was good news.

Then in the spring of 1664, Plymouth learned that royal commissioners would be sent to New England. Although the restoration government had at first tried a conciliatory approach to the Massachusetts Colony, reports reaching England had continued to indicate that the leaders of the Bay Colony would permit no interference from England in their avowed purpose of constructing a Puritan commonwealth. Once he had put his own house in order, Charles II, like his father before him, was determined to establish royal control over the Massachusetts Colony. Anxious also to dislodge the Dutch from their foothold in New York, the king appointed four commissioners, gave them a small detachment of troops, and ordered them in 1664 "to secure in the first place possession of Long Island," then to visit the New England colonies and ascertain their "true state." While the commissioners' major focus of interest in New England was to be Massachusetts, they were also to visit Connecticut, Plymouth, and Rhode Island, and examine their charters and inquire into their laws.[3]

The occasion of the visit seemed to offer a new and propitious chance to raise the matter of a royal charter. Pondering the news that commissioners were coming, and believing their visit might be critical to the future prospects of the colony, Governor Prence

2. *Cal. of State Papers, Col. Ser., 1661–1668,* #102. New Haven was still a separate colony in 1660 but was incorporated into Connecticut in 1662.
3. Ibid., #713.

decided to summon all the freemen to attend the June 1664 Election Court. In this court the freemen voted to petition the crown for a new charter and gave the magistrates and deputies authority to expedite the matter.[4]

Eight months later the commissioners stopped at Plymouth, and the General Court, especially convened in their honor, presented Plymouth's request for a charter. Declaring the colony too poor to send an agent to England, the Court asked the commissioners act in Plymouth's behalf. Unfortunately for Plymouth Colony, in the two years which had elapsed since John Winthrop, Jr. and Roger Williams had successfully petitioned the king, policy in England had changed to favor tighter control over the New England colonies. The commissioners, therefore, answered that if Plymouth Colony would allow the king to appoint its governor from three men nominated by the freemen to a three to five year term, they could promise a favorable response to the petition. The General Court rejected this offer. Men accustomed to voting each year for their governor were not willing to give up that right even in return for a royal charter.[5]

Although the colony rejected this quid pro quo, it asked one of the commissioners, Robert Cartwright, to petition for a charter. Impressed by Plymouth's loyalty to England and by the friendly reception given to him, Cartwright agreed. Once again, however, Plymouth seemed indifferent to pushing the matter to a conclusion. Before he sailed for England, Cartwright wrote to Prence and urged the Plymouth Governor to forward a map of the colony. Cartwright continued that if he could persuade the king that it was possible for men to be so negligent in the pursuit of their own interest, he would have done his duty, and if he was not successful, "you may in part blame yourself who will not see me furnished with necessaries thereunto." [6] On the trip back to England, Cartwright's ship was seized by pirates and all his possessions and papers taken.[7] God seemingly had intervened to save Massachusetts, but He had forgotten Plymouth. While Cartwright's efforts to obtain a charter for Plymouth might well have been unsuccessful anyway, the loss of his papers made it certain. In 1677, Plymouth's legal right of existence still rested on the Bradford Patent of 1629.

4. *Ply. Col. Rec., 4*, p. 62.
5. Ibid., *4*, p. 92, *Cal. of State Papers, Col. Ser., 1661–1668*, #1103.
6. *Winslow Papers*, 61, #26.
7. Ibid., #28.

When Governor Winslow sat down to write the king in June 1677, he knew, of course, the lack of a royal charter clearly defining Plymouth's bounds weakened his claim to the Mount Hope lands; nevertheless, he attempted to make the best case he could. To counter the rumor that Plymouth provoked the war, the Governor insisted that Plymouth was not responsible and had only attempted to maintain his majesty's interest. Winslow continued that the Bradford Patent gave Plymouth undisputed title to Mount Hope Peninsula. To make the king more receptive to this argument, Winslow thoughtfully enclosed King Philip's crown, his gorge (apparently some kind of a staff), and two Wampanoag belts. Several weeks later Nathaniel Morton, on order from the General Court, wrote an account of the war, acknowledged neglect in not writing sooner, and forwarded it to Whitehall. Plymouth sat back and waited for results.[8]

The colony waited for some time. Unfortunately Winslow had chosen to entrust the Indian "rarities" to his brother-in-law, Major Waldegrave Pelham of Ferriers Hall, and they were never received at Whitehall. Pelham, Winslow later believed, was so delighted with these spoils of war that he had decided to keep them for himself. Winslow's letter and Morton's account of the war which accompanied the Indian artifacts also disappeared.[9] For two years the king and Privy Council awaited news from Plymouth, and Winslow and the General Court waited for news from England.

In 1679, Plymouth received a letter from the crown chastening the colony for neglecting to communicate the details of the war. Winslow's distress upon opening this letter—and his wrath for his brother-in-law—can hardly be imagined. The Governor broke the news to an adjourned session of the General Court sitting early in July, and at the Court's request forwarded a letter to the king along with copies of the documents sent in 1677. In this letter Winslow did not attempt to blame his brother-in-law for the miscarriage of letters but suggested that their loss might have been due to a change in administrative personnel in England.[10]

8. *Cal. of State Papers, Col. Ser., 1677–1680,* #314, #333.

9. Ibid., #1131; Massachusetts Historical Society *Proceedings,* 7 (Boston, 1864), pp. 482–83.

10. Massachusetts Historical Society *Proceedings,* 7, p. 482; *Cal. of State Papers, Col. Ser., 1677–1680,* #1042; *Ply. Col. Rec., 6,* p. 20.

The letters sent from Plymouth in July were read before the Privy Council on September 26th. Henry Coventry, the Secretary of State charged with responsibility for the American Colonies, informed Winslow that the king was "very sensible" of Plymouth's loyalty, and very thankful for the presents he had never received. The Secretary continued that no action as yet had been taken on the Mount Hope lands but that the question had been referred to a committee. Coventry forwarded a request for answers to a number of specific inquiries about the colony; he also commended Edward Randolph, then about to leave on his second visit to New England, as a man "the king believeth of very well." [11]

Governor Winslow had already made the acquaintance of Edward Randolph. Randolph, a member of the gentry who had fallen 'upon hard times and turned to the government for employment, a person whom his recent biographer calls "a man with a head for details and an eye for the written record," had first come to New England in 1676.[12] On a mission to represent the interest of his cousin Robert Mason (Mason was petitioning for a restoration of his proprietary rights to New Hampshire), Randolph also investigated the military, political, and economic conditions in the New England colonies. What Randolph found in Massachusetts did not please him, and he had so reported to England. The colony did not enforce the laws of trade and navigation; the General Court, in violation of the Massachusetts Charter, had enacted legislation contrary to the laws of England; most of the clergy and men in civil service, he believed, were seditious.[13]

Randolph's impressions of Plymouth were more favorable. He paid a visit at Governor Winslow's suggestion, and on June 17, 1676, wrote home to Secretary Coventry that Winslow was "a stout commander, well-beloved," and would act in response to instructions from England. Three months later Randolph referred to the Plymouth Governor as a man "of loyal principle" and one who had voiced criticism of the intransigence of the

---

11. *Cal. of State Papers, Col. Ser. 1677–1680*, #1131; C.O. *1*, vol. 43, #128. The quotation is from the original.

12. Michael G. Hall, *Edward Randolph and the American Colonies* (Chapel Hill, 1960), p. 2.

13. Ibid., Chapter 2.

Massachusetts government. Randolph reported that in Winslow's opinion New England would never be secure to the king until it was reduced under his immediate government by the crown's appointment of a governor general, a reorganization to which Plymouth would readily submit.[14]

Winslow was highly embarrassed when Randolph's report of this conversation became public. Agents sent to England to defend Massachusetts against Randolph's accusations stated that Winslow denied any criticism of the Bay Colony, that Massachusetts had acted "fairly and neighborly," and that Plymouth had no desire for a change in the government of New England.[15] Governor Leverett of the Bay Colony evidently accepted Winslow's repudiation of this conversation and wrote a surprisingly sympathetic letter to the Plymouth Governor suggesting that Randolph's purpose was not so much to exalt one and depress the other as to split apart good friends.[16] In spite of Winslow's subsequent denial it is probable that Plymouth's Governor was anxious to do business with Randolph, and it is quite likely that he may well have expressed some criticism of Massachusetts policy. Winslow already had the reputation of being a "moderate," which meant in the language of the time that he favored submission to the sovereignty of the crown.

Edward Randolph returned to England in September 1676. Three years later he sailed again for America to assume duties as customs collector for the New England colonies. Randolph carried explicit orders to see that the Acts of Trade and Navigation were enforced, but he had no soldiers or ships of war to support him. His reception in Massachusetts was chilly and the two years which followed were ones of frustration.[17]

Randolph was more welcome at Plymouth, and in July 1680 the colony made him a freeman.[18] The information reaching Plymouth from England (and which Randolph himself probably brought) that a decision would soon be forthcoming on the Mount Hope lands gave some basis for hope; after nearly three

14. *Cal. of State Papers, Col. Ser., 1675–1676,* #953, #1037.
15. Ibid., 1677–1680, #740.
16. Winslow Papers, *61,* #108.
17. Hall, *Randolph,* Chapter 3.
18. *Ply. Col. Rec., 6,* p. 46.

years of silence, the colony knew that its claim had finally received official notice. Then in early summer, a letter from Secretary Coventry arrived indicating that the crown had granted Plymouth Colony title to Mount Hope. Writing in the name of the king, Coventry explained that the major consideration in giving Plymouth title was "your loyalty and good conduct in that war." The Secretary continued that the king was in fact so pleased with Plymouth's loyalty that, upon proper application, he had agreed to grant the colony a charter.[19]

Coventry's statement to Governor Winslow commending Plymouth Colony for its loyalty and good conduct reflected the belief at Whitehall that the colony should receive some mark of favor for an attitude in marked contrast to the stubborn hostility of the Massachusetts government. In 1679 the Committee for Trade and Plantations, studying the disposal of the Mount Hope lands, recommended that "this occasion of favor may be improved to other good purposes of a more immediate dependence on your Majesty not only in the colony but by their example to the rest." In addition, the committee recommended that Plymouth Colony be invited to submit a new application for a charter. The king approved, and Secretary Coventry's letter to Winslow followed.[20]

Opening Coventry's letter at Marshfield, Winslow must have experienced a sense of great satisfaction. His policy directed toward establishing a friendly relationship with the crown's principal representative in New England, Edward Randolph, and through Randolph with the responsible officers of government in England, seemed vindicated. Loyalty to the crown did bring its own reward although it had undoubtedly exposed Winslow to sharp criticism at home. The Massachusetts government had elected to challenge any extension of royal authority over the Bay Colony, and the failure of the Plymouth Governor to support this position represented a significant breach in the Puritan ranks. Winslow must have known when he tried to conciliate Randolph that he would alienate some persons in his own colony

19. *Cal. of State Papers, Col. Ser., 1677–1680*, #1256; *Hinckley Papers*, pp. 32, 33.

20. *Gay Transcripts*, 2, pp. 4, 5; C.O. 5, vol. 904, pp. 10–15; *Cal. of State Papers, Col. Ser., 1677–1680*, #1168, #1174, #1206, #1237. The quotation is from the Gay Transcripts.

and in Massachusetts. But Winslow also knew that the interests of Plymouth Colony were not identical to the interests of Massachusetts.[21]

When the General Court convened at Plymouth in June 1680, news had already arrived from England that the king had granted the colony title to Mount Hope and invited an application for a royal charter. The Court commissioned Winslow to carry forward the proceeding; and in July, the Governor wrote to thank the king and to report that the colony intended "very speedily, to send some person or persons to wait upon your majesty with [a] copy of our old and (indeed) imperfect grant, and to make our humble address for obtaining your majesty's free and royal tender." [22] During the summer Winslow drafted a petition and the abstract to a charter. The abstract asked that the governor, assistants, and freemen be declared a body politic with every person, freeman or not, to enjoy all the liberties and immunities as if born within the realm of England. In September, Winslow sent these documents to England.[23]

But between July and September the colony government decided against sending money to dispatch an agent, and instead asked Lord Culpeper, on his way home to England from Virginia, and William Blathwayt, Secretary to the Board of Trade, to handle the business. This procedure was followed even though Edward Randolph had written urging Winslow that if Plymouth wanted to see its hopes for a charter carried forward to a successful conclusion, Winslow himself must go to England; and even though the General Court had voted unanimously in June to send an agent. The petition stated that the Plymouth government had decided to depend upon Culpeper and Blathwayt because of "our paucity of fit men." [24]

Culpeper appeared before the Lord Commissioners of Trade

21. Thomas W. Perry, "New Plymouth and Old England: A Suggestion," *William and Mary Quarterly, 18* (April, 1961), pp. 251–65.

22. *Cal. of State Papers, Col. Ser., 1677–1680,* #1421; *Hinckley Papers,* pp. 40, 41; *Ply. Col. Rec., 6,* pp. 36, 37.

23. *Hinckley Papers,* pp. 48–52; Gay Transcripts, *2,* pp. 41–47. The quotation is from the Gay Transcripts.

24. *Edward Randolph: Including his Letters and Official Papers,* Tappan and Goodrick, editors, Prince Society Publications, *24–28, 30, 31* (Boston, 1898–1909), III, p. 65; *Ply. Col. Rec., 6,* pp. 36, 37; *Hinckley Papers,* p. 52. Winslow's health may have already begun to fail, and this may explain why he did not go. He died in December.

and Plantations in April 1681. He testified that Plymouth was "very well inclined" toward the crown and therefore should be encouraged. But Culpeper continued that he himself believed New England could not be brought into a satisfactory relationship with the home government until a governor general was sent over.[25]

Edward Randolph agreed. From Boston, where he reported his reception was more like that of a spy than one of the crown's officers, Randolph had written to Governor Winslow in February 1680 proposing a reorganization of New England. Randolph informed the Governor that he believed Charles II intended to contract the number of governments into two or three, and that the consolidation of Plymouth and Massachusetts and the appointment of Winslow as governor would be of great benefit to the country. Winslow's pay—Randolph's entrance into government service was at least partially for financial reasons, and he therefore presumed other men could be similarly tempted —was to be about £400 a year, or eight times the salary paid to the governor of Plymouth.[26] Winslow's answer to this letter is not preserved, but it was the following June that Randolph became a freeman of Plymouth Colony.

Before Randolph returned to England to press the cause of consolidation, Governor Winslow was dead. At age fifty-two, he died in December 1680. He was the last of the Plymouth governors to challenge Massachusetts and carry forward policies in conflict with Massachusetts objectives.[27] As a final act of respect to its deceased governor the Plymouth General Court in June 1681 voted £40 to pay his funeral expenses; the court also chose Thomas Hinckley, elected to the office of assistant annually since 1658 and as deputy governor in 1680, to succeed him.[28]

Governor Hinckley continued the measures initiated by his predecessor to obtain a charter. In the summer of 1681, James Cudworth, Plymouth's new deputy governor and a septuagenar-

25. C.O. *391*, vol. 3, p. 260; *Cal. of State Papers, Col. Ser., 1681–1685*, #82.

26. Winslow Papers, *61*, #113.

27. The nineteenth century historian, John Gorham Palfrey, described Winslow as not "a New-England patriot of the highest type." Palfrey continued, "The bold and generous policy of Massachusetts had no effectual support from him." Palfrey, *The History of New England, 3*, p. 423.

28. *Ply. Col. Rec., 6*, pp. 58, 63. Hinckley indicated that Winslow died on November 18th, but Thomas Prince believed the date was December 18th. *Hinckley Papers*, p. 53.

ian, sailed for England to present Plymouth's case to the crown.[29] In the months which followed the colony waited anxiously for news, but no news came. Governor Hinckley replied in May 1682 to a letter from William Blathwayt, written in October, to thank Blathwayt for his continuing efforts on behalf of the colony, and to explain Plymouth's failure to pay the annual quitrent of seven beaver skins owed as a condition of the Mount Hope grant. Hinckley apologized for a mix-up in the medium of payment, and expressed his disappointment that as yet he had heard nothing from Cudworth.[30]

Four months later Hinckley learned from Joshua Moodey of New Hampshire that Blathwayt continued to work for the new patent; "and it had received despatch ere this, had not one of your magistrates told him, about Christmas last, that he was bound to the West, and desired him to suspend any further instances at the council till his return." Moodey's letter went on that Cudworth had not reappeared, but that Blathwayt now intended to press the matter and to send Hinckley a draft of the new charter for approval. In the meantime the Plymouth Governor should send a copy of the Bradford Patent, since a copy forwarded by Governor Winslow in 1680 had been mislaid and could not be found.[31] Moodey's news was disappointing; even more disappointing was the report which Hinckley now had, or would soon have, that James Cudworth was dead and that the colony would again have to depend on the good will of busy men for whom the issue of a charter to Plymouth was a matter of little consequence.[32]

Ever hopeful and determined to maintain a favorable image, the Plymouth Governor wrote again to Blathwayt in November 1682 to assure him the colony retained confidence in him and to ask that he continue his efforts to secure a new charter. As further encouragement Hinckley thoughtfully enclosed fifty guineas.[33] Hinckley also began to look for another agent to replace the deceased Cudworth, and in February 1683 the General Court requested the Duxbury Church to allow its minister, Ichabod Wiswall, to go to England on colony business. Although the Court

29. *Hinckley Papers,* footnote, p. 74.
30. Ibid., pp. 65–67.
31. Ibid., p. 73.
32. Hinckley heard of Cudworth's death some time between May and November 1682.
33. *Hinckley Papers,* pp. 74–81.

delicately phrased the request for Wiswall by asking that Duxbury "lend him to the Lord for a little season," the church voted
against his release and Wiswall stayed in Duxbury.[34]

Duxbury's reluctance to approve the departure of Wiswall
proved of little consequence. After a long period of indecisive-
ness, the King in Council had decided to act against the Massachusetts government. In January 1683 Randolph received word
to return home for consultations on the continuing refusal of
Massachusetts to enforce the Acts of Trade and Navigation and
failure to act in accordance with the laws of England. Randolph
wrote Governor Hinckley that he must see him before sailing "to
adjust the matters of our Colony," but Randolph had been away
from England for several years, and the hopefulness of his note
did not reflect policy in Whitehall.[35] A more accurate appraisal
of Plymouth's prospects came from William Blathwayt, who
wrote in the autumn of 1683 that while continuing to work for a
new charter, "I must deal plainly with you, that it is not probable
any thing will be determined in that behalf until his majesty do
see an issue of proceedings in relation to the Massachusetts
Colony." Blathwayt continued: Massachusetts was to "be
brought under such an actual dependence upon the Crown as be-
comes his majesty's good subjects. From hence it will be that
your patent will receive its model." [36]

Blathwayt also counseled Hinckley to trust Randolph, who returned to New England in the autumn of 1683, bringing with
him a writ of quo warranto against the Massachusetts Charter.
And Blathwayt urged the Plymouth Governor follow Randolph's advice in preparing a new petition to the crown. Hinckley
followed these recommendations, and when Randolph returned
to England in December 1683, he carried with him one more
Plymouth address to the king, the third such petition in three
years.[37]

It is possible, although I think highly unlikely, that Blathwayt
and Randolph were already practically certain that Plymouth
Colony would be joined to Massachusetts; that for some reason,

34. Ibid., pp. 84–87; *Ply. Col. Rec., 6,* p. 99.
35. The date given in the *Hinckley Papers* for this letter is January 1682. Since
Randolph was recalled in January 1683, the date should read 1682, or 1682/3 as it
was usually written then. *Hinckley Papers,* p. 83.
36. Ibid., pp. 91, 92.
37. *Cal. of State Papers, Col. Ser., 1681–1685,* #1389.

perhaps hoping that Hinckley would continue to give the charter application financial support, they engaged in conscious deception. Probably, however, while both knew that some reorganization of the Massachusetts government was forthcoming and that such a reorganization, as suggested by Culpeper and Randolph himself, might involve a consolidation of existing governments: until the vacating of the Massachusetts Charter in October 1684 they were not certain what form that reorganization might take. When Randolph, carrying the writ of quo warranto, sailed for New England, he also carried an option which did not require going forward with the quo warranto proceedings, but only authorized the king to make certain changes in the Massachusetts Charter.[38] Had the Massachusetts government chosen that option, Blathwayt and Randolph may have believed that Plymouth Colony would be offered a similar charter. At least this possibility seems to have been considered in Blathwayt's statement: "from hence it will be that your patent will receive its model."

But Massachusetts had not chosen this option, and with her choice probably ended any chance for Plymouth to obtain a new charter. In any major reorganization of New England, Plymouth was likely to be consolidated with Massachusetts, especially now that Thomas Hinckley, whose sympathies for Massachusetts policies were well-known, was governor.[39] In retrospect, the prospects for consolidation after 1683 are much clearer than they were at the time, particularly in Plymouth, where Governor Hinckley was totally ignorant of decisions reached in England until long after the event. Thus Plymouth continued to hope in 1684 and through 1685 that its request for a charter would be met. Meanwhile, under Governor Hinckley's guidance, Plymouth Colony turned to some internal reorganization of its own.

38. Hall, *Randolph,* p. 79.

39. See Governor Cranfield's comment, C.O. *5,* vol. 904, p. 86; *Cal. of State Papers, Col. Ser., 1681–1685,* #1024.

15

"A New Booke of Lawes"

WHEN Thomas Hinckley succeeded Josias Winslow in June 1681, the General Court was the effective governing instrument over all matters which seemed to have colony-wide application. Of much less significance was the Court of Assistants; once without statutory limitation to its power, this court, by the time Hinckley became governor, was principally a court for settlement of civil suits in excess of forty shillings and for trial of major crimes.

More important in the daily lives of most inhabitants than either the General Court or the Court of Assistants was the system of town government which had developed on the local level. In the 1630s pressures to establish local self-government had grown with the development of new towns; and in 1636 the General Court had authorized the purchasers and freemen of the towns of Plymouth and Scituate "to make such orders for their convenient and more cõfortable subsistance as shall by them be thought most meet and convenient provided they be not contrary to the publick ordnances of the Governm ᵗ." [1] Several years later the Court authorized all towns in the colony to make town orders as necessary and to establish penalties to a limit of ten shillings for noncompliance.[2]

In March 1643 the Court for the first time voted to allow the election of local officials to assume resonsibility for the per-

1. *Ply. Col. Rec., II*, p. 18.
2. Ibid., p. 32.

formance of certain functions in the town. The Court authorized each town to choose three or four men to assess the property of taxpayers.[3] But the Court was still unwilling to authorize the election of men to assume general responsibility for governing the towns. And legislation empowering the towns to elect selectmen did not pass until 1665; in voting it the Court, in fact, only gave legal status to established common practice.

Taunton, settled by Massachusetts men familiar with town government in that colony, had elected seven selectmen since 1643. In 1642 the forty-six purchasers of Taunton had paid a twelve-shilling tax to extinguish the debt to the Indian owner and took over title to the town's lands. This meant in effect the seven commissioners appointed by the General Court to distribute the township lands were out of a job. But while the forty-six purchasers were anxious to assume control of the township's lands, they were not anxious to assume full responsibility for the continuing settlement of the town. In December 1643 the town met and agreed to elect seven men—they were not yet called selectmen—to manage "town affairs." The seven men were to be chosen annually and meet six times a year. The town gave them power to distribute lands "from time to time as needful" with a limit of ten acres to an individual. They were supposed to supervise the admission of new inhabitants into the town although the purchasers reserved the right of final approval of a prospective settler. They were also given authority to determine trespasses and debts under £3, and, if the consent of the General Court was obtained, to grant warrants to distrain or attach property for such debts or trespasses. The town agreed that an inhabitant owning one house lot could not buy another without its consent.[4]

The choice of selectmen in the town of Plymouth began in 1649 when the town met and agreed that since all the inhabitants could not "redyly com together" the town would elect seven men to manage its affairs. The town specifically authorized the seven to lease lands to needy persons and to tax for the relief of families "in absolute need." They were also required to oversee the wintering of cattle at Sepecan (Rochester). By 1673 their authority also included the power to call to account "such younge men or others as live Idelely and disorderly . . . and to take

3. Ibid., p. 42.
4. Taunton Proprietor Records, Chapter 3.

Course for their Reformation as shalbe by them thought meet."
The town authorized the selectmen to expel persons who were
not settled residents and who did not meet their approval.⁵ This
system of town government adopted in Taunton in 1643, in Plymouth in 1649, and written into colony law in 1662, was firmly
established in Plymouth Colony at the outbreak of King Philip's
War.

The establishment of a judicial system on the local level seems
to have proceeded in a similar ad hoc fashion. During the two
decades following the Pilgrim landing, the Court of Assistants
was the principal court of justice in the colony. But after the settlement of Massachusetts and the concurrent settlement of new
towns in Plymouth Colony, some expansion of the judicial system
became necessary. In 1640 the General Court directed that a
court be set up on Cape Cod to hear a particular case and the
following year this court was permanently established to hear all
civil actions in which the damages sought did not exceed twenty
shillings. (One of the first defendants was one of the men appointed to it.) ⁶ In 1643 Taunton authorized its selectmen to
settle minor disputes, and a few years later a court with jurisdiction in cases up to £10 began to hold sessions in Rehoboth forty
miles west of Plymouth.⁷

Formal establishment of a uniform local court system in Plymouth Colony did not take place until 1665 when the General
Court ordered the organization of "select courts" in every town.
Composed of three or five selectmen, whose election now required confirmation from the colony government, these local
courts had the authority to adjudicate all civil suits of forty
shillings or less; their jurisdiction also included cognizance of
litigation between the Indians and the English arising from
damage to Indian crops by marauding livestock.⁸

The select courts were not an unqualified success even in assur-
ing an impartial judgment between white settlers, and after they
had been in operation for a few years the General Court began
to pass legislation curtailing their power. In 1670 they were for-
bidden authority to grant an attachment against a settled inhabitant. Five years later their jurisdiction was limited to the

5. *Plymouth Town Records, I*, pp. 29–31, 138, 139, 143.
6. *Ply. Col. Rec., I*, p. 155; *Sandwich Town Records*, pp. 4, 5.
7. Taunton Proprietor Records, Chapter 3; *Ply. Col. Rec., II*, p. 55.
8. *Ply. Col. Rec., II*, p. 213.

township in which the court convened, and they were ordered not to interfere with colony officers executing colony business. They were directed to reduce the expenses involved in trying a case and limited as to the number of sessions which could be held in one year.[9] Such limitations placed upon them undoubtedly reflected a belief in the General Court that, under the control of local officials, the select courts could become the legal support of local interests.

In the administration of justice on the local level, one other institution played an important role in Plymouth Colony. As with justices of the peace in England, men elected to the office of assistant sat individually in judgment on cases of petty crime. As in England (but unlike Massachusetts), a single magistrate before 1685 could not hear civil suits.[10]

Such then were the governing and judicial structures in Plymouth when Thomas Hinckley became governor. They were, he apparently thought, inadequate.

A month after Hinkley's election, the General Court appointed the Governor and Deputy Governor Cudworth a committee to revise and settle the laws of the colony.[11] Cudworth himself soon sailed for England and the committee was subsequently enlarged to include other magistrates; but departing from earlier practice at both Plymouth and Massachusetts Colony, no deputies were added. The progress of the committee during the succeeding three years is unknown; but the passage of this amount of time and the addition of other men to the committee suggest that the proposed revision of the laws may have encountered some opposition in the General Court. In 1685, however, a new edition of the laws was published in Cambridge. Patterned in format and often in text after the Massachusetts laws of 1672, the codification of 1685 established a legal system more complex and comprehensive than that which had formerly regulated colony life. But the most fundamental change was the creation of county courts, one for each of the three counties.

Massachusetts had established county courts in 1636. Since

9. Ibid., pp. 227, 238. Selectmen's judicial powers in 1685 are found on p. 22 of the *Book of General Laws* (1685).

10. *Book of General Laws* (1685), p. 46. Previous legislation provided for the trial of civil actions before three magistrates.

11. *Ply. Col. Rec., 6,* p. 68.

this was shortly after settlement of the colony, and since county courts were in many respects similar to the courts of quarter sessions in England, the county courts caused little disruption in the existing system of government.[12] But their introduction into a colony which had existed without them for sixty-five years, and in which few men remembered the English courts of quarter sessions, disturbed an equilibrium of power to which men were accustomed.

Until the creation of the county courts, the General Court had exercised control over the raising of all taxes except for those matters which were primarily of local concern; the care and maintenance of highways, the levying of town rates for the support of the poor and for the support of the ministry, the building and improvement of the meeting house, and the multitudinous other housekeeping duties which were left to the individual towns. Of course the General Court had assumed a supervisory responsibility over some town activities, particularly in the payment of town deputies and the support of the minister. For the most part, however, the towns were left to manage their own affairs; and when interference did come, as it occasionally did, a town at least knew that the interference came from a body in which it was itself directly represented.

The county court now came between the town and the colony government, and from each the court drew certain power. Responsibility for building highways and bridges in the county was taken from the individual towns and centralized in the county government. To finance the highway program and the expenditures required to run county administration (including the building of county prisons), the county court had the power to tax and to enforce collection. The county court was also charged with responsibility for supervising the state of religious worship in the county towns and of ensuring the adequacy of the minister's salary. The law setting up the county courts provided that a quorum of three men be present for the court to meet, and that the judges who sat on the court be assistants or "county associates" appointed by the General Court.[13]

Because freemen alone could vote in the election of the colony assistants and because the General Court controlled the selection

12. For the establishment of the county court system in Massachusetts, see Haskins, *Law and Authority in Early Massachusetts,* pp. 32, 33.

13. *Book of General Laws* (1685), pp. 19–22; *Ply. Col. Rec., 6,* p. 194.

of the county associates, neither the townsmen nor the towns as political entities were represented on the county courts. Thus, while the decentralization of government brought certain conveniences, some men saw their rights of self-government being curtailed and protested. The town of Scituate informed the General Court that county government would lead to a three-fold increase in public charges and signified tyranny by depriving men of their right to taxation by consent. A complaint from seven Dartmouth men was more specific; insisting that they had already contributed to the cost of building a prison at Plymouth, they protested a tax to build a new prison at Bristol, the county seat.[14] The Dartmouth men were apparently not the only people to protest the building of a county prison and the assessment of a county tax to pay for it. Enough opposition developed in the colony to cause the General Court in June 1686 to order the deputies from the county towns to meet with the county courts and vote the money.[15] Men could at least know their elected representatives had some voice in the matter, a principle of some importance to men who were accustomed to being taxed only by their elected representatives. But the law establishing the county courts was not repealed.

The creation of the county courts in 1685 also changed the structure of the colony's judicial system, for the new courts were institutions of justice as well as instruments of county government. In their judicial role, the courts did not constitute a substantive break with the past. Under the law defining their jurisdiction, they were given the authority to hear and determine all civil and criminal cases except for divorce and crimes punishable by death, mutilation, or banishment. They were supposed to sit twice a year, although for a court to be held at least three cases must be awaiting trial. All cases proper to the cognizance of the county court except for defamation and battery were to be heard before it and not in any other court. Provided that he gave bond to satisfy all damages, a man could appeal the decision rendered in the county court to the next Court of Assistants. The county courts in turn were the courts of appeal from cases tried in the select courts.[16]

14. Scituate Town Records, pp. 28, 28a; Deane, *Scituate,* pp. 102, 103; Dartmouth Town Records, Dartmouth, Massachusetts, *I,* p. 7.

15. *Ply. Col. Rec., 6,* p. 193.

16. *Book of General Laws* (1685), pp. 6, 7.

The establishment of county courts and publication of a new edition of *Colony Laws* testified to the growing complexity of jurisprudence in Plymouth Colony. In part, this greater complexity reflected an attempt to spell out in fuller detail the requirements of human behavior, but it also reflected an increasing emphasis on procedural law.

Growth in the complexity of law, the new attention to detail and to procedural safeguards, proceeded in the first instance from the growing complexity of society itself. As population had increased and the knowledge which men had of one another had diminished, more complicated legislation became necessary to adjust controversy and to protect the rights of persons accused of breaking the law; the clash of competing interests demanded that ways be found to formalize disagreement and resolve it according to a proscribed set of rules. But there was also another explanation. Committed to preserving a way of life which seemed increasingly threatened by the weakening of traditional patterns in America, the leaders of Plymouth Colony turned to the example of Massachusetts and tried to meet their responsibilities, as they understood them, by legislating an ever-enlarging number of rules for human behavior.

The early settlers of Plymouth did not include, so far as is known, anyone with formal legal training. There was no one, for example, like Governor Winthrop of Massachusetts, who once sat as a justice of the peace on the court of quarter sessions and held an appointment as an attorney in the court of wards and liveries; or like Richard Bellingham of the Massachusetts Colony, who received a legal education and served as recorder of the city of Boston before he came to New England. Lacking the formal legal experience of such men and anxious to draw from their own understanding of English laws a set of rules applicable to the American environment, the early inhabitants of Plymouth made their law brief and uncomplicated.

Although the Pilgrim fathers had passed some legislation as early as 1623, the first codification of law came in 1636. This codification set forth the powers of the government and the oaths required of individuals holding office. Capital offenses (eight) and criminal offenses (three) were listed; also included were laws relating to inheritance, the conveying and granting of land, fees allowed certain officials for performing their duties, and laws regulating the setting of traps, the killing of wolves, the payment of damages for trespass done by cattle, etc.[17] In the opinion of a recent scholar, the laws establishing civil marriage, equal descent to children, provision for widows, and the recording of land deeds represented "marked advances on English law" For the most part, however, the legislation found in Plymouth Colony in 1636 was rooted in the English experience.[18]

The codification is also important for what it did not include: the colony had not yet begun to attempt regulation of private life by the legislative process. There were no laws pertaining to profanation of the Sabbath, to the wearing of clothing, to the support of the churches, to the playing of cards, or the prohibition of "night-walking." [19] The omission of such legislation did not mean inhabitants were necessarily allowed to ignore the requirements of human behavior expected from men who lived in a Puritan community: the law authorized a grand jury to inquire into "all such misdemeanors of any person or persons as tend to the hurt and detriment of society Civility peace and neighbourhood." [20] The omission meant rather that punishment, as was the case in many criminal offenses, was left to the discretion of the magistrates; it probably also meant a need for legislation of this kind did not as yet exist both because a major challenge to Puritan standards had not occurred and because the standards themselves were not always precisely defined.

In the fifty years which followed the codification of 1636, Plymouth Colony became increasingly dependent upon written law to spell out the rules for human behavior. The *Book of Laws* published in 1685 included legislation which prohibited the playing of cards, regulated the wearing of clothing, and prevented "night-walking" except by "known peaceable and orderly inhabitants." To the legislation written in 1636 stating that the right to marry for one living under a parental roof required parental approval, the General Court by 1685 had added "that whosoever shall go about to inveigle or endeavour to steal the affections of any Man's Daughter, Pupil or Maid servant without his consent," should be fined not more than £5 or suffer corporal pun-

17. *Ply. Col. Rec., II,* pp. 6–24.
18. George L. Haskins, "The Legacy of Plymouth," *Social Education, 26,* #1, January 1962. The article was published separately by Plimoth Plantation. See Haskins, *Law and Authority,* Chapter 10, for English precedents.
19. *Ply. Col. Rec., II,* pp. 6–24.
20. Ibid., p. 18.

ishment.[21] By 1685 "Sabbath" had become one of the subhead-ings in the *Book of Laws,* and the offenses included "unnecessary servile work," "unnecessary traviling by Land or passing by Water," "bearing Burthens," "carrying of Packs," "Buying or Selling," "Sports," and "Recreation." The law also prohibited walking or riding about a town, and the visiting of neighbors un-less on an errand of mercy.[22] And by 1685 the General Court had added idolatry, blasphemy, and rebellion by a child more than sixteen years of age to the number of capital crimes; they had been capital offenses in Massachusetts since 1648.[23]

The new *Book of Laws* also indicated that people were less willing to give the magistrates as much discretion in the applica-tion of justice. Men wanted to know what they could and could not do; they wanted to know explicitly what the penalties were when they broke the law, and they wanted certain protections guaranteed them when they appeared in court. Except for the right to trial by jury, the codification of 1636 had not included a single statute relating to procedural justice. But by 1685 a grow-ing number of legal safeguards, most of them enacted earlier in the Massachusetts Colony, protected the interests of defendants brought into court. Persons arraigned for a capital crime were allowed to challenge twenty jurymen without stating a reason, and all persons accused of breaking the law were entitled to un-limited number for cause. No person could be damaged "but by virtue of some express law." No one could be indicted for a petty crime more than one year after the offense. No one could be found guilty without the testimony of two witnesses "or other sufficient Evidence or Circumstances equivolent thereunto." An accused had the right to be represented by counsel in civil cases provided the attorney was a person of good repute. And no one could be restrained pending trial so long as he could put up bail except in capital crimes, contempt of court, or where an express act of the General Court prohibited it. In its attempts to define the penalties for major criminal acts and for petty crimes and misdemeanors, the General Court also added to the protection of a man brought before a court of law.[24]

Much of the sumptuary and procedural legislation which ap-

21. *Book of General Laws* (1685), p. 47.
22. Ibid., pp. 57, 58.
23. Ibid., pp. 9–11; *The Lawes and Liberties of Massachusetts* (1648), pp. 5, 6.
24. *Book of General Laws* (1685), pp. 2, 6, 36.

peared in the codification of 1685 was not new. It had evolved slowly since 1636 and particularly in the period after 1650. Much of it was borrowed directly from Massachusetts; and in some cases the wording of laws in the two colonies was almost identical.[25] Thus Governor Hinckley, in the new codification of colony laws (to the extent that it expanded the quantity of legislation), only consummated a process which had been under way for some time. But to the extent that he changed the structure of the government itself, he introduced a significant change. This change, however, had little opportunity for trial before it was replaced by an even more sweeping break with the past, a break which Hinckley himself bitterly opposed.

25. Plymouth Colony prepared four codifications of law: 1636, 1658, 1672, 1685. The codifications of 1672 and 1685 were published at Cambridge; the other two are found in the *Ply. Col. Rec., II*. I have compared the 1685 edition with the *Massachusetts General Laws and Liberties* (Cambridge, 1672).

16

"The State of Things as Now They Stand With Us"

IN APRIL 1685 news reached Plymouth that Charles II was dead and that his brother, James II, formerly Duke of York, had succeeded to the throne of England. Still without knowledge of what action had been taken on the address sent to England in 1683, Governor Hinckley immediately wrote the Lords of the Privy Council asking the continuance "of our wonted liberties, both civil and religious, especially our religious." And in June the General Court petitioned the new king to carry out the promise made by his brother in 1679 to grant Plymouth a new charter. The colony remained hopeful.[1]

But events in England had advanced to the point where no further consideration would be given Plymouth's application for a charter. Edward Randolph had returned to England in early 1684 to report that Massachusetts refused to accept any changes in the existing charter. Randolph's information set off proceedings to vacate the charter; on October 23rd it was formally withdrawn.[2] Massachusetts was now without legal government and the crown had to decide what form the reorganization of New England should take.

Randolph, whose recent experience in the New England colonies was unequaled by any royal official and whose own plan for consolidation had existed several years, worked during the summer and early autumn of 1684 on the reorganization. He wanted

1. *Hinckley Papers,* pp. 134–38.
2. Hall, *Randolph,* pp. 82, 83.

the appointment of a governor general and council for all New England, but he did not recommend representative government be done away with altogether. He believed the towns should continue to have some voice in their government through their elected representatives.[3]

Randolph's work on the reorganization was interrupted in October when the customs commissioners sent him to Holland. Upon his return to England he learned Charles II had appointed Colonel Percy Kirke as governor general of New England. Kirke had established a reputation as a martinet while in command of the British garrison at Tangier, and the rumor had spread that he would take a regiment of troops with him to New England. Randolph also learned to his dismay (for in spite of his shortcomings, he was in some ways a political realist) that the king had directed there be no elected assembly in the new government.[4] The Committee for Trade and Plantations had already set the boundaries for the new government which Kirke was to administer. Plymouth Colony and the Narragansett Country, west of the Island of Rhode Island, were included; since neither had a charter this could be done merely by administrative decree.[5]

The death of Charles II and the succession of his brother brought one change in plans for the reorganization of New England. James II hoped to reduce all his American colonies to the common denominator of royal colonies, and thereby ensure stricter compliance with imperial policy. He accordingly pressed ahead with the project to consolidate the New England colonies under one government and he approved the decision to deny the inhabitants an elected assembly. But, much to the relief of Randolph who had publicly opposed the appointment and worked to have it changed, the king withdrew the name of Percy Kirke for governor general. Kirke was instead sent to put down Monmouth's rebellion. To replace Kirke, James II appointed Sir Edmund Andros who had served as the Governor of New York from 1674 until 1681.

3. Ibid., p. 84.
4. Ibid., p. 87.
5. *Cal. of State Papers, Col. Ser., 1681–1685*, #1928, #1941, #1953. Hall says that the Committee had also decided to include Connecticut and Rhode Island if quo warranto proceedings could be brought against their charters. But the *Calendar of State Papers, Col. Ser., 1681–1685* does not include an entry to this effect. Hall, *Randolph*, p. 87.

A year had passed since the invalidation of the Massachusetts Charter. To avoid further delay in establishing a new government and to prepare for the transition to a royal governor, Randolph urged the creation of a temporary council to govern Massachusetts until a new governor could be appointed and reach New England.[6] Randolph nominated Joseph Dudley, one of the men in Massachusetts who favored conciliation toward England to head this new government as president of the temporary council. And Randolph suggested his own appointment to the office of Secretary and Registrar of the Colony. The crown approved this plan, and early in 1686 Randolph sailed for New England carrying with him the king's commission to establish the new government. On May 25th, the judgment against the Massachusetts Charter was read publicly and the proclamation constituting Dudley and the council as temporary government of the colony published "by beat of drum and sound of trumpet." [7]

Randolph's arrival in New England did not terminate Plymouth's existence as a separate colony; that would await the arrival of Sir Edmund Andros himself. But the consolidation now was only a matter of time, and in September 1686, Randolph, who was busy preparing for the new government to be set up under Andros, proposed the names of Hinckley, John Walley, William Bradford, Barnabas Lothrop, and Nathaniel Clark as the men from New Plymouth who should become members of the governor's council.[8] All but Nathaniel Clark were colony magistrates and Clark had been secretary of the General Court in 1685.

On December 20, 1686, Governor Andros, accompanied by two companies of royal infantry, landed at Boston. Orders were immediately sent to Plymouth, Rhode Island, and Connecticut to submit to the authority of the new governor, and councilors appointed by Andros, including the five nominated from Plymouth by Randolph, were directed to appear in Boston on December 30th for a meeting of the governor's council.[9] Connecticut refused and remained outside the Dominion until summer, but Plymouth and Rhode Island complied with the governor's orders, and on December 30th the councilors from the two colonies

6. Hall, *Randolph,* pp. 88, 89, 93.
7. C.O. *5,* vol. 785, pp. 1–3.
8. Mass. Archives, *126,* #77.
9. *Randolph Papers, 6,* p. 209.

dutifully presented themselves at Boston. Of the five who came from Plymouth, several must have suffered misgivings about the future. For all but one, the two years which followed gave substance to their early pessimism.

Some New Englanders preferred the Dominion government to the four independent governments which had existed before; but many did not. To the bureaucrat settled comfortably in Whitehall, the centralization of government at Boston and the replacement of cumbersome democracy by a governor and council loyal to the crown seemed efficient and practical. To many of the inhabitants of Plymouth Colony, "efficiency" and "practicality" brought unwanted complications and hardships into their lives. For not only was the right of representative self-government now taken from them, but the center of government for all New England was established in Boston.

This centralization was no small inconvenience. Even a trip from Plymouth to Boston was time-consuming, and in winter could only be undertaken at some hazard. But under the Dominion government, trips to Boston often could not be avoided. An order published under the authority of Governor Andros required all civil court cases involving sums in excess of £10 and all land suits be heard before the Superior Court of Common Pleas. The superior court did not sit in Barnstable County, and persons who lived there and who wished to bring suit had to appear before the session of the court held in the town of Plymouth. And if a writ was needed to force the defendant or witness to appear in court, the plaintiff had to travel to Boston, since writs for superior court could be obtained only from the secretary of the colony.[10] The centralization of government also caused hardship in the probate of wills. Governor Andros ordered all estates in excess of £50 have their final probate in Boston. This requirement occasioned inconvenience, expense, and delay, and a Barnstable County grand jury sitting in 1687 listed it as a major grievance of the Andros government.[11]

The inconvenience experienced by the average citizen multiplied for the man who was supposed to participate in the government. The session which Andros convened in December 1686 was in fact the first and last at which all members of the gover-

10. *Hinckley Papers,* pp. 158, 159.
11. Ibid., p. 168.

nor's council from Plymouth were present. The expense of
coming to sit in council for eight or ten days at a time they soon
found excessive, particularly since their presence or lack of it
seemed to matter little. The Thomas Hinckley, who at first conscien-
tiously tried to attend meetings, returned to Boston for an
adjourned session only to find that significant action on the probate of wills had taken place at an unscheduled council meeting
called the previous week. As it became clear that Andros preferred to work with a few men he could trust, and as the hostility
to the Dominion government increased, some of the Plymouth
councilors, wishing to dissociate themselves from the government, stopped coming altogether, and after March 1688,
Nathaniel Clark was the only member from Plymouth present
when the council met.[12]

More burdensome to the people of New England than the inconvenience attendant upon the centralization of authority at
Boston were the policies carried out by the Andros government.
Within a month after the arrival of Andros, New England for
the first time knew the burden of a tax imposed without the consent of elected representatives. When news of the tax reached
Taunton, the town voted to inform the new governor that Taunton "did not feel free" to raise the money without the assent of an
elected assembly. But Taunton, which rushed its minutemen to
Boston in April 1775, was not prepared to begin a revolution in
1687; and on Governor Andros orders, Shadrock Wilbor,
Taunton's town clerk and writer of Taunton's defiant statement
on the tax, was jailed for "scandalous and seditious writing." In
jail, Wilbor's spirit wilted and he eventually petitioned the governor that he had only carried out the will of the town and that he
was very sorry and asked a pardon. After languishing five weeks
in a prison which he found "very cold," Wilbor was released under Andros' order, since Taunton had by then paid the required
tax.[13]

While all New Englanders could protest the levying of taxes
without their consent as a denial of their rights as Englishmen,
Plymouth also protested that the methods of taxation imposed
upon her citizens a particular hardship. On January 4, 1687, less

12. Ibid., p. 157; Mass. Archives, *126*, #186, #205, #209, #221, #225,
#238–41; *127*, #121; *Randolph Papers, 4*, pp. 201, 206, 208, 229, 263. See also
Proceedings of the American Antiquarian Society, 13 (Worcester, 1901), pp. 463–99.
13. Mass. Archives, *127*, #59, #142, #236.

than two weeks after his arrival in New England, Governor Andros re-established an old Massachusetts law and ordered a tax of one shilling on every adult male and one penny for every twenty shillings on all estate real and personal. The governor's order did not change established taxation practice in Massachusetts, for the poll tax and taxes on all real and personal estate were familiar. But in Plymouth they were not and Thomas Hinckley complained "that it seemed neither just or legal to impose that law, made by another Colony, on us in our Colony, who never had any hand in the making of it, nor never had any such use or custom amongst us as to rate every head above sixteen years old at £20 . . . nor to rate our houses, built only to sleep and shelter ourselves, and occasionally our friends." Hinckley insisted that the valuation placed on property under the old Massachusetts law was unrealistic and unrelated to current prices. "For, except here and there some special horse, a man may buy five horses and mares for £5, the price set upon the head of one, and two oxen for £5, the rate set on the head of one, and two sheep for 10s., the price set on the head of one." Furthermore, the Andros government had pegged the price of corn at 20d. a bushel. Corn frequently circulated as a medium of exchange, and Hinckley complained that the devaluation from 2s. 6d. to 20d. had contributed to Plymouth's economic distress.[14] Hinckley's statements were not a case of special pleading: after the fall of the Dominion government in 1689, Plymouth Colony placed the valuation of one horse at £2, an ox at £2 10s., a sheep at 5s., and corn at 2s., and later 2s. 6d., a bushel.[15] A few months after the imposition of the tax rate of 1687, Thomas Hinckley wrote bitterly to England that "poverty is like to come upon us like an armed man." [16]

For the towns on Cape Cod, the establishment of the Dominion government brought a particular grievance. Subject to a small tax imposed by the colony government, Cape Cod towns enjoyed the privilege of disposing of small whales (blackfish) washed up on town beaches, and with whale oil in great demand, the fish constituted a source of revenue for the towns. But after incorporation of Plymouth into the Dominion, these fish became the property of the crown. On one occasion, Hinckley himself

14. *Hinckley Papers,* pp. 155, 175.
15. *Ply. Col. Rec., 6,* pp. 220, 221, 253.
16. *Hinckley Papers,* p. 154.

tried to obstruct the sheriff from seizing a drift whale, an effort which created enough response in Boston to bring a sharp note from Secretary Randolph.[17]

Plymouth Colony also protested the restriction upon local government imposed by Governor Andros preventing the use of town meetings as a forum for airing opposition to the Dominion government.[18] Long-accustomed to meeting for the resolution of local problems, New England towns now found themselves limited to one town meeting annually, and that limited to the choice of selectmen for the coming year. Before publication of this order, the towns in Plymouth Colony often met twice or more in a given year. Furthermore, the fact that a town could meet to discuss and act in a local emergency was in itself important: in 1689, when faced with a number of crises, the inhabitants of Marshfield met six times.[19]

Limitation of the town meeting to election of officers in effect deprived people of the power of local self-government. Under the act for regulation of the choice of selectmen, inhabitants of a town were required to assemble on the third Monday in May to choose any number of "fit persons" not exceeding eight. One-half were to be men who had served the previous year and one-half to be new. If any town should refuse, then any two justices of the peace (who were appointed by the governor) could designate the selectmen. The selectmen, once chosen to office, acted as overseers of the poor and with the consent of two justices of the peace, but without reference to the voters of the town, could levy a tax for the relief of the poor. They were also charged with the maintenance and repair of bridges, churches, schools, watchhouses, cages, and were authorized on a warrant from two justices of the peace to assess the inhabitants for expenses incurred in discharging their responsibilities.[20] Residents of the town had no voice in the assessment of these taxes. The appointed officers of the crown, the justices of the peace, had replaced them as a check on the powers of their elected officials.

Governor Andros also upset the inhabitants of Plymouth Col-

---

17. Prince Papers, Massachusetts Historical Society, Boston, *70, #32*; Mass. Archives, *128, #*134.

18. *Hinckley Papers,* p. 178.

19. Marshfield Town Records; Bridgewater Town Records; *Plymouth Town Records;* etc.

20. Scrapbook *#*2, p. 104.

ony (and many other New Englanders) by his efforts to change the system of land holding. With the exception of Mount Hope, for which the colony annually paid seven beaver skins, Plymouth settlers had never paid quitrents on their lands. In the patent issued in 1621 the Council for New England had waived the collection of quitrents for seven years, and in the patent granted to Governor Bradford in 1630, the Council had granted title without obligation except for the customary payment of one-fifth of all gold and silver ore.[21]

When Governor Andros sailed for New England, however, he carried instructions from the Board of Trade to attempt establishment of the quitrent system in New England. The Board believed the collection of quitrents would provide the Dominion government with a steady source of revenue; it also believed such a system would drive home to the independent New Englanders their dependence upon the king. But the Board knew an attempt to change a system of land holding in force for more than fifty years could produce strong hostility, and the implementation of this policy was left in the hands of Andros himself.[22]

Andros knew he must proceed with caution, and therefore attempted to establish the new system in an indirect way. He directed that all new grants bear an annual obligation of two shillings six pence for every 100 acres, and he started the rumor that men already in possession of their lands should petition for a confirmation of their grants on similar terms. Finally, he instructed his councilors to send in their own petitions to set an example.[23]

The prospect of asking Governor Andros to confirm a grant, held freely for many years and which, even if no conflicting claims existed to delay confirmation, would henceforth require the payment of an annual quitrent, was a dismal one indeed. Some question, however, existed as to whether the earlier grants were valid under English law. William Bradford, as a direct patentee of the Council for New England, presumably had the legal power to distribute land; but in 1640, Bradford had surrendered his patent to the General Court. Whether the general court of a colony, which had never obtained a royal charter,

21. The Peirce Patent is printed in Bradford, *History, 1,* pp. 246–51. The Bradford Patent is in *The Compact with the Charter and Laws of the Colony of New Plymouth,* William Brigham, ed. (Boston, 1836), pp. 21–26.
22. Viola Barnes, *The Dominion of New England* (New Haven, 1923), p. 177.
23. Ibid., p. 188.

could grant legal title to land was doubtful; that towns could not make grants since they were not legal corporations was certain.[24] For men who held their land through a grant from either the General Court or a particular town, the new policy of Governor Andros presented a dilemma.

A few men decided to petition the governor for a confirmation of title.[25] But the great majority of people decided to wait and see what would happen. John Saffin, one of the proprietors of Mount Hope, wrote from Boston in December 1687 to Thomas Hinckley and urged men not to ask for confirmation until necessary "it being deemed then soon enough." Saffin continued that it would be "good prudence and policy for the respective towns and particular persons, that have considerable tracts of land to the southward of these parts, to make their application to the survivor of Rhadamanthus [Bradford] to procure a piece of paper or parchment called a release, which may corroborate their titles and quiet their possessions long since derived from the west-country Council." Saffin suggested this be done "without noise or clamor."[26] A number of Plymouth towns later followed Saffin's advice, but apparently after the overthrow of Governor Andros.[27]

The specific actions of Andros in regard to certain town lands increased Plymouth's distrust of the Dominion government. By assuming title to all undistributed land earlier granted to a particular township but not as yet laid out, and by granting some of these lands himself, Andros invited bitter protests from some of the towns. Such protests were forthcoming from Sandwich, where Thomas Tupper, one of the original grantees of the town, complained that the inhabitants wanted to divide a neck of land which the town had earlier agreed to use as commons; and from Scituate, where the town insisted that three 100-acre plots Andros had granted to Humphrey Johnson belonged in part to others and in part were town commons; the Scituate petition noted that no one in town owned more than fifty acres in a single great lot.[28]

In one case involving the town of Plymouth, the controversy

24. Ibid., p. 184.

25. Ibid., p. 201. Ten petitions were received from Plymouth.

26. *Hinckley Papers*, p. 188.

27. Bliss, *Rehoboth*, pp. 125–29; Daniel Ricketson, *The History of New Bedford, Bristol County, Massachusetts* (New Bedford, 1858), p. 56; Bowen, *Rehoboth*, *I*, pp. 47–68.

28. Mass. Archives, *126*, #321, 322; *127*, #247; *128*, #11.

between the governor and the inhabitants became so acrimonious that it resulted in the fining of several persons. Northeast of Plymouth in Duxbury Bay, lies a small island where the scouting party from the *Mayflower* had rested before exploring the mainland. In the years which followed, although several individuals owned the island for a period of time, the town eventually regained title, and in 1687 considered the island lands as part of the town commons. Nathaniel Clark, former secretary of the colony and now one of Governor Andros' councilors, however, wanted the island for himself; and in December 1687 a notice from the governor was posted at Plymouth directing that any persons having claim to this "vacant and unappropriated" property appear before the council the first Wednesday in February.[29]

The town acknowledged receipt of this order and answered that "they are Resolved to defend their Rite in the above said land to their utmost." To implement their resolution, the town choose a committee which began to raise money (through a tax on the inhabitants) to bear the expense of a court test.[30] Infuriated by the town's response, Governor Andros ordered the arrest of the committee for raising money contrary to law and summoned them before superior court in Boston. In the summer of 1687 they were convicted, fined, ordered to pay cash, and bound over in good behavior until the next session. Meanwhile, Councilor Clark obtained title to the island, and Edward Doty, to whom the town of Plymouth had granted wood-cutting rights, was arrested and charged with trespassing. His case was also bound over for trial before the superior court sitting in Boston.[31]

Plymouth Colony had other complaints about the Dominion government. The removal of colony records (including land records) to Boston provoked bitter comment from Hinckley, who mentioned the "expensive journeys and screwing fees" which had followed. Probate fees, Hinckley also complained, were too high, forty or fifty shillings, "ten times more" than colony residents were accustomed to paying.[32] More important, Governor An-

29. Ibid., *127*, #298.
30. *Plymouth Town Records, I*, pp. 192, 193.
31. Mather Papers, 7, #10, #25; Mass. Archives, *129*, #286; Gay Transcripts, *2*, p. 100.
32. *Hinckley Papers*, pp. 176, 177.

dros had disestablished the Congregational churches and made them dependent upon voluntary support for their existence. John Cotton informed his son, Rowland, in 1687 that the raising of £50 through subscription to pay his salary was uncertain and that he might not be able to continue support for Rowland's education at Harvard.[33] Cotton, however, was either too pessimistic or found the money somewhere else, for the boy stayed in college. Scituate chose not to observe the freedom of conscience granted by Andros and attempted to collect the minister's salary as before through a tax upon all the inhabitants including several who were Quakers. The governor's council intervened and put an end to proceedings against Edward Wanton, a Quaker who refused to pay. Edward Randolph wrote Hinckley suggesting it was perhaps as reasonable that Congregationalists be taxed to support the Church of England.[34]

Plymouth Colony's complaints against the procedures of the Dominion government began in February 1687, only a few weeks after the arrival of Governor Andros in New England. Hinckley had written directly to Governor Andros in February asking all the inhabitants be required to support the clergy in their respective towns. And Hinckley had also asked that revenue obtained from fishing monopolies granted for the Cape Cod fishing grounds be applied to the support of grammar schools in Plymouth Colony. Hinckley pointed out that this had been the practice followed by the General Court.[35] Neither of these requests was granted.

Despairing of redress in Boston, Hinckley turned to England. In June 1687 he wrote to William Blathwayt "to represent to your honor the state of things as now they stand with us." Hinckley's letter contained a catalogue of complaints that were repeated in an address to the crown drawn up in October 1687. Stating that until the arrival of Sir Edmund Andros the inhabitants of Plymouth Colony had accounted themselves "in a very happy condition," the October petition continued that after his coming they were "cut off in one day (as it is interpreted) from all their civil liberties which they prescribe to have enjoyed for

---

33. Prince Papers, *70*, #30.
34. *Randolph Papers, 4,* p. 87; Mass. Archives, *11*, #40.
35. *Hinckley Papers,* pp. 149, 150.

more than threescore year." Hinckley concluded by requesting "some marks of your princely favor on this your first-born English plantation in this your domain of New England." Neither Hinckley's letter to Blathwayt nor the address to the king brought relief, except possibly for the removal of the financial limitation of £10 on cases heard in the inferior courts.[36]

But events were underway in England which were soon to bring relief to New England. James II, in his attempt to govern England without Parliament, in his revival of the Court of High Commission, and in his own Roman Catholic sympathies, had increasingly alienated himself from his subjects. In early summer 1688, James brought to trial seven bishops of the Anglican Church on charges of seditious libel. This act infuriated popular feeling, and in June a number of Whig and Tory leaders issued an invitation to William of Orange, Stadtholder of Holland, and his English-born wife, Mary, heir presumptive to the English throne, to lead a revolution against the king. By early autumn, preparations had begun in Holland for an invasion of England, and on November 5th, William landed on the Devon coast at the head of an army of 12,000 men. Within a month, and without fighting a major battle, the forces of William prevailed, and on December 22nd, James left England for France never to return.[37]

The report of William's invasion reached New England on April 4th. John Winslow, who brought the news from Barbados —and who was thrown in jail by Andros, but not before the news was out—also brought a copy of the Declaration issued by William from the Hague before landing in England.[38] The Declaration stated that William was coming to depose arbitrary power and to restore parliamentary government. The Declaration seemed to New Englanders to confirm their own thinking about the kind of government that James II had instituted over them. Their beliefs had already received support in January 1689, when information had reached Massachusetts and Plymouth of two developments in England: the attorney general rendered an opinion that the Massachusetts Charter had been illegally vacated; and the king had published a proclamation "for restoring

36. Ibid., pp. 154 ff., 169, 171, 183. Barnes, *Dominion*, 183. Hinckley sent another petition, apparently to Increase Mather, in July 1688; Mather Papers, 7, #10.
37. George M. Trevelyan, *The English Revolution* (Oxford, 1938), Chapters 3, 4.
38. Barnes, *Dominion*, pp. 239, 240.

corporations to their ancient charters, liberties rights and franchises." [39]

Two weeks after the arrival of Winslow, rebellion broke out in Boston. Cotton Mather may have been an instigator, but for reasons that are not difficult to understand—no one knew how the revolt would be received in England—contemporary accounts stress the spontaneity of the uprising. The precipitant of revolution was the mutiny of a company of soldiers on garrison duty on the Maine frontier who left their posts and marched toward Boston. The troops arrived late in the afternoon of April 17, and on the following day were joined by militia from Boston and the surrounding towns.[40]

When the population rose against him, Governor Andros took refuge in the fort. He promptly refused a summons to surrender but agreed to meet at the Boston Town House with some of the clergy and leaders of the former government to discuss the situation. Arriving at the Town House, Andros demanded an explanation of the arming and assembly of the militia. The committee of leaders and clergy responded by ordering his arrest and imprisonment. The fort surrendered a few hours later and on the following day the Castle Island garrison in Boston Harbor came to terms and laid down its arms.

Massachusetts had overthrown Governor Andros, but no word had yet reached Boston as to the success of William. This news arrived several weeks later. In the meantime, New England reverted to the constituent governments which existed in 1686.

---

39. Trevelyan, *Revolution*, p. 102; Barnes, *Dominion*, pp. 234, 288, 239; *Cal. of State Papers, Col. Ser., 1685,* #1879. The quotations are from Barnes, *Dominion,* p. 234.

40. Barnes, *Dominion*, pp. 241, 242.

17

"This Poor Colony"

Nᴇᴡs of the overthrow of Governor Andros on April 18th reached Thomas Hinckley at Barnstable several days later. Hinckley promptly called for a meeting of delegates from all towns in the colony to discuss resumption of colony government; and in May the delegates gathered at Plymouth.

Hinckley, possibly because he was reluctant to assume responsibility for reestablishing the former government, seemed to have considered the May meeting as informal, and resisted any change in the structure of government which existed before Plymouth became a part of the Dominion of New England. Several of the colony towns had other ideas and instructed their delegates to press for changes in the system. Duxbury directed its delegates to press for a liberalization of the franchise requirement, allowing anyone who could vote in town meetings (not just the freemen) to participate in the election of the governor and assistants. Marshfield went even further and suggested that anyone the town thought suitable should be permitted to vote. Scituate again protested against the county courts established in the reorganization of 1685 and urged a return to the earlier form of government.[1] Nothing came of these proposals; they were apparently shelved and forgotten, and the delegates adjourned after agreeing to call for the election and summoning of the General

1. *Copy Of old Duxbury Records*, p. 179; Marshfield Town Records, *1*, p. 187; Deane, *Scituate*, 105, 106; for Scituate's earlier protest against the county courts, see Chapter 15, p. 206.

Court in June. To Governor Hinckley the recommendations for change may have seemed unnecessary and irresponsible. But coming, as they did, from two of the oldest towns in the colony, they anticipated the political restlessness which developed in Plymouth Colony in 1689 and 1690, and which led to the breakdown of government in 1691.

As representatives from the towns rode into Plymouth early in June, the legality of their meeting as a general court was clearly in question. Following the instructions he received from England, Governor Andros had incorporated Plymouth into the Dominion of New England without taking even passing notice of the Bradford Patent. To men who had worried for many years about the legal basis of their colony's existence, and who had repeatedly tried to reassure themselves that they were in fact a legal entity, the action of Governor Andros had seemed a confirmation of their worst fears: the legal status that Plymouth claimed under its patent was obviously not recognized in England. Realizing that the action taken to join Plymouth to the Dominion had shaken the confidence of some citizens in the authority of the old government, and lacking instructions from England, the General Court tried to reestablish its authority and reassure the doubters. The Court ordered a resumption of the old government under the *Book of Laws* published in 1685, and directed that the original charter be committed to public record. Towns that had not yet chosen selectmen, or where the present selectmen were not acceptable (presumably because they were not freemen), were asked to make a new choice. The Court also acted to nullify the action of Governor Andros in granting title to Clark's Island in Plymouth Bay to Nathaniel Clark. Clark, "by sundry of the inhabitants of the town of Plimouth declared to be a publicke enemy to (and disturber of the peace of) this colony," was placed in £200 bond, and title to the island was restored to the town of Plymouth.[2]

To clarify the confusion about Plymouth's authority to organize a government, the Court directed Governor Hinckley to prepare and forward a petition to the King requesting the reestablishment of the colony and a return of its public seal. Hinckley in turn asked Reverend Samuel Lee of Bristol to draft the petition. Scholarly Samuel Lee, a recent arrival in the New World, and

2. *Ply. Col. Rec., 6*, pp. 207-11.

one who would shortly return to England, was not a practitioner of the plain style: "Whereas the infinitely glorious Sovereign of heaven and earth, by whom kings reign and princes decree justice, hath raised your majesty up, like to those valiant judges of Israel, to deliver them from their oppressions and idolatries . . . we, your majesty's most Western subjects, do humbly beg the orient star of your benign influence may not disdain to pour down some bright rays of your generous favor to cherish the parched plants of this great wilderness." In more specific terms, Lee asked that the king grant Plymouth a charter and, in particular, one that would allow it to require support of the churches.[3]

Hinckley forwarded the address to England and sent along a covering letter to Sir Henry Ashurst. Hinckley wrote that poverty and wickedness had prevented many from supporting the churches and that the colony needed a charter if it was to have an effective instrument of government.[4] On August 13th, Ashurst replied that the petition had been read before the king in council, and the king had returned the "very gracious answer" that he would look out for his colonies in New England. Ashurst concluded: "you are in possession of your ancient liberties by charter; and I hope you will leave them free to your posterity."[5] This news, which arrived in the early autumn of 1689, was welcome because the General Court had already begun to encounter increasing opposition to its authority.

In part at least, this opposition to the Court occurred because of external pressures placed upon the colony. The summer of 1689 had seen a number of serious reverses for the English in the war against the French in Maine. This war had broken out in 1688 along the Canadian boundary where an uneasy peace had existed since King Philip's War. Governor Andros, later accused of negligence in failing to carry the war to the enemy, sent troops to the boundary, but after his overthrow in April 1689, some of the militia performing garrison duty along the northern frontier packed up and returned home; other companies were recalled because the new government in Boston distrusted the loyalty of their officers.[6]

3. *Hinckley Papers,* pp. 199, 200. Thomas Prince believed this address was written by Lee and I have relied on Prince's judgment.
4. Ibid., pp. 201, 202.
5. Ibid., p. 206.
6. Francis Parkman, *Count Frontenac and New France under Louis XIV* (Boston, 1902), p. 234.

The consequences of this withdrawal became all too apparent in the spring and summer of 1689. First came news that an Indian raiding party had surprised a fortified house at Cocheco and butchered the owner. This was followed by reports of other disasters: 100 Christian Indians from missions established by the Jesuits attacked the garrison at Pemaquid in August, and after the fort surrendered, some of the prisoners were slaughtered. The garrison at Pemaquid, on orders from Boston, had recently been reduced from 156 men to thirty.[7] The same month Haverhill, forty miles north of Boston, reported an Indian alarm. Letters reaching England that summer reported that Massachusetts was desperately trying to reinforce the frontier, but that many of the soldiers drafted for service refused to go. In this deepening crisis Massachusetts turned to her sister colonies for help.[8]

In the months which immediately followed the break-up of the Dominion, Plymouth Colony had not taken an active part in the prosecution of the war. Governor Bradstreet of Massachusetts wrote Benjamin Church in July offering him command of a company of friendly Indians and requesting Governor Hinckley's aid in recruiting the Indian soldiers. Church agreed to go, but in the summer of 1689 he and the volunteers he led were the only soldiers from Plymouth Colony to see service on the northern frontier.[9]

The discouraging news from Maine, the report that the zone of conflict seemed to be extending south into Massachusetts itself, and the proposal of the Bay Colony that a meeting of representatives from all the New England colonies assemble in Boston in September to review the conduct of the war, all forced the Plymouth government to consider the colony's active participation in the defense of the northern frontier. In August, Governor Hinckley summoned a special session of the General Court for this purpose. The Court approved a united front in repelling the enemy, and ordered representatives to attend the September meeting in Boston, although cautioning them to be certain the colony was not charged beyond its proportion. Still without official word from England (Ashurst's reply had not yet arrived) and reluctant to raise a tax without an official mandate establish-

7. In fact, the number of men left in the fort may have been only eighteen. See ibid., p. 235, footnote 1.
8. C.O. 5, vol. 855, #29.
9. *Hinckley Papers*, pp. 203–05.

ing its legal authority, the government directed the deputies and selectmen to use their influence to persuade people to lend fiscal support for the war. Efforts were also undertaken to enlist volunteers for service in Maine. Both enterprises achieved at least partial success, for the reinforcements rushed to the front in late summer included Plymouth troops, and in several of the towns people came forward and offered to advance money to pay for the expenses of equipping and paying the soldiers.[10]

But there were other people in the colony who were less willing to cooperate with the government. The General Court had ordered the reinstatement of militia officers who held commissions in 1686, and in several of the towns the execution of this order encountered stiff opposition. On August 13th, Major John Walley, commanding the Bristol County militia regiment, reported dissatisfaction which he was having difficulty containing. Walley informed Governor Hinckley that at the county seat at Bristol, unrest had agitated the militia company on training day, but that he had succeeded in quieting it. The following morning, Walley continued, he had visited Swansea where it had taken very persuasive arguing to convince the militia to submit to their old officers for "there were a young crew that were very heady." From Rehoboth came news "of some unhandsome doing," and at Taunton the division within the town was so bitter that the only acceptable recourse became the establishment of two different companies.[11]

The extent to which this unrest in Bristol County reflected opposition to Plymouth's participation in the war is not clear; its immediate cause in several towns was unquestionably the reinstatement of former company officers. But there was probably more to this challenge to authority than a dissatisfaction with commanders (who were in fact originally nominated by the votes of the militia); certainly the subsequent breakdown of civil authority in Bristol County suggests that this was the case. In October 1689 the General Court, interpreting Ashurst's letter as a confirmation of its legal authority, passed a tax for support of the war. Walley had warned that some towns in Bristol County might oppose collection of this tax, and in December his fears

10. *Ply. Col. Rec., 6*, pp. 212–15; Marshfield Town Records, *1*, p. 189; *Hinckley Papers*, pp. 214–16.
11. *Hinckley Papers*, pp. 208, 209, 235; *Ply. Col. Rec., 6*, p. 237.

were confirmed: Bristol, Dartmouth, Swansea, and Eastham in Barnstable County, refused to pay.[12]

The war news in December also was bad. England and France were now officially at war, but while this meant the resources of Britain would be thrown into the struggle, few responsible persons expected large-scale use of English forces in North America. The formal declaration of war, however, could bring stepped-up activity on the part of the French, and representatives of the New England colonies meeting in Boston in December urged measures be taken to have the militia in readiness and that fortifications in the seaport towns be repaired and strengthened.[13] Sub-zero temperatures and a deep cover of snow had temporarily brought operations along the Maine frontiers to a halt; but there was every expectation that warfare would resume on a greater scale in the spring, that more men and more supplies would have to be thrown into the fight, and that French warships and privateers would raid along the New England coast.[14]

In early February, even before the first signs of winter's breaking, the enemy struck. Setting out from Montreal late in January, a party of 200 men marched south toward the English settlements along the Hudson River. On the eighth of February, the war party camped in a driving snow storm a few miles from Schenectady, and after night had fallen, fell upon the settlement. The inhabitants, many of whom were asleep, were quickly overwhelmed, and the next day Schenectady was burned to the ground. According to reports reaching Boston, seventy people died, including several children frozen to death during the retreat of the survivors to Albany.[15] A few weeks later, a raiding party attacked and overran the fort garrisoned by Massachusetts troops at Salmon Falls, Maine. No watch had been kept, and the enemy achieved complete surprise; more disheartening was the report that during the pursuit of this raiding party, forty militia-

12. *Hinckley Papers,* p. 223; *Ply. Col. Rec., 6,* p. 226.

13. Mass. Archives, 35, #106. England declared war on France in May 1689, and this news must have reached New England in June or July. Apparently news of the existence of a formal state of war had not been widely disseminated, for in December the commissioners recommended that "his Majesty's declaration of war against the French be forthwith published."

14. C.O. *5,* vol. 855, #60.

15. Parkman, *Count Frontenac,* pp. 222–29; C.O. *5,* vol. 855, #77, #94. Governor Bradstreet wrote to Hinckley in March that "sixty of them were butchered in the place." *Hinckley Papers,* p. 230.

men had bolted after the first volley and jeopardized the safety of their comrades.[16]

When news of the attack on Salmon Falls reached Plymouth, the Council of War ordered the colony into a state of alert. A guard was to be maintained in every town during the hours of darkness, and a day watch authorized when local town war councils believed it necessary, particularly in the seaports. The council also directed that carriages be built for the great guns guarding Plymouth Harbor and the guns mounted and placed.[17]

Protected from attack to the north and west by neighboring towns, Plymouth could afford to take a defensive position. Massachusetts and New York, whose frontiers were the target areas for French and Indian raiding parties, could not, and in the spring and summer of 1690, both colonies tried to mount offensives into enemy country. In Massachusetts favorable consideration was given to the idea of a frontal assault upon the fortified harbor at Port Royal, Nova Scotia. This port served as a supply base for French cruisers operating in the North Atlantic, and during the winter of 1689–90 it was decided that, to protect Massachusetts' extensive mercantile trade, Port Royal must be reduced. In the letter advising Governor Hinckley of the massacre at Schenectady, Governor Bradstreet asked for Plymouth's support in the Port Royal expedition.[18]

Plans were also afoot in the colony of New York, and in March, Governor Leisler called for commissioners from all the colonies south to Virginia to meet May 1st in New York City and discuss the possibility of a joint attack upon Montreal. Plymouth was invited to send a representative, and Hinckley, probably more as a result of the urging of Massachusetts than for other reasons, asked Major John Walley to go. Hinckley informed Governor Leisler that because it had been impossible to convene the General Court or the Council of War, Walley was not authorized to commit Plymouth to a course of action.[19]

Out of this conference came the decision to push forward an attack upon lower Canada. New York would supply 400 men for this army, Massachusetts 160, Connecticut 135, and Plymouth was asked to provide sixty, a request which Governor

16. C.O. *5*, vol. 855, #80.
17. *Ply. Col. Rec., 6,* pp. 237, 238.
18. *Hinckley Papers,* p. 230.
19. Ibid., pp. 232, 233, 239, 242–44.

Hinckley and the Council of War agreed to meet. Despite Major Walley's warning that the militia of Bristol County were in "ill posture," plans were drawn up for raising Plymouth's quota, and in June the press for troops began. These soldiers, however, never marched to the aid of New York; they were instead diverted to a projected attack upon Quebec.[20]

The expedition which sailed from Boston in April to seize Port Royal had persuaded the French Commander, Meneval, to surrender without a fight. In return, according to the French, the commander of the New England forces, Sir William Phips, promised not to seize private property and to send the French garrison either to Quebec or to France. Discovering that some booty had been surreptitiously taken from the town and hidden while the terms of the surrender were arranged, Phips believed himself released from his promise to respect private property and plundered the town.[21] Emboldened by a success which seemed to promise an economical way to wage war, the leaders of the Massachusetts Colony decided to follow up the raid on Port Royal and undertake the capture of Quebec. Plymouth was asked to furnish support and agreed, and in June the General Court directed that two hundred soldiers, including fifty Indians, be raised for service in Canada.[22]

Under the command of Sir William Phips, the Quebec expedition weighed anchor from Nantasket Roads on August 9th. Provisioned for only four months, without experienced St. Lawrence River pilots, commanded by persons totally lacking in military experience, this force of 2200 men arrived off the mouth of the St. Lawrence in September. Although surprise was an important element in his chances for success, Phips did not press an attack; for nearly three weeks the fleet remained anchored within three days' sail of the city. Meanwhile the French worked strenuously to fortify their town. The governor-general, Count Frontenac, arrived from Montreal to take personal command of the defense and troops were summoned from lower Canada. On the morning of October 16th, when the New England ships sailed into the Basin of Quebec and dropped anchor, Quebec had become a fortified town garrisoned by nearly 2700 regulars and militia.

The forces available to Phips were neither strong enough nor

20. Ibid., pp. 250–53; *Ply. Col. Rec., 6*, pp. 231, 232.
21. Parkman, *Count Frontenac*, pp. 248–52.
22. *Ply. Col. Rec., 6*, pp. 248, 249.

commanded with sufficient skill to overcome French resistance. A bombardment by the ships in the squadron expended the major part of the ammunition without doing significant damage, and a landing force placed ashore under the command of Major John Walley of Bristol was repulsed. Convinced that his cause was hopeless, Phips re-embarked the landing force, and while small-pox and fever raged aboard the ships, the fleet sailed for home. On the way it encountered gale-force winds off the New England coast and some of the ships were blown far off course, eventually landing in the West Indies; several were never heard from again.[23]

The failure at Quebec in the autumn of 1690 considerably aggravated the deepening financial crisis in Plymouth Colony. One of the four towns delinquent in paying its taxes earlier in the year subsequently sent in its arrears and the three other towns had probably also paid.[24] But resistance to support of the war continued, and in February, Governor Hinckley informed Increase Mather that "some few leading men" were trying to persuade people neither to obey the present government nor to pay taxes assessed by it.[25] Discounting the importance of this opposition and the shortage of hard money in the colony, the General Court in November ordered £1350 raised "for the payment of all known debts of the colony relating to the present war, and otherways, excepting the charges about armes for the expedition to Canada." The Court ordered half of the tax paid in money.[26] In November, "known debts" did not include soldiers' wages, since the Court apparently hoped that they would be paid in booty brought home from Quebec. The news of late November that the assault had failed disappointed this hope, and the Court agreed on December 7 to raise an additional £1350 for the payment of soldiers who fought in Canada and along the Maine

23. Parkman, *Count Frontenac,* Chapter 13. For contemporaiy accounts, see the Journal of Major Walley printed in Thomas Hutchinson, *History of Massachusetts* (Cambridge, 1936), *I,* Appendix XXI. Accounts of the defeat forwarded to England are found in C.O. *5,* vol. 855.

24. *Ply. Col. Rec., 6,* p. 246; the colony records do not prove that the taxes were paid, but there is no entry after that of December 1689, indicating that they were not paid. In the event the three towns had continued to refuse payment, I assume some further action would have been taken and an entry made to that effect.

25. *Hinckley Papers,* pp. 228, 229.

26. Hinckley himself notes the shortage of money, ibid., p. 243; *Ply. Col. Rec., 6,* pp. 253.

frontier. The £2700 tax bill voted by the Court in November and December represented about seven and one-half per cent of the total assessed property valuation in the colony.[27]

The increased tax burden which support of the war required was reflected in comparative figures of pre-war and wartime rates. In 1684, Scituate paid £45-16-4 in taxes; in 1685, £81-16-3; the following year the assessment was £54-15-7; in 1689, the rate was £90. The next year, 1690, Scituate's tax jumped to £328-10-0. The figures for Eastham show a similar increase. In December 1689, Eastham paid a tax of £46; a year later the figure had risen to £187-19-0.[28] Probably more than any other single factor, this sharp rise in the burden of taxation contributed to the loss of civil authority in the colony. Some towns were simply unwilling to shoulder their part of the burden and remained so until after Plymouth became a part of the Province of Massachusetts Bay. One town, Little Compton, even then remained recalcitrant and yielded only after a military expedition marched to enforce compliance.

After the defeat in Canada opposition to the government increased, and in the early months of 1691 the colony seemed headed for a complete breakdown in authority. On January 31, John Cotton wrote to his son Rowland that "our condition here calls with speed for a general court—if it would have been sooner it had been well." [29] A few days later Cotton wrote Governor Hinckley: "Sir, I doubt not of your faithfulness and solicitous care to promote the best interest of this poor Colony, who hath not only deserved ill from the hands of God, but have so demeaned themselves to the authority of their own choosing as not to deserve from man to say 'I will be your Healer;' yet, good sir, I hope you will overlook all such discouraging considerations, and at this day stand forth and play the man." [30] But Hinckley, discouraged by the failure of the inhabitants to support their soldiers in the field and their churches at home, had begun to lose heart and was either unwilling or unable to supply the leadership which the colony so desperately needed. By summer the situation had deteriorated further; when the annual Election Court met in June, representatives from Dartmouth,

27. *Ply. Col. Rec., 6*, pp. 255, 251, 252.
28. Scituate Book of Accounts, pp. 63–73; Eastham Town Records, *1*, pp. 55, 56.
29. Prince Papers, *60*, #2.
30. *Hinckley Papers*, p. 279.

Swansea, Little Compton, and Freetown were absent. Three weeks later the town of Bridgewater voted it would pay nothing further towards the expenses of the colony until the other towns paid the taxes due for the previous year.[31] Bridgewater's ultimatum stated what was already clear: the General Court had ceased to function as an effective instrument of government.

The impact of the war was, of course, the critical factor in this breakdown of civil authority: the pressing of men for duty away from home, the casualty lists—Scituate alone lost eight men in the attack upon Quebec—the heavy financial burden, and the disappointments of defeat became finally more than some men would endure. In addition to war, other factors contributed to civil instability. The absence of a charter gave some an opportunity to challenge the authority of the government, an opportunity which a few, for reasons of their own, were quick to exploit. One who did so was Colonel Henry Sloughter, who had succeeded Jacob Leisler as Governor of New York in March 1691, and who may have hoped that Plymouth would be incorporated into his own colony. Governor Hinckley bitterly complained in November to the government of Massachusetts that Sloughter had been fomenting trouble in Plymouth Colony by urging the inhabitants not to pay their taxes.[32]

Less tangible but also important to the disintegration of authority was a temper of general restlessness which gripped New England after the overthrow of Governor Andros. The Dominion seemed to have unleashed powerful forces that had been pent-up, and New England was never quite the same again. The old order went into eclipse for nearly three years and some people, including a few who had opposed Andros, were anxious to prevent the return to a society in which the traditional patterns were reestablished. The requests of Marshfield and Duxbury for a loosening of the franchise requirements and hostility to the General Court's reinstatement of the old militia officers gave warning of discontent. But Plymouth's government was seemingly impervious to these warnings and to the significance of the civil disobedience which followed. By 1691 it was too late, and in the crisis caused by failure in domestic leadership and the pressure of a resolute foreign enemy, civil authority collapsed, and in September 1691, Plymouth Colony became a part of the Province of Massachusetts Bay.

31. *Ply. Col. Rec., 6,* p. 263; Bridgewater Town Records, *1,* p. 117.
32. Mass. Archives, *35,* #208.

Even before the overthrow of Governor Andros, Massachusetts agents had been at work in England attempting to persuade James II to recall the governor general, dissolve the Dominion, and restore to the colony its former liberties and privileges. Disguised to prevent his apprehension by the Andros government, Increase Mather had stolen away from Boston in April 1688 to take ship for England, there to present the case for Massachusetts to the crown. Four times Mather succeeded in obtaining an audience with the king, and by autumn Mather had obtained promises of relief from the tyranny of Governor Andros. But before these promises could be carried out, James II was forced to abdicate and William, Prince of Orange, and Mary, his English wife, became King and Queen of England.[33]

Early in January, Mather received his first audience with the new king and received a promise that William III would look into the matter of New England's grievances. Through William's secretary, he was also successful in persuading the king against formally reconfirming the appointment of Governor Andros. Apparently suspicious that an attempt to overthrow Andros might follow news from England of the flight of James II, Mather was anxious that such an attempt not take place against a duly constituted officer of William III and thus prejudice his own efforts to bring about a restoration of charter government.[34]

On February 8th, Mather presented a petition to the Privy Council for a restoration of charters of the four New England colonies; four days later this petition was referred to the Committee for Trade and Plantations. Mather argued his case before this committee, and by the end of the month he had persuaded the committee to give its recommendation to the crown that Governor Andros be replaced and that money be raised only with the consent of representatives elected by the people. On March 14th, Mather gained a second audience with the king and heard William promise that Andros would be removed. But persuasive as he apparently was, the New Englander was unable to convince either the Committee for Trade and Plantations or the king that the Dominion should be broken up and restored to its constituent parts; and early in May, Mather was summoned to appear before the Privy Council and show cause why the king

33. Kenneth Murdock, *Increase Mather* (Cambridge, 1925), p. 187. The formal coronation of William and Mary did not come until February 1689.
34. Ibid., pp. 214, 215.

should not appoint a general governor for all New England.[35]

News reaching England of the revolution in New England, however, introduced a new element. By overthrowing Andros, proclaiming William and Mary King and Queen, and reverting to separate colony status, New Englanders had taken the initiative away from the crown; and by committing these acts in the name of loyalty to the Prince of Orange and the cause of Protestantism in general, they in effect forced the crown either to repudiate their loyalty or acquiesce in dismemberment of the Dominion. The consequence of the removal of Andros was thus to force some rethinking in England about the New England colonies.

This rethinking and the final resolution of the problem lasted two years, during which time pressures were constantly brought to bear in England to influence the result. From Massachusetts came a number of letters complaining about the restoration government headed by Governor Bradstreet and asking the king to settle a general governor for all New England. Written by merchants and others who were anxious to prevent the permanent reestablishment of the old regime, these letters were exceedingly pessimistic about the state of the colony, and urged a new union of all the New England colonies. A letter written on July 10, 1689, reported that "the dicided state of the territory once formidable is now dissolved." Another letter written from Marblehead four days later stated that although many were pressed for military service in Maine, few would go. And from his cell in the Boston jail, Edward Randolph, his days of triumph over, reported that violation of the Acts of Trade and Navigation had again become common. Randolph warned that only the appointment of a governor by the crown would ensure enforcement of the navigation system.[36] At the same time, Increase Mather and other agents appointed by the Massachusetts Colony were at work in England to counter the effect of these unfavorable reports. That they were in the end fairly successful in obtaining a charter which granted most of their desires is no small tribute to their skill and to their use of the fairly limited funds available to them in their efforts to secure a new charter.

35. Ibid., pp. 215, 216; C.O. *5,* vol. 1, pp. 4, 5; C.O. *324,* vol. 5, p. 45. *Acts of the Privy Council of England, Colonial Series* (6 vols. London, 1912–1923), *2,* pp. 283, 289.

36. C.O. *5,* vol. 855, #29, #37, #43, #53.

The leadership of Plymouth Colony remained strangely apathetic to the resolution of this matter in England. After the petition to the crown was forwarded in June 1689, Plymouth took no further action to secure a charter for a year, although it alone of the four New England colonies had never been successful in obtaining a charter, and it was therefore the most vulnerable to incorporation into a larger unit. This failure to act was not a result of insufficient information. In September 1689, Increase Mather wrote to Governor Hinckley that if Plymouth wanted a charter, money must be forwarded to England at once, for Sir Henry Ashurst, who presented the General Court's petition to the Privy Council in August, could do little without funds to pay the fees and to obtain the interest of people who could help. Mather warned, "You may do it too late: you cannot do it too soon." [37]

Acting on Mather's advice, Governor Hinckley proposed to the General Court that money be raised for this purpose. To what extent Hinckley himself tried to persuade the General Court to adopt this course is unknown; in the light of his subsequent attitude, I should suspect—there is no evidence—that he did not overexert himself. Regardless of Hinckley's position, the Court did not appropriate any money for this purpose. And in February 1690 the Governor wrote Mather that Plymouth was unwilling to raise funds unless there was an immediate prospect for a charter, in which case the Court had agreed it would engage itself for "what is proper." At the same time, a letter went to Ashurst thanking him for presenting Plymouth's petition the previous summer and noting that a combination of general poverty, war, and drought made it impossible to forward any money. [38]

When Hinckley wrote Ashurst and Mather, he already knew that Plymouth, apparently through no effort of its own, would soon have one of its own residents on the scene in England. The Massachusetts government had recently asked Ichabod Wiswall, minister of the Duxbury Church, to join Mather as an agent for the Massachusetts Colony. Wiswall consented to go, and some understanding probably existed between him and Hinckley that Wiswall would also act for Plymouth's interest. But if there was such an understanding when Wiswall sailed in 1690, Duxbury ei-

37. *Hinckley Papers*, p. 211.
38. Ibid., pp. 225–29.

ther did not know about it or disapproved. The town bitterly protested the use of Wiswall and demanded that the Massachusetts government supply and support a substitute during his absence.[39]

Opposition to incorporation into the Bay Colony and the failure of Plymouth to press its own case for a charter became a matter of concern to the Massachusetts authorities in 1690. Cotton Mather wrote angrily to Governor Hinckley in April that only the industry of his father had prevented Plymouth from being attached to the Colony of New York. He continued that friends at Whitehall had assured his father that a petition for a separate charter for Plymouth would not only fail but would prejudice the chance of a charter for Massachusetts. Acting on this advice, Increase Mather had proceeded to have Plymouth included in a draft of the Massachusetts Charter. Wiswall promptly protested and bluntly informed Mather that Plymouth "would all curse him." Wiswall's plea sufficiently moved the solicitor general, who was charged with the responsibility of drawing up the charter, to exclude Plymouth. Cotton Mather, in a self-righteous manner, added that he supposed Plymouth would probably be annexed to New York again, and "if you find yourselves plunged into manifold miseries, you have none to thank for it but one of your own." [40] Mather's prophecy was in fact inaccurate; and May his father wrote from England that the bill for restoring the Massachusetts Charter had expired because of the unexpected prorogation of Parliament.[41]

Cotton Mather's letter to Hinckley, which arrived in the spring of 1690, produced no known response in the form of greater activity to obtain a charter. And in October, Elisha Cooke, who joined Mather in England as an agent for the Massachusetts Colony, wrote Governor Bradstreet that it seemed strange Plymouth Colony had not renewed its application for a charter in the past year. Wiswall, the same month, sent a letter to Governor Hinckley stating that if Plymouth wanted a charter, the colony must act at once to petition the king and to enlist the support of men who could bring influence to bear. Wiswall was

39. Mass. Archives, *II*, p. 51. Murdock says that Wiswall was sent as Plymouth's agent, but the evidence he cites does not support this.
40. *Hinckley Papers,* pp. 248, 249.
41. Ibid., pp. 254, 255.

still hopeful and believed the prospects for annexation to either New York or Massachusetts had temporarily diminished. But Wiswall insisted money was needed to gain a favorable decision, and reminded Hinckley of Ecclesiastes 10:19—"A feast is made for laughter, and wine maketh merry; but money answereth all things." [42]

Wiswall's letter and the entreaty of John Cotton to Governor Hinckley to check the drift into civil anarchy, "to stand forth and play the man," led to the summoning of the General Court in February. Reluctant to make the decision on a question which related to the very survival of the colony and which depended upon the willingness of the people to give their financial support, the Court voted to refer the matter to the separate towns. The inhabitants must decide whether they wanted to "sit still and fall into the hands of those that can catch us," or whether concerted efforts should be made to secure a new patent. The Court warned that the minimum cost of a new patent would be £500 sterling or about £700 New England money. [43]

A number of towns wanted to try for a charter and agreed to provide limited financial support. Eastham, for example, voted their "unanimous minds" that efforts to secure a charter should be undertaken. The town asked one of its citizens to advance £25 to the colony treasurer, and promised to mortgage two islands to him as security for repayment. Yarmouth agreed to sell eight acres of meadow to cover its share of the expense. The town of Plymouth decided that "the utmost endeavors" should be used to secure a charter and promised to bear its share of the cost. Barnstable, Bridgewater, Taunton, and Duxbury promised their support. And Major Walley, writing to Wiswall about this time, reported the people were very anxious to secure a charter and were prepared to raise a considerable sum if they were certain that the money would not be wasted; but Walley added they would not risk more than £200 on an uncertainty. [44]

In spite of initial enthusiasm, raising £200 proved beyond the capability of the colony. While some men contributed liberally,

42. Massachusetts Historical Society, *Proceedings, 45* (Boston, 1912), p. 653; *Hinckley Papers*, pp. 276–78.
43. *Ply. Col. Rec., 6,* p. 259.
44. Eastham Town Records, *1,* p. 59; Yarmouth Town Records, *2;* Plymouth *Town Records, 1,* p. 202; Barnstable Town Records, p. 156; Bridgewater Town Records, *1,* p. 116; Taunton Town Records, p. 19; *Copy of Old Duxbury Records,* p. 182; *Hinckley Papers,* pp. 286–87.

others refused "partly by reason of the great charge of the war and their low condition, and partly and especially being discouraged by some leading men telling them that they would but throw away their money." Of the goal of £200, only £150 was collected, and although Hinckley himself urged sending this sum, the General Court reasoned that some men should not carry the whole burden while others did nothing. The Court, therefore, ordered the money returned.[45]

Progress on a Massachusetts Charter meanwhile went forward. On January 1, 1691, the king referred a new draft to the Committee for Trade and Plantations. Shortly thereafter, William III left for Holland. When he returned to England in April, the matter was discussed by the king in council, and in May the attorney general drew up a draft which reflected the decisions reached at this meeting. Through the summer months, hearings on the charter continued before the subcommittee of the Privy Council. In their testimony, Mather and his colleagues argued for including Maine, New Hampshire, and Nova Scotia in the Massachusetts Colony; there is no evidence they also argued for the annexation of Plymouth, although Wiswall later accused Mather of being one reason for the disappointment of Plymouth's hopes.[46] A June draft of the charter included Maine and New Hampshire, but not Plymouth.[47] Wiswall himself may have been the restraining influence in blocking the incorporation of Plymouth into Massachusetts in June, but Wiswall's influence waned during the summer, and on September 2nd the Privy Council agreed to annex Plymouth to the Massachusetts Colony and instructed the attorney general to prepare a new draft of the charter. On October 7, 1691, with some further revision but with Plymouth annexed, the charter passed the Great Seal, and in the spring of the following year writs were sent from Boston to the Plymouth towns requiring the election of representatives to the Massachusetts Assembly scheduled to sit in June.

45. *Hinckley Papers*, pp. 292–97.
46. C.O. 5, vol. 856, #166; *Hinckley Papers*, p. 299.
47. C.O. 5, vol. 856, #166.

18

"The Government Over Us is Yet in the Hands of Saints"

IN THE last analysis, the annexation of Plymouth took place for reasons beyond the colony's control. The failure to secure a charter before 1686 meant Plymouth was more vulnerable than either Rhode Island or Connecticut, and the absence of an interested and powerful supporter in England meant that no one who had personal contact with the men in power was prepared to argue its case. More important, the recurring reports of military failure in the war against the French indicated that consolidation was in the best interests of the crown and also of the inhabitants of New England: the charter itself stated that Plymouth had been incorporated into the Massachusetts Colony "to the end that our good subjects within our colony of New Plymouth in New England may be brought under such a form of government as may put them in a better condition of defense." [1] There is little doubt that the Privy Council, in placing Plymouth under jurisdiction of the Massachusetts government and justifying its action in these terms, meant what it said. The council was in fact so alarmed by the military situation in New England that it urged the appointment of Sir William Phips, the new governor of the Massachusetts Colony, as commander-in-chief of all the militia of Connecticut, New Hampshire, and Rhode Island.[2] The conclusion seems almost certain that Plymouth's case for a char-

1. C.O. *5*, vol. 905, pp. 298–364.
2. *Cal. of State Papers, Col. Ser., 1689–1692*, #1916.

ter was lost in spite of any and all efforts that she could have made on her own behalf.

Yet the fact that these efforts were not seriously made, that the colony did not do its utmost to maintain a separate existence, is of no little interest, for the failure casts some light upon the dependence of the colony upon its leadership. If it was true, as Walley wrote in 1691, that the people in the colony were "very desirous" for a new charter, then the question must be asked: Why were serious efforts not undertaken to persuade the crown to continue Plymouth as a separate colony? Part of the answer was that many people who wanted a charter were in fact unwilling to pay for it. The difficulty encountered in trying to collect £200 in the spring of 1691 is some indication that this was so. But more is needed by way of explanation than this. Many of the towns, when asked to contribute, in fact did so willingly and the money subscribed was raised voluntarily and without any pressure or direction from the General Court. And why did Plymouth wait so long? Why did efforts to collect this money wait until 1691, two years after the break-up of the Dominion of New England? Clearly not because of a lack of information, for as early as 1689, Increase Mather informed Governor Hinckley that an attempt to secure a charter would succeed only if given generous financial support.

Evidence is admittedly fragmentary, but that which survives indicates Governor Hinckley and some of the colony assistants welcomed the annexation of Plymouth to Massachusetts. Certainly this was so by late 1691. In October, after the new charter had passed the Great Seal but before the news reached New England, Governor Hinckley wrote Increase Mather that it would be "well pleasing to myself and to sundry others of the most thinking men" if Plymouth were annexed to Massachusetts.[3] It cannot be proven that Hinckley's thinking in 1690 or even early 1691 was the same as it was by October 1691. But in light of the governor's apathy in pressing Plymouth's case in England, a reasonable assumption is that it was. Ichabod Wiswall wrote Hinckley from England in July 1691: "When some consider the spirit which animated the first planters to venture their all, in attempting so great hazards for the enjoyment of civil and religious privileges. . . . That Plymouth, under its pres-

3. *Hinckley Papers,* p. 287.

ent circumstances, should sit silent so long (may I not say, sleep secure?) is a great riddle." Wiswall complained in a subsequent letter: "When I parted from your honor, Feb. the 6, *anno* '89, I little then imagined that it would have been August the 29, '91 before I should receive one line from you." He continued: "There is a time to speak, and a time to keep silence. We might have been happy, or, at least not so miserable, had some been able or willing to be taught their proper seasons." [4] Wiswall could hardly have helped wondering if Hinckley really wanted Plymouth to maintain a separate existence.

By October 1691, and probably earlier, Hinckley was convinced that the willingness of people to support religion and education had reached such an alarmingly low level that only annexation to Massachusetts could save the two institutions from extinction. Committed to the traditional Puritan belief that the duty of the state was to nourish and support religion and learning, Hinckley believed disintegration of civil authority in Plymouth meant the end of a scheme of society which he passionately believed gave meaning to life itself; rather than see this scheme jeopardized, he preferred to give up the independence of his colony.

Hinckley, moreover, seemed unable to give the colony leadership and direction in the perilous days it faced in 1690 and 1691. Lacking the ability "to stand up and play the man," as John Cotton so bluntly urged in early 1691, Hinckley preferred to drift, to wait and see, and to hope. That he was not a strong governor is borne out by the testimony of contemporaries. Governor Craddock of New Hampshire reported back to England in 1683 that Hinckley was weak and incapable of governing effectively.[5] Craddock himself had recently come from England, and his criticism must be judged with some scepticism; colonial administrators coming out from England were seldom complimentary about rude colonials. But Craddock was not alone in his judgment of Hinckley. Cotton Mather, in *Magnalia Christi Americana,* wrote of the Plymouth Governor in the most scathing terms; and John Cotton, in his letters to Rowland Cotton and to Hinckley himself, deplored the absence of leadership in the colony.[6] Certainly, from the evidence available, there is no indication that the

4. Ibid., pp. 285, 299.
5. *Cal. of State Papers, Col. Ser., 1681–1685,* #1024.
6. Cotton Mather, *Magnalia, I,* p. 117; *Hinckley Papers,* p. 279; Prince Papers, ⟩ *60,* #2.

Governor responded with energy or resolution to the disintegration of civil order in 1690 and 1691. He in fact seems rather to have abdicated his responsibilities.

The situation in which Governor Hinckley found himself was admittedly difficult. The colony was poor and the conditions of economic life were unfavorable to the payment of heavy taxes. A determination on the part of several of the towns not to pay for the continued support of the war, and the rioting in Bristol County to stop the tax collectors, confronted Hinckley with a grave dilemma: he could acquiesce in civil disobedience in a few towns with almost certain knowledge that once this happened, support of the government would be jeopardized elsewhere; or he could enlist the militia of the loyal towns and march on the people who refused to meet their tax payments. This latter alternative, particularly in the light of the failure of the king to give his government positive backing, Governor Hinckley was unwilling to do.

Given the lack of encouragement from England, the policy of avoiding bloodshed may have been wise, but it was difficult to reconcile with Plymouth Colony's participation in the war against the French. In spite of the desperate poverty of the colony, Hinckley and the General Court had fully committed Plymouth to the support of Massachusetts. Certain that the cause of Massachusetts was the cause of all New England (which it was), Hinckley and the Court were not sufficiently cold-blooded to turn their backs on the Bay Colony and, right or wrong, the decision to help Massachusetts followed. But it was at least inconsistent for the colony to draft her sons and send them off to battle while the government refused to compel their support by the people who stayed home. To men taken from their families and sent off to fight, and in some cases to die, the acceptance of civil disobedience on the home front must have brought feelings of anger and betrayal.

The failure of the government to use force against delinquent taxpayers represented a choice between two unpleasant alternatives. More difficult to explain as a political act was the passage of legislation in June 1690 to support creditor interests in the colony. Governor Hinckley knew hard currency was in short supply and that his colony faced conditions of serious economic distress. Instead of lightening the load of the debtor, however, the General Court changed the law to the benefit of the creditor. Previously the law allowed a debtor to surrender his livestock and goods if he was unable to pay in money. Stating that this sometimes resulted in great damage to the creditor, the Court required that henceforth the creditor should have the liberty of having a writ served on the estate, or on having the debtor committed to prison until the debt was paid.[7] While creditor interests had undoubtedly suffered under the old law, the enactment of this legislation at a time when the government was struggling to survive, and had already lost the confidence of many people, showed a surprising insensitivity to political requirements.

They were requirements which an earlier governor, confronting even more difficult times, had never forgotten. Governor Bradford had known that for his little colony to survive, the government must retain the confidence of its people, that while strong executive leadership must be given, ultimately that leadership could function only within limits acceptable to the families living at Plymouth. Because Bradford accepted this, and because he proved a tower of strength in moments of crisis, Plymouth Plantation had survived to become the second permanent settlement of Englishmen in the New World. In part at least, because Governor Hinckley was not an equally forceful man, and because he did not seem to understand that governing in the absence of an efficient police force requires political sensitivity, a government which had endured for seventy years collapsed in the years 1690 and 1691.

Only nostalgia could lead one now to feel regret at the passing of Plymouth Colony. Incorporation into the stronger and wealthier Province of Massachusetts Bay was without doubt in the interest of many of Plymouth's inhabitants, and in time it was surely in the interest of all their descendants. Except for a spasm of revolt at Little Compton, where the experiment of not paying taxes continued for a time, the annexation of Plymouth was carried forward without apparent difficulty. For most people, except for a different system in the assessment of taxes and some difference in the eligibility requirements to vote, the change of government had little immediate impact.[8] And for those who believed in

---

7. *Ply. Col. Rec., 6,* 246.

8. Massachusetts law authorized persons with a 40 shilling freehold (property that would rent for 40 shillings annually) or £40 sterling in property to vote in Province elections, and £20 ratable estate to vote in town elections. After 1685,

Puritanism and the way of life it required, incorporation into Massachusetts could not be counted as a catastrophe. In April 1693 the Plymouth Church held a day of Thanksgiving that the government was still in the hands of the saints.

Plymouth Colony required that no one could vote in town meetings except freemen or freeholders of £20 ratable estate or nonfreeholders of £30 ratable estate; and only freemen were authorized to vote in the election of the governor and assistants. Thus, under the Massachusetts Charter, more people could vote than under the old Plymouth government. On the other hand, Massachusetts' taxing procedures were apparently more demanding than those which had earlier existed at Plymouth. Massachusetts used poll taxes and taxed buildings; Plymouth Colony had taxed neither.

Index

Newhaven

Gilford

Mattabesick

Wultfield

16

Northamton 14

Hatfe 13

Hartford Winsor

Seybrook

12

Springfield

15 Hadly

Newlondon

Pequid Country

Sqbaog

wajis Hille

Stoniton

Nipmuk

17

Quentigamog

Lancaster 21

Naragansset

31 Malborough

23 G

Sudbury

32

canonicus 19 Fox

8
mendam

Waler Town

37 Concord

Bull Garrisonhouse 18

Mccfield

Dedz

Cambridg 39

Woturm

25 Wickford

Warwick

20 Providence

Foxbury

a

Newport

Dorchester Boston

RHODE ISLAND

Mount: Hop 1 2

Swangey Seaconk

Brantry

Lyn

Pocasset 6

7 Tanton

Weymoth

Sale

Marblehead

Hingom

Plimouth

ituat

Dartmouth 3

n sole Burrough

Sandwich

Martins Vineyard

Yarmoth

Cape Cod

Nantuket